Revised
Edition

Principles of
Effective
Communication

Christian Liberty Press   Arlington Heights, Illinois

A publication of

Christian Liberty Press

502 West Euclid Avenue
Arlington Heights, Illinois 60004

www.christianlibertypress.com

Scripture references are conformed to The Holy Bible, New King James Version ©1982, Thomas Nelson, Inc., so that modern readers may gain greater comprehension of the Word of God.

Shewan, Edward J., Garry J. Moes, and Kathleen A. Bristley
    APPLICATIONS OF GRAMMAR, BOOK 4
    ANALYSIS FOR COMMUNICATING EFFECTIVELY
    Includes glossary and index
    1. English Language—Grammar and Composition

Copyediting by Diane Olson

ISBN 1-930367-28-7

Printed in the United States of America

Preface

This book is intended to lay a proper foundation for the student's effectiveness in communicating with the English language. The student will learn the basics of English grammar, including the definition and usage of verbs, nouns, adjectives, adverbs, and other parts of speech. In addition, the student will examine how these are to be properly used in phrases, clauses, sentences, paragraphs, and composition. The *Applications of Grammar* series is designed to develop students' skills in using the rules of grammar to communicate effectively for the glory of God.

While some today would discard the need for grammar, this text affirms that the learning of grammatical rules and their proper usage is foundational to good communication. The distinctions between words, their relation to each other in a sentence, and the rules that govern language are the basic building blocks of writing well.

This text is designed to be read carefully by the student so that he may review the grammar knowledge he has already learned and build upon it with new writing skills. Each lesson should be read carefully and reviewed as necessary. Some of the words used in the text may be new to the student's vocabulary, and their spelling unfamiliar. Therefore, a glossary and index are located at the back of this volume to provide students and teachers with additional reference material.

Many of the lessons will require use of a dictionary. While an unabridged dictionary would be useful, a standard, full-sized, collegiate-level dictionary will be more useful. Small, pocket-size, or greatly abridged desktop editions will likely not provide the amount of information which the student will need to complete many of the lessons in this book. It would also be helpful if the student had access to a set of encyclopedias or other reference works. These will be useful in the several writing assignments included in this textbook. If your school or home does not have adequate resources of this nature, you should visit your local library.

THE AUTHORS

Edward J. Shewan is a writer and editor for Christian Liberty Press. He graduated from Valparaiso University with a B.S.E.E. degree in 1974. After a year of mission work in Africa, he attended the Moody Bible Institute's Advanced Studies Program in 1976. Subsequently, he served in Chicago city churches for ten years. In 1983 he graduated from Trinity Evangelical Divinity School with the M.Div. degree. Ed is married and has three daughters. He is the author of *How to Study: A Practical Guide from a Christian Perspective* and *Writing a Research Paper*, both of which are published by Christian Liberty Press.

Garry J. Moes is a free-lance writer, textbook author, and editorial communications consultant from Murphys, California. He earned his B.A. in journalism from Michigan State University, East Lansing Michigan, and did postgraduate research at Scandinavian Christian University's Nordic College of Journalism in Sweden. He was a writer, reporter, and editor for The Associated Press for twenty-one years, and has been an essayist, international correspondent, and executive editor for several Christian periodicals.

Kathleen A. Bristley is a free-lance writer and copyeditor for Christian Liberty Press. Kathy has worked on a number of publications for the Orthodox Presbyterian Church, including *Pressing Toward the Mark: Essays Commemorating Fifty Years of the Orthodox Presbyterian Church*. She attended Covenant College and is the mother of four sons.

Table of Contents

Wks. 1,2

Wks. 3,4

Wks. 5,6

Wks. 7,8

Unit 4 The Mechanics of Good Writing - - - - - - - - - - - 109

Unit 5 Colorful Writing - 139

Unit 6 Nouns and Pronouns - - - - - - - - - - - - - - - - - - 161

Test

Introduction

THE CHRISTIAN VIEW OF LANGUAGE

Students often wonder why they have to study grammar and composition when they already know how to talk and write. Although basic communication skills may be evident, every student needs to thoroughly learn not only how language works but how to use it accurately. In order to speak and write well, students must acquire a proper understanding of grammatical definitions, functions, structures, and rules so that they may verbalize their thoughts with clarity and precision. Few skills are more important to Christian students than the ability to effectively communicate through the written and spoken word.

The student will be able to study language more purposefully if he begins with an understanding of the Christian view of language. Sadly, some students merely study language and grammar because they have been made to do so. They fail to grasp that, because we are made in God's image, good communication is essential to our service for God. As an image bearer of God, the student should consider how the Bible can direct his study of language. Through faith in Jesus Christ he can be reconciled to God and learn how to use language to the end for which it was created. Because language did not originate with us, we do not have the right to use it any way we wish. We must be guided by the Bible. Language skills are not neutral; they must be oriented toward reading, writing, and speaking the truth in love. Linguistic abilities should be developed as part of the student's chief end to glorify God and enjoy Him forever.

GOD IS THE ORIGIN OF LANGUAGE

> In the beginning God created the heaven and the earth. And the earth was without form and void; and darkness was upon the face of the deep. And the Spirit of God moved over the face of the waters. And God *said* ... (Genesis 1:1-3).

God is the origin of language, for the three Persons of the Trinity spoke to each other before time began. When the Father, the Son, and the Holy Spirit speak to each other eternally, their communication is perfect; there is never one word of misunderstanding! The Son of God is called the *Word* of God and the Holy Spirit searches the mind of God and communicates with spiritual words (1 Corinthians 2:10-13). When God created the heavens and the earth, He spoke it into existence by the Word of His power. When He spoke, He uttered a series of sounds—audible symbols which communicated His meaning and brought the creation into being. When God spoke, His Word conveyed both infinite power and eternal meaning—*infinite power* because He manifested His absolute will, and *eternal meaning* because He expressed His infinite mind. His infinite wisdom is revealed in creation, and the creatures He has made serve the purpose of communicating His glory. Thus the rock, for example, is used as a picture of God's unchanging character. Creation itself was designed to provide the basic terms and environment for language.

GOD GAVE MAN THE GIFT OF LANGUAGE

When God created man in His own image, He gave him the gift of language—the ability to communicate with words. He gave man the ability, like Himself, to convey meaning with his words, but He did not impart the infinite creative power of His speech. Thus, God's Word is the final authority, and men are to speak in submission to that Word. The language of man is to be subject to God, for man by his speech has no power to create or change what God has made. Yet there is a great power to human speech. It not only sets on fire the course of our lives but the course of history as well (James 3:6).

Because language is a gift of God, it has a purpose. It was given first of all as the means by which God would communicate to man. As such, it has a high and holy place in our lives. From the beginning God chose to communicate with man. The first words spoken to Adam and Eve were His charge, "Be fruitful, and multiply, and replenish the earth..." (Genesis 1:28). God's desire to communicate with Adam and Eve in the Garden of Eden was central to their fellowship. They "heard the voice of the Lord God walking in the cool of the day..." (Genesis 3:8). Secondly, language was given so that man would respond to God. God created mankind to praise His name and answer His call. Thirdly, it was given for men to communicate with each other in subjection to God's word. People were given the ability to talk to one another and thereby develop marriage, the family, and other social relationships. The primary instrument for building these relationships is verbal communication. God's purpose for language should direct our study of it.

RULES FOR COMMUNICATION

For many students, rules are a burden to be disregarded. But the student who is willing to submit to God's order will seek to develop precision in communicating. Because God is a God of order and truth, He has demonstrated the proper use of language in His speech from the dawn of history. For people to communicate properly and effectively with one another, God not only gave language but with it the basic principles of good communication. This does not mean that we have a divinely revealed set of rules from God, but we can learn from the Bible's use of language and build upon the principles that have been learned in the past. In particular, the Bible and the Christian religion have had a central role in molding the English language.

Consequently, the study of grammar—the body of rules for speaking and writing—should be based on the fact that God is the Creator of language and thereby the originator of its order. Good grammar reflects His logic and manifests the orderly structure of His mind. By learning the rules of proper usage, the student will know how to make his thoughts known and communicate in a compelling manner. His purpose is not simply to be able to communicate, however, but to use language effectively to communicate God's truth.

Language and grammar are not mere human conventions which spring from chance evolution to fill a human need. Language expresses a people's culture, religion, and history. This is why language changes over time. Each language has its own characteristics and rules of usage. But every language displays an underlying unity with other languages. Every language is a verbal system of communication. Each has similar patterns of grammar, though not expressed in exactly the same way. Yet at bottom, the basic principles of grammatical structure are common to every language, which is why writings from one language can be translated into another. While the basic principles of grammar may be adapted in unique ways, these are derived from the original language given by God to man.

LANGUAGE CORRUPTED BY SIN

After our first parents sinned, the same Voice that spoke the world into existence now stood in judgment over mankind. And the language that had been given as a gift to man by the Father of Truth had now been distorted by the Father of Lies. That which was created to praise and worship God had now been used to rebel against the Author of language. Man's fellowship with the Living God had been broken and he no longer desired to hear Him speak.

In addition, the Bible tells us that after the Great Flood, men united by a common language sought unity apart from God at the Tower of Babel. Seeing this, God confused their one language by dividing it into many, and scattered them over the face of the whole earth. Language was thus changed by God to keep men from disobeying His mandate. Because of these different languages there are now barriers between men when they communicate; and sin has continued to pervert the use of language, making it an instrument of lies and manipulation. Today, there are those who would reject all form and grammar and seek to justify any use of language and any breaking of the rules of grammar. As a result, confusion reigns in many quarters, and many people have great difficulty clearly articulating their thoughts in speech and writing.

THE RESTORATION OF LANGUAGE IN JESUS CHRIST

God chose to restore language in His Son. Jesus, as the second Adam, was sent into the world to undo the sin of the first Adam and its consequences (Romans 5:19). Jesus, who is the Word, was with God in the creation because He is God (John 1:1-3). Jesus is the *logos* or revelation of God to man, for God has spoken to us in His Son (Hebrews 1:2). There is no other name under heaven given among men, whereby we must be saved (Acts 4:12). God's will to communicate with man was one factor that motivated Him to restore language to its rightful state in Christ Jesus. By His death and resurrection, Christ not only provides forgiveness of sin, but also newness of life to those who receive Him by faith. As the Truth, Christ calls His disciples to speak the oracles of God (1 Peter 4:11), lay aside lies, and speak truth to one another (Ephesians 4:25). Jesus is the true source of the meaning of all things. He declared, "I am the Alpha and Omega, the beginning and the ending, saith the Lord, which is, and which was, and which is to come, the Almighty" (Rev. 1:8). As R. J. Rushdoony states:

> Christ's statement has reshaped Western languages and grammars, and, through Bible translation, is reshaping the languages of peoples all over the world. Bible translation is an exacting task, because it involves in effect the reworking of a language in order to make it carry the meaning of the Bible. This means a new view of the world, of God, time and language.… Our ideas of grammar, of tense, syntax, and structure, of thought and meaning, bear a Christian imprint.[1]

Students who profess the Christian faith should have a unique appreciation of the role of verbal communication. It is the Christian, above all, who should seek to be clear and accurate in his use of the written word. His God-given duty is to use language with integrity and accuracy for the sake of promoting the gospel and Kingdom of Jesus Christ. Noah Webster saw this in his day when he wrote:

> If the language can be improved in regularity, so as to be more easily acquired by our own citizens, and by foreigners, and thus be rendered a more useful instrument for the propagation of science, arts, civilization and Christianity; if it can be rescued from the

---

1.   Rousas J. Rushdoony, *The Philosophy of the Christian Curriculum* (Vallecito, CA: Ross House Books, 1985), p. 49-50.

mischievous influence of ...that dabbling spirit of innovation which is perpetually disturbing its settled usages and filling it with anomalies; if, in short, our vernacular language can be redeemed from corruptions, and...our literature from degradation; it would be a source of great satisfaction to me to be one among the instruments of promoting these valuable objects.[2]

To show that the Christian has the marvelous opportunity to employ language and its power for the service of the gospel, Gary DeMar asserts:

> Ideas put to paper and acted upon with the highest energy and uncompromising zeal can change the world. Even the worst ideas have been used for this very purpose. If minds are going to be transformed and civilizations changed, then Christians must learn to write and write well. Writing is a sword, mightier than all the weapons of war because writing carries with it ideas that penetrate deeper than any bullet. Writing about the right things in the right way can serve as an antidote to the writings of skepticism and tyranny that have plundered the hearts and minds of generations of desperate people around the world ...[3]

Language as the gift of God needs to be cultivated for serving God. It will not only help the student in academic studies, but in every area of communication, at home, at church, and on the job. Proper English skills are a great asset in serving Christ effectively in one's calling. The student's skill in using English will make a good first impression when he sits for an interview and as he labors in the workplace. The student should take advantage of the time and opportunity he now has available to develop proficiency in English communication. May God bless you as you seek to glorify Him, not only by learning the proper use of English, but in using God's gift of language to spread His Word to every nation.

---

2. Noah Webster, *An American Dictionary of the English Language* (New York, NY: S. Converse, 1828); reprint by (San Francisco, CA: Foundation for American Christian Education, 1987), preface.

3. Gary DeMar, *Surviving College Successfully* (Brentwood, TN: Wolgemuth & Hyatt Publishers, Inc., 1988), p.225.

Unit 1
Thinking
and Writing

INTRODUCTION

Applications of Grammar, Book 4, is designed as a review of the basic elements of effective writing and a reenforcement of the fundamentals of grammar. This course is essentially divided in two parts—**composition** and **grammar**. The first part emphasizes the *thinking process* and develops a sound *writing strategy*. These basic elements of effective writing are then applied to writing an essay, a research paper, and an article of opinion. The second part focuses on grammar, highlighting various grammatical issues that are challenging or prone to errors.

As you approach this course, you must keep in mind that there is a vital connection which exists between *thought* and *language*—both being gifts of God which were given to mankind at creation. It is your responsibility, therefore, to master how you *think* and *communicate* so that you might use these God-given abilities with power and for His glory, as He intended them to be used. In this unit, you will learn how to use **thought** to write effectively. You will learn to **think before you write**. As God thought and then spoke the universe into existence, you too must begin with the thinking process before you proceed to the writing process.

WRITING WITH A PURPOSE

Writing should be done with a **purpose**—a purpose that conforms to God's Word. As you study the principles of composition and grammar, you should also seek to *glorify God* in the simplest essay to the most sophisticated paper.

The **key to effective writing** is *a deep understanding of the greatest story of all time*. This story encompasses all the conflicts of history, beginning with the wonderful yet tragic story of God breathing life into man, and man rebelling against his Creator. It then flows through the lives of the people of Israel, reaching its powerful climax in the drama of the cross. "For He made Him who knew no sin to be sin for us, that we might become the righteousness of God in Him" (2 Corinthians 5:21). The story advances in the life of the church as it comes into conflict with the kingdom of darkness, coming to a grand finale at the return of Christ as King.

Every endeavor to write effectively does not need to embrace all aspects of God's great story, but each effort should **mirror key aspects** of that drama. *God must be glorified in Christ by your thoughts and, subsequently, your words*—whether they reveal the great truths of salvation and how they change lives; or how biblical values triumph over the world's values; or the conflict between the children of darkness and the children of light; or, indeed, the struggle that each child of God fights in this world. This is what distinguishes effective writing that is *Christian*. Writing that is truly Christian arises from a heart that knows and loves the Lord, demonstrating a devotion that pleases Him and a creativity that is subject to the Lordship of Christ.

THE THINKING PROCESS

Putting your thoughts down on paper does not take place in one sitting; nor is it something that you should try to accomplish in a hasty or haphazard manner. Whenever you write, even the simplest paragraph, you are involved in *an ongoing process* which includes using your mind, making decisions, and organizing your thoughts *before* you write them down in a meaningful and orderly way. Start by taking time to let your creative thoughts flow. Quiet your heart and let your thoughts soar the heights of your imagination and search the depths of your soul.

In the first part of this unit, you will answer the following questions: "What is my goal in writing?" "Who is my audience?" "What is my topic?" "What is my stance toward the topic?" and "How am I going to support my topic?" This is the **thinking process** that precedes the process of writing. Subsequently, in the rest of the unit, you will learn how to develop a sensible **writing strategy**, using *public resources* to write an essay of about 750 words.

LESSON 1: WHAT IS MY GOAL?

Whenever you write poetry, prose, or any other sort of literary piece, you **write with a goal in mind**. Naturally, there may be other underlying purposes, but it is your main goal that guides your thoughts as you put them down on paper.

There are **four basic writing goals**, each with its own distinctive perspective: (1) to tell a story (*narrative*), (2) to inform or explain (*expository*), (3) to describe something (*description*), and (4) to persuade or convince (*argumentative*). The following table defines and gives examples for each of these goals:

WRITING GOAL	DEFINITION	EXAMPLE
Narrative	tells a story or recounts a chain of events	recounting the first time you sang a solo in church
Expository	reveals information or explains	explaining electromagnetism
Descriptive	describes a person, place, or thing	describing the Grand Canyon
Argumentative	persuades or convinces	persuading your parents to let you go on a short term mission project

◼ *Narrative*

Narrative writing is the telling of a story or recounting of a chain of events. Often you tell a story about what happened to you. It does not need a plot, characters, or setting, because you are only concerned about conveying to your reader a short synopsis of what happened to you. On the other hand, if you are writing a short story, biographical narrative, or novel about one or more people, you would include the above elements of a story.

◼ *Expository*

Expository writing reveals information or explains. This kind of writing *gives reasons for something happening, presents facts on how something works, explains an idea,* or *gives a definition* in a detailed manner. For example, you may want to **give reasons** why you learned to drive before you were fifteen or why you were late to an activity or why your family is planning to move to a new location. These kinds of explanations are easy to write because they are derived from your experience, but explaining an *idea* or *how something works* is more involved.

To Present Facts

To present **facts on how something works** calls for your ideas to be given in a logical way. Your reader needs enough information so he will be able to follow your train of thought and grasp what you are saying.

To Explain an Idea

To explain an **idea** or concept is probably the most difficult kind of expository writing. It is much more complex because you are trying to communicate something that is *abstract*—as opposed to something *concrete* like the anatomy of the human body.

To Give a Definition

In expository writing, giving a **definition** of a particular term involves more than merely re-stating an entry from your dictionary. It tries to explain the meaning of a word in a more conversational way. This informal approach includes the detailed explanation of the various denotations and connotations of the word.

■ *Descriptive*

Descriptive writing describes a *person, place,* or *thing.* Describing the external aspects of such subjects is relatively easy, but seldom adequate. A superficial description may be sufficient for a medical profile, travel brochure, or sales advertisement, but it is not a complete picture of the entity under consideration. Revealing the deeper, inner qualities or aspects of the person, place, or thing should be your goal.

Describing a Person

A description of a **person** does not merely reveal his physical features; it includes insights into the inner qualities of that person. When describing a person, include particular faults, strengths, and idiosyncrasies which put "flesh" on the bare "bones" of his outward appearance.

Describing a Place

Describing a **place** attempts to capture the essence of that location by choosing words that paint a plausible picture in detail. It is as if you transport your reader to the very place that you are describing. Remember to appeal to the five senses of touch, taste, smell, hearing, and sight, to bring the description to life.

Describing a Thing

A **thing** is described in much the same way as a place. You appeal to the five senses to help your reader "see" or "feel" the thing you are describing. It is also helpful to compare that thing with something else that has similar aspects or qualities. **Similes** and **metaphors** are devices that may be used to look at such things side by side (*See page 144*).

■ *Argumentative*

Argumentative writing tries to persuade or convince. This type of writing *influences, reasons,* or *gives opinions.* If you desire to persuade someone, you must take him through the specific steps which you have taken to reach your conclusion. In essence, you are engaging your reader with reasoned arguments that you set forth in writing. An **argument** may be defined as follows: a claim that should be relevant to proving or establishing the arguer's conclusion. Each argument is used to build or refute a case in support of one's side of a debatable issue.

The first task in argumentative writing is clarifying what the **debatable issue** is and what **approach** is going to be taken. Often in a given argument, the approach to a particular issue is difficult to pin down and even the issue itself is unclear. Seek therefore to have a clear-cut understanding of what the debatable issue is and what approach you will take. We will primarily focus on the *persuading* approach, but the others may apply in certain circumstances; *quarreling*, though common, is the only approach that is unacceptable at all times. The following chart describes the various approaches to this type of writing:[4]

APPROACH	SETTING	METHOD	GOAL
Quarreling	emotional conflict	personal attack	"strike out" at other
Debating	public contest	verbal victory	impress audience
Persuading	difference of conviction or opinion	internal and external proof	persuade others
Inquiring	lack of proof	argumentation based on knowledge	establish proof
Negotiating	difference of interests	bargaining	personal gain
Seeking information	lack of information	questioning	find information
Seeking action	need for action	issuing imperatives	produce action
Gaining knowledge	lack of knowledge	teaching	impart knowledge

According to Douglas Walton, there are four stages to argumentative communication: the *opening stage, confrontation stage, argumentation stage,* and *closing stage.* In the opening stage the approach that will be taken is clarified and the "rules of argumentation" agreed upon. These may be specific rules as used in a court of law or informal guidelines of customary, polite conversation or discussion.

In the confrontation stage, the debatable issue is announced, agreed upon (if there is another party involved), or clarified. The argumentation stage is the stage where the agreed method (see chart above) is used to argue a given position. Finally, the closing stage is the point where you achieve your goal.[5]

✎ **EXERCISE A** Identify the *writing goal* for each of the following topics. In the blanks at the left, write *N* for narrative, *E* for expository, *D* for descriptive, and *A* for argumentative.

_____ 1. How to arrange a bouquet of flowers

_____ 2. A terrifying experience while traveling to a strange place

_____ 3. Why Christians should run for public office

_____ 4. What Victoria Falls (in southern Africa) looks like

_____ 5. A biographical sketch of the Apostle Peter

---

4.   This chart is adapted from Douglas N. Walton's *Informal Logic,* page 10, Table1.0, "Types of Dialogue."

5.   Ibid., pages 9–11.

✎ **EXERCISE B** Write a short paragraph (3 to 4 sentences) for each goal of writing: *narrative, expository, descriptive,* and *argumentative.* Use the topics suggested or choose ones of your own.

Narrative—Tell about the first time you drove a car or placed in a sports event.

_____

_____

_____

_____

_____

_____

Expository—Explain the idea of entropy, how to "surf" the Internet, how to audition for a part in a play, or how the pyramids were built.

_____

_____

_____

_____

_____

_____

Descriptive—Describe the Golden Gate Bridge, your favorite dessert, or the appearance and personality of your best friend.

_____

_____

_____

_____

_____

_____

Argumentative—Persuasively write on why everyone should exercise at least three times a week, why vaccines may be harmful, or why materialism often destroys families.

_____

LESSON 2: WHO IS MY AUDIENCE?

Whenever you write, you must consider who is reading what you have to say. Since your audiences will vary in age, background, and interest, you cannot write in the same way all the time. Content and language is affected by your audience.

■ What Do They Know?

First, you must determine what information your audience already knows about your topic. For example, if you were to present a paper on the issue of voter registration with members of the local election board, you must consider the level of knowledge the members possess about this problem. Most likely, they would be more informed than the average citizen.

■ What Don't They Know?

Second, you must discover what information your audience does *not* know about your topic. If you are writing a paper on embryonic stem-cell research, for example, you need to ascertain what background or technical information is needed for your audience to understand the topic and what terms need to be defined.

■ What Type of Language Do They Use?

Third, you must consider the type of language that you will use so that your audience will be able to receive the information readily. If you are leading a children's club, you would choose words that are age-appropriate; but if you were leading an adult Bible study, you would use terms that would communicate on a higher level. Your *presentation* would also vary in such situations—either using a formal, didactic approach or an informal, inductive approach.

■ What Biases or Convictions Do They Hold?

Fourth, before you begin writing, you should consider what biases or convictions your audience may hold. Everyone has strong feelings either *for* or *against* various topics, which will affect the way you write. For example, if your audience holds the same biases that you do, then your writing will be more congenial than with a hostile audience that disagrees entirely with your perspective.

✎ **EXERCISE A** Choose one paragraph from a magazine or book on a topic in which you are interested. You should have some background knowledge of or experience in the topic. After you have made your selection, rewrite the paragraph for two of the following audiences. Identify the audience of your choice at the beginning of each of the two versions.

1.   High school students with no previous knowledge of the topic

2.   College students with some knowledge of the topic

3.   Adults with extensive knowledge of the topic

✎ **EXERCISE B** Fill in the following chart for the topics given in the first column. Determine what various audiences know or don't know about the topic, type of language that should be used, and any biases or convictions that may be held.

TOPIC	AGE LEVEL	WHAT THEY KNOW	WHAT THEY DON'T KNOW	TYPE OF LANGUAGE	BIASES OR CONVICTIONS
Embryonic stem-cell research	high school students	potential cures for various diseases	kills embryonic life; very poor success rate[a]	clear, direct terms; firm but loving approach	it is "okay" to kill embryos to "save" lives
How to write a poem	junior high students	rhyming words end every other line of a poem	poetry does not have to rhyme; poetic meter		
Pursuing missions	Christian college students	missionary stories; the Great Commission			
Training for the Olympics	(your age)				
(Topic of your choice)					

a. Research on umbilical cord, placenta, and adult stem cells, which does not involve the same moral dilemma, is much more successful, practical (no storage needed), and cost-effective than embryonic stem-cell research.

LESSON 3: WHAT IS MY TOPIC?

A written composition is a group of sentences and paragraphs that are tied together by one, unifying idea that has been developed sufficiently. This sole, unifying idea is called the **topic**. For example, the main idea in a paragraph is stated in a **topic sentence** which normally comes *at* or *near* the beginning of a paragraph; occasionally, however, it may come in the middle or at the end. The topic sentence reveals to the reader the main idea which is going to be developed in the paragraph.

■ *Choosing My Subject*

Always consider what your audience knows and what interests them, when choosing your subject. A **subject** is an unrestricted, familiar area of knowledge. By way of illustration, let's say you decide to write about the subject of the overuse of antibiotics; you would probably focus your thoughts toward concerned parents or individuals with various health challenges rather than disinterested high-schoolers. BEWARE: Even if your subject is age-appropriate, you must use the proper forum for discussing it. For example, you may write about the excessive use of antibiotics, but you would not submit your article on the subject to *PC Magazine*.

■ *Limiting My Subject*

After choosing your subject, you need to limit it. A limited subject is called the **topic**. Since a topic for a paragraph is more limited than one for a term paper due to space constraints, make sure that your topic is not too general for the form of writing you are using, or you will not be able to properly develop the main idea for your readers. The easiest way to limit a subject is by dividing it into smaller subdivisions. Depending on what subject you choose, it may be helpful to divide your subject into time periods, episodes, examples, aspects, functions, or causes.

✎ **EXERCISE A** Identify the following items as *subjects* or *topics*. In the blanks at the left, write *S* for subject and *T* for topic.

_____ 1. Conflict in the Middle East   _____ 5. Wycliffe Bible Translators

_____ 2. A character sketch of Patrick Henry _____ 6. New York Stock Exchange

_____ 3. How to defend your faith   _____ 7. Trials of the pioneers

_____ 4. Sir Winston Churchill   _____ 8. Making origami flowers or birds

---

✎ **EXERCISE B** Choose three of the following subjects and divide each of them into five subdivisions, or topics.

1. The World Wide Web   5. War Between the States

2. Music for Worship   6. Oceanic exploration

3. The War on Terrorism   7. The Great Awakening

4. Urban Outreach   8. Modern literature

Subject 1: _____

         a. _____

         b. _____

         c. _____

         d. _____

         e. _____

Subject 2: _____

   a._____

   b._____

   c._____

   d._____

   e._____

Subject 3: _____

   a._____

   b._____

   c._____

   d._____

   e._____

LESSON 4: WHAT IS MY STANCE TOWARD THE TOPIC?

■ *How Will My Point of View Affect My Writing?*

There is no such thing as **neutrality of thought**. All of us have a point of view toward any given subject, consequently, our point of view will be reflected in how and what we write. As Christians, we should not shrink back from the truth found in God's Word and how that truth affects the way we *think* and the way we *write*. We are not and cannot be neutral when it comes to thinking, acting, speaking, writing, or any other God-ordained undertaking. As Greg Bahnsen rightly states in *Always Ready*:

> Attempting to be neutral in one's intellectual endeavors (whether research, argumentation, reasoning, or teaching) is tantamount to striving to erase the antithesis between the Christian and the unbeliever. Christ declared that the former was set apart from the latter by the truth of God's Word (John 17:17). Those who wish to gain dignity in the eyes of the world's intellectuals by wearing the badge of "neutrality" only do so at the expense of refusing to be *set apart* by God's truth. In the intellectual realm they are absorbed into the world so that no one could tell the difference between *their* thinking and assumptions and *apostate* thinking and assumptions....
>
> —Greg L. Bahnsen, *Always Ready: Directions for Defending the Faith*

The point of view that you bring to your writing is called your ***worldview***—what you believe and the way you approach life. If you are a Christian, you hold to the truth that the Bible is the Word of God; it does not *become* the Word of God, or *contain* the Word of God, but it **is** the Word of God. Likewise, you view the world as being created by God—He spoke and the universe came into existence in six 24-hour days (Genesis 1). This is the basis of your Christian worldview and should be reflected in the way you think and write.

Nevertheless, it must be added that in our writing we should be objective and fair in considering all the facts. This means fairly representing an opposing worldview as you bring God's Word to bear on the truth with respect to that particular view. It is the duty of all writers to understand and interpret the facts as clearly and fairly as possible.

■ *How Will My Attitude Affect My Writing?*

Your attitude toward your topic also affects both the details you include and the language you use. Your attitude may reflect approval, sarcasm, boredom, humor, bitterness, or fear—this is called *tone*. To some extent, the topic determines the tone you want to achieve. You can achieve that tone by using various methods—using figurative language, omitting distracting details, adeptly adding rhythm, or carefully building sentences to reach your goal.

In writing, you cannot use the colorful techniques of speech—speaking in a sarcastic tone, shouting, whispering, modulating pitch in your voice, using gestures or facial expressions. You must depend on the words you use and the way you place them, how you construct your sentences and arrange your ideas in the composition. This takes effort; it does not happen automatically.

✎ **EXERCISE** In two or three paragraphs, describe your *worldview* and how it will affect your writing. In one paragraph, also explain how your *attitude* will affect your writing.

LESSON 5: HOW AM I GOING TO SUPPORT MY TOPIC?

Your goal for writing normally determines what kinds of information you will gather to support your topic. In this lesson, you will learn various means of gathering such information. For example, *to describe* your car, you would simply explain its looks, features, power, etc. *To reveal information* about Islam, however, you would provide knowledge gathered through research.

1. GATHERING RAW MATERIAL

■ Observation

The most basic means of gathering raw material to support your topic is by using your abilities to observe specific details either directly or indirectly. **Direct observation** is made through your own senses; **indirect observation** is made through the senses of others.

Direct Observation

This kind of observation is done through your **five senses**. The aim of *descriptive* and *narrative* writing is to give pleasure by calling up an image of what has been seen, heard, felt, and enacted. These literary forms are distinguished from superficial descriptions or narrations found in catalogs, textbooks, advertisements, and the like.

Indirect Observation

Observation not made directly through your own senses is called *indirect*. This raw material is gathered through listening to or reading about what other people observed or experienced. Most of the information that you gather for writing comes from indirect observation.

■ Brain Power

Another means of gathering raw material to support your topic is by using your abilities to generate specific details through *brainstorming, clustering,* or *answering the five "W's" and the "H."* These methods of generating supporting details use brain power—your mental abilities to think of and organize ideas which relate to your topic.

Brainstorming

Brainstorming is the free flow of ideas or suggestions which will be used as the specific details that support your topic. In this method of gathering raw material, write down every word, phrase, or concept that comes to mind as you focus your thoughts on the topic. By the time you are finished, you will have a long list of words or phrases. Let your imagination "run wild," noting every idea that crosses your mind. Do not stop until you have exhausted all possibilities.

After generating your list, evaluate the items you have written down. Begin by circling or noting those items which seem to best support your topic. You may see certain patterns or related ideas coming together. Note any such developments next to the list.

The important thing to remember is that brainstorming will help you **generate a list of ideas** which may be used to support your topic. The actual outlining of your ideas will be discussed later. Always make sure that your subject has been limited to a workable topic.

Clustering

Clustering is similar to brainstorming except that the ideas which come to mind are placed in a diagram instead of a list. The topic is first written in the center of a piece of paper and a circle drawn around it. As new ideas come to mind, they are written down and circled; lines connect them to the topic itself or other related ideas on the diagram. As new ideas are added, certain *controlling ideas* will emerge that will have various subordinate ideas connected to them.

The **topic** is placed in the *center of the diagram* so the other ideas may easily be connected to it. Next, the **controlling ideas** are connected directly to the topic, and then all the **subordinating ideas** are connected to the controlling ideas. This means of "clustering" ideas gives you a definite picture of how your specific ideas relate to your topic and how they fit into your writing.

Who? What? When? Where? Why? and How?

A third method of generating details for your topic is by **answering the five "W's" and the "H."** These six basic questions—Who? What? When? Where? Why? and How?—are used to gather more information for your topic. *Who* is the person, or group, about whom you are writing? *What* are the facts concerning your story? *When* do the events occur? *Where* do the events of the story take place? *Why* did the events occur or did the person involved act as he did? *How* did the events take place? Keep in mind that every question may not apply to every topic.

✎ **EXERCISE A** On a separate sheet of paper, use the *brainstorming, clustering,* or *answering the five "W's" and the "H"* to gather raw material for the topic of your choice.

2. CLASSIFYING RAW MATERIAL

Now that you have formulated your topic and gathered your raw material, the next step in the thinking process is organizing your ideas into specific categories. This means you need to classify the raw material under various subheadings based on how they relate to each other.

■ Why Classify Your Raw Material?

Classifying raw material helps to determine missing or extraneous details that need to be added or deleted. It also guides in balancing out the various items so that the composition will be properly proportioned.

■ How to Classify Your Raw Material

Your raw material may be classified by using the following four steps: (1) search for elements that have something in common, then group them under an appropriate heading; (2) categorize your ideas and headings according to importance—those items which are more important will be developed later in the writing stage; (3) develop an outline by using subheadings under your main idea; (4) discard any items that do not fit under your subheadings or divisions.

✎ **EXERCISE B** On a separate sheet of paper, classify the raw material you gathered in the previous exercise using the four steps described above.

3. ARRANGING RAW MATERIAL

Up to this point, you have established your topic, considered your audience, set the tone, and gathered and classified your raw material. Next in the thinking process, you need to focus on the best order to present your material. Your raw material should be arranged by *chronological order, spatial order, order of importance, comparison or contrast,* or *analogy.*

■ *Chronological Order*

At times, your goal (narrative, expository, descriptive, or argumentative) will suggest the order you will follow. For example, if your goal is *to narrate* an experience that happened to you or someone else, then you would use **chronological order**. Likewise, if your goal is *to describe* the various steps it takes to bake a cake, you would follow a logical time sequence.

■ *Spatial Order*

Another means of arranging your raw material is the use of **spatial order**. This approach describes where certain items are in relation to one another. Using spatial order, you would seek to lead your readers from one part of a scene to the next in a smooth, orderly fashion.

■ *Order of Importance*

Expository or argumentative writing demands a different type of order—**order of importance**. This arrangement of raw material allows the writer to build on progressively more powerful reasons which support the main idea. Usually the most important argument is placed at the end, as in the closing statements of a jury trial. This is what the reader will remember best. An exception is in journalistic writing, where the most important item is normally placed first.

■ *Comparison or Contrast*

Another means of ordering your raw material is by **comparison** or **contrast**. Similarities and differences between two aspects of a topic are revealed by *examples, facts, happenings,* and *specific details*. You may order your raw material by (1) comparing or contrasting each element of your topic point by point or (2) introducing all the elements of one side of your topic first, then stating all the contrasting elements second.

■ *Analogy*

A final means of ordering your raw material is by way of analogy. An **analogy** is an expanded comparison where parallels are drawn between two unlike topics. This approach helps explain a topic that is unknown by comparing it with a topic that is known.

✎ **EXERCISE C** On separate sheets of paper, write five paragraphs using each of the five means of arranging raw material for a topic. Suggested topics are given, or you may choose ones of your own.

1. **Chronological Order**—Explain how to build a model car, ship, or spacecraft.

2. **Spatial Order**—Describe the sanctuary at your church.

3. **Order of Importance**—Give reasons why abortion is immoral.

4. **Comparison or Contrast**—Compare or contrast a book you have read with its film adaptation.

5. **Analogy**—Compare alternative medicine to traditional medical practices.

LESSON 6: WRITING STRATEGY

Now that the foundation of *right thinking* has been laid, you will be able to build a sound *writing strategy*. This strategy involves words, phrases, clauses, and sentences which are the building blocks of grammar. These aspects of grammar will be covered later in this workbook, but here we want to focus on the most basic component in the writing process—**the paragraph**.

ROUNDED DEVELOPMENT

A *paragraph* may be defined as the rounded development of the *main idea*, or *topic of the paragraph*. It is a definite part, or sub-topic, of the larger topic about which you are writing. The paragraph undergoes construction basically like the building up of the main idea within the whole composition. In that sense, the treatment of the paragraph topic is a **rounded development**—the arrangement and expansion of the main idea according to a definite plan.

The paragraph also gives the reader a sense of completeness and adequacy (i.e., order, as the whole composition has order). At the same time, it must remain a functional component. The paragraph must therefore satisfy these two requirements: (1) it must deal effectively with its own topic, and (2) it must present the topic in clear relation to the whole composition.

PARAGRAPH STRATEGY

Effective paragraphs are organized and developed according to a definite plan. This plan includes the *main idea, topic sentence, body of the paragraph*, and *summarizing sentence*. Each aspect of this strategy will be stated briefly under the "overview" section, then discussed in detail.

■ *An Overview*

The Main Idea

First, every good paragraph must have a **main idea**, or *topic*. This requires some thinking on the part of the writer, who should ask himself: *What is the one main idea I want to express and develop in this paragraph?* The mental step of identifying the topic of a paragraph is very important for beginning writers. Experienced writers understand this main idea as a matter of intuition and know, without much forethought, when the progression of ideas requires a new paragraph.

The Topic Sentence

The main topic will usually be expressed in one sentence within the paragraph known as the **topic sentence**. Most often, the topic sentence will be the first sentence in the paragraph. However, it may appear at any point within the paragraph, depending on how the writer chooses to develop his thoughts around his *main idea*. Experienced writers, however, may write a paragraph without a topic sentence, since the main idea emerges from the paragraph as a whole. As a beginning writer, though, you should make it a regular practice to include one.

The Body of the Paragraph

The middle of the paragraph is known as the **body of the paragraph**. In the sentences that comprise the body, the writer will *develop* the main idea stated in the topic sentence. There are a number of different ways to develop a paragraph. We will discuss these ways in a later lesson.

The Summarizing Sentence

A **summarizing sentence** is often included in a well-written paragraph. It usually comes at the end of the paragraph and restates the idea set forth earlier in the topic sentence. This sentence is especially useful if the paragraph is long. Not every paragraph, however, requires one.

THE MAIN IDEA

The *main idea* is the conscious determination of the writer to make every part of his writing move in *one* direction and conform to *one* clear intention. It is like a coach who stands by the writer's side and helps him stay on course. Since the main idea states the limits of the discussion, it should be consulted for where to begin and end your paragraph.

It will help in selecting your raw material, choosing vocabulary, setting the tone, and, above all, giving unity to the paragraph. In short, the main idea enables the writer at every point to *control* his writing. His paragraph will not ramble; it will not be vague and disordered but will become *one* thing—an entity.

■ *The Writer's Challenge*

All writers must ask one question: *What do I wish to say?* This challenge is one of control, which may be a task that is imposed upon you when asked to write a book report, theme, or term paper. At this point a number of questions may overwhelm you: What subject shall I choose? How shall I begin? How much shall I write? What should I include and exclude? Should I write conversationally or must I try to be "literary"?

The answer to all these questions is: "That depends!" Nothing can be decided until the aim of your writing has been determined. Until you are sure for what goal you are aiming, you will not know whether to take a bat, club, racket, or paddle into the game.

One Definite Idea

The first step in writing a paragraph is for the writer to determine his aim. He must centralize his thoughts around **one definite idea**. That is, each paragraph should have a precise topic sentence.

Choosing a manageable topic or a specific aspect of an idea, rather than a vague generalization, is the best place to begin. If you are interested in basketball, for example, you have a vast field of fact and opinion from which to draw raw material; but if you decide to start with a vague idea of saying "something about basketball," you will not be able to write a good composition. You must choose a definite topic for your paragraph.

The Topic Statement

If you are going to limit your topic, you must decide *before you begin to write*. It is best to write it out on a piece of paper so that it stands before your eyes; this will help you clarify your thoughts. It should be *one* sentence that is as simple and concise as you can make it. It should answer the question: "What am I trying to say in this paragraph?"

Many writers carefully plan their compositions by creating a **topic statement**, either mentally or on paper. This statement is an expression or mental construction of the main idea. This statement may or may not become the topic sentence of a paragraph (or composition), but it guides the writer as he creates an outline of the material he plans to use and develop in his paragraph. An *outline* is a series of brief, specially arranged phrases expressing each point to be discussed in the paragraph or composition.

THE TOPIC SENTENCE

The **topic sentence** is important in creating unity within the paragraph because it expresses the central thought among the sentences. Since it contains the heart of the idea developed within the paragraph, it provides a yardstick by which to measure whether the other sentences relate to that central thought.

Although it is called a topic "sentence," it may not be a full sentence in some cases. The main subject of the paragraph may be stated as: (1) one of the clauses in a compound sentence, (2) the main clause of a complex sentence, (3) a phrase, or (4) a single word. A **simple sentence**, however, is probably the most effective way to express the paragraph's main idea. It is almost always more effective to express the main idea in a topic sentence than to force the reader to infer the central thought from an implied topic statement.

■ *Vary Your Topic Sentences*

If your composition is longer than one paragraph, you may consider using a variety of sentence types for your topic sentences in each paragraph. Usually, simple declarative sentences are the clearest way to express your topic. On the other hand, you may wish to consider using *compound, complex,* or *compound-complex* declarative sentences—or even *interrogative, exclamatory,* or *imperative* sentences—for variety. As stated above, it may also be effective to use a powerful word, phrase, or clause as the vehicle for expressing your topic.

■ *Vary The Position of Topic Sentences*

Clearness and directness of communication usually mean putting the topic sentence at the beginning of the paragraph. This is especially true if your main goal is to inform or to argue your position. Other forms of writing, with other goals in mind, may allow for the possibility of placing the topic sentence elsewhere in the paragraph. For example, you may generate a sense of suspense or anticipation by placing the topic sentence last. At other times, you may wish to introduce or hint at the main idea in the beginning, then state the topic in the middle and follow-up with additional details or supporting information. In some cases, you may find it is useful or necessary to restate the main idea by having two or more topic sentences. REMEMBER: A *summarizing sentence* may serve this purpose as well.

THE SUPPORTING SENTENCE

Since a **paragraph** is defined as the *rounded development of the main idea,* it cannot consist of a bunch of disconnected sentences that are merely placed without rhyme or reason. The paragraph is made up of **supporting sentences** that develop or expand the main idea of the paragraph. The *content* of the paragraph is fixed by its relationship to the composition as a whole, and its *form* is determined by how the specific details are treated, thus giving the paragraph its rounded development.

The organization of the sentences in the paragraph is basically affected by the order in which the ideas are presented. The order of ideas, in turn, is established by the nature of the topic and how the writer chooses to develop it. For example, he may use *chronological order* if the sequence of ideas calls for order of time or *spatial order* if certain items are in relation to one another. *Order of importance* may be applied instead if reason is used to determine the arrangement of the writer's arguments. *Comparison or contrast* or *analogy* may be used to order ideas that are too difficult or abstract for his audience to understand or follow.

Many methods may be used to logically develop your paragraph so that the supporting sentences you write will strengthen the topic of the paragraph; the paragraph as a whole will thus strengthen the larger composition. In the next lesson, we will look at several of these methods.

THE SUMMARIZING SENTENCE

The **summarizing sentence** rounds off the discussion of the topic in much the same way that a closing paragraph does for the whole composition. The purpose of the summarizing sentence is to give the reader a sense of completeness and closure. It should sum up your discussion in a concise and meaningful way. The sentence may briefly restate your topic with an emphatic generalization or a pithy appraisal of what has been said.

In writing a summarizing sentence, the writer should work towards making the best possible impression on his reader—last impressions are often resolute and lasting. Remember as well that every sentence, whether the last or the first, is to be judged by what it does within the whole paragraph. It is superfluous to make up a special sentence at the end of the paragraph if the paragraph brings itself naturally to a close without it. The concluding sentence should not appear to be added as an afterthought or as a bombastic recapitulation.

✎ **EXERCISE** Using the above writing strategy, write a paragraph on the topic of your choice. Be sure to include a *topic sentence*, *supporting sentences*, and a *summarizing sentence*.

_____

_____

_____

_____

_____

_____

_____

_____

_____

_____

_____

_____

_____

_____

_____

_____

LESSON 7: TOPIC BUILDERS

In well-written paragraphs, the topic is developed or expanded, not merely restated in sentence after sentence. There are any number of ways in which a topic can be developed in a paragraph. If you carefully and creatively write your topic sentence, it will often suggest the best and most appropriate approach for expanding the topic. The most common methods of developing a topic in a paragraph are given below, but you may discover a new method or combine several approaches.

EXAMPLES AND ILLUSTRATIONS

Development by **examples and illustrations** means to use supporting sentences which provide examples or specific instances of the main idea expressed in the topic sentence. Try to find examples which are likely to be familiar to your intended readers. If your topic is not likely to be familiar to your readers, concrete examples and illustrations will help them better understand the subject at hand. It is not always necessary to list numerous examples or illustrations. Sometimes, just one good example will develop your theme.

PARTICULARS AND DETAILS

Developing a paragraph with **particulars and details** means to provide specific, concrete information explaining the broader idea expressed in the topic sentence. The sum of these details will give the reader a more definite understanding of the wider topic under discussion. REMEMBER: These details must relate clearly to the topic, or they will distract and confuse the reader.

The kinds of details you provide depend on the type of writing you are doing. If you are writing a *narrative*, you should supply details that will help you tell your story. If your composition is *descriptive*, details that further describe your subject should be given. If your composition is *expository*, your details should be to further explain your subject.

INCIDENT

The method of development by **incident** uses a specific historic or biographical occurrence, episode, or event to develop the topic sentence.

REASONS

Development by **reasons** is often the method used to develop paragraphs in argumentative writing. In most cases, the topic sentence will be a statement of opinion or position. The topic is then developed by giving reasons for the opinion or information.

CONTRAST OR COMPARISON

Sometimes you can make your topic more clear by showing how it is like something that may be more familiar to your readers. Alternatively, you might develop your topic by showing how it is different from something else.

CAUSES OR EFFECTS

A topic may be developed by showing its **causes** or its **effects**. A *cause* is something that produces a result, and an *effect* refers to the result that the topic produces.

DEFINITION

In a paragraph using this method of development, the writer is trying to answer the question: *What do you mean?* Development by **definition** does not always require the use of dictionary-style statements. The meaning of a topic can be given in many different ways, including some of the other methods of development already discussed. For example, the paragraph you are now reading is one which attempts to provide the definition of a particular topic—the topic in this case being "the meaning of the term *development by definition.*"

CHRONOLOGY OR SEQUENCE

The method of developing a topic by **chronology or sequence** is used almost exclusively in narrative-style writing, in which a story—fictional or non-fictional—is unfolded. Of course, stories are not always told in the order in which the events evolved; but the sequence of events, in whatever order, is usually the backbone of the narrative.

DIVISION

In the **division** method of development, the writer discusses a topic which has two or more parts. In developing the topic, the writer deals separately with each part of the topic in the same paragraph. In the most common approach, the topic sentence names two or more points. The body of the paragraph then uses the "First…," "Secondly…," "Thirdly…," "Finally…" format to deal with the separate points mentioned in the topic sentence.

✎ **EXERCISE** Develop each of the following topic sentences into a brief paragraph using some or all of the approaches discussed in this lesson. (Fill in the blanks with words of your choice.)

1. _____ is a harmful habit.

2. _____ has (have) become an essential part of modern life.

3. It is not difficult to make a _____.

    _____

    _____

    _____

    _____

    _____

    _____

    _____

    _____

    _____

    _____

    _____

4. God's glory can be seen in _____.

    _____

    _____

    _____

    _____

    _____

    _____

    _____

    _____

    _____

    _____

    _____

LESSON 8: UNITY AND COHERENCE

PARAGRAPH UNITY

A paragraph, by definition, is a meaningful sentence or group of sentences that are related to one another by a common idea. This means that a paragraph requires **unity**—"oneness." All elements of a paragraph must be relevant to the central thought if unity is to be achieved. The requirements for achieving unity are simply stated in this *twofold rule*:

1. Include all material that is essential to the development of your topic.

2. Likewise, eliminate all material that is not essential to the development of your topic.

■ *Including Essentials*

Inexperienced writers often fail to include enough information to fully communicate their main idea to the reader. Sometimes the paragraph is just too brief, but the length is not the most important consideration. *Underdevelopment* is the absence of important ideas and details necessary to the expression of a complete and unified theme.

■ *Excluding Non-essentials*

Unity of a paragraph can also be destroyed by the inclusion of **too many details**, especially those that do not directly relate to the topic or those that connect only superficially. Good discipline in writing requires that the writer should focus carefully on his topic and eliminate anything that might distract or mislead a reader away from the target theme.

Unity does not require that only one method of paragraph development be used, but every approach must contribute to the effective communication of the central idea. You may combine two or more of the methods discussed in the previous lesson for developing your topic—as long as the various approaches are appropriate and necessary.

Unity does not mean *sameness*. Avoid meaningless and unnecessary repetition of the topic sentence. If you repeat your topic, be certain that the repetition has a specific purpose and effectiveness. To be effective, the repetition should add needed clarity or details, moving the reader's mind in a positive, intended direction. Do not bore the reader or lead his mind in circles.

PARAGRAPH COHERENCE

It is one thing to obtain information and to properly narrow or expand it. It is another thing to properly arrange it in a paragraph. Information that has substance can be presented ineffectively if it is not correctly and logically arranged. This means that a paragraph requires **coherence**.

■ *Logical Order*

The human mind does not always process information logically; often our thoughts occur to us in a haphazard way. Perhaps you have heard people say things like, "I should have mentioned earlier..." or "Before I go any further..." or "Let me back up...." This is usually an ineffective way *to write*. In writing, we should strive to put ideas in **logical order**.

Good writing has been compared to a dinner that is arranged in *courses*—each course coming in an order that enhances tastiness and digestion; one course would conclude before another begins. Paragraphs should also follow a logical pattern, where related elements go together.

Clear Progression

The arrangement of sentences in a paragraph depends on the material you are using. There is no absolute rule about arrangement, except this: *thoughts must follow a recognizable line of progression*. Sentences should follow some order that leads to where you want the reader to go. The three main kinds of **clear progression** are as follows:

1. Time (chronological) order

In this arrangement, the writer arranges his sentences in time sequence. Events are discussed in the order in which they occurred (or in reverse order). Another technique is the "flashback" —starting in the present, then reverting to a time in the past, followed by progress back to the present. Time-related order serves best in narrative writing, but it may also be used in descriptive writing, or in writing that explains processes.

2. Space (spatial) order

In this arrangement, which is used almost exclusively in descriptions, sentences are written in a way so as to describe subjects according to their position in physical space: from near to far, from far to near, from left to right, from right to left, from inside to outside, or from outside to inside. This type of arrangement can also apply figuratively, as material is familiar (near) or unfamiliar (remote) from the knowledge, interest, or environment of the reader.

3. Logical order

There are two types of logical order: *inductive* and *deductive* order. In inductive order, the writer first states particular points and then draws a general conclusion from them. In deductive order, the writer makes a general statement and then draws particular conclusions or individual truths from that general statement.

Effective Position

The order of a paragraph should not only be clear and progressive, but sentences should also be placed in positions which enhance their effectiveness. There are three **effective positions** which are possible in ordering a paragraph.

1. Beginning and ending positions

Usually, it is most effective to place the most important sentences at the beginning or end of the paragraph. First and last impressions are usually the strongest.

2. Climax

When a paragraph contains a series of related ideas, sentences can be arranged so that the most important idea or the conclusion of the series of ideas comes at the end of the series. Each stated idea leads to a more important one and the most important or dramatic one comes at the end. The reader is encouraged to keep reading until he discovers the climax idea.

3. Miscellaneous order

When a paragraph contains several related ideas, but none of them is more important than the other, the writer may arrange his sentences in any way that he believes will be most interesting to the reader.

■ *Proportion and Length*

A writer should not only strive for unity and coherence in writing a paragraph, but also for good *proportion* and *length*. *Length* becomes more significant when a composition consists of several paragraphs. Usually, it is best to avoid making one paragraph extremely long and another extremely short, although a short paragraph may occasionally produce a special effect.

More importantly, though, the writer should strive for good *proportion*. This means that the *ideas* within a paragraph should be developed according to their relative importance; in other words, *paragraphs* should be written with careful attention to how they relate to one another and to the composition as a whole.

1. Strive for correct proportion.

One error, for example, would be to write a 500-word composition with an extremely long introductory paragraph and a transitional paragraph that together use 400 words, leaving only 100 words to develop the main idea of the composition.

In a paragraph containing several related ideas of differing importance, greater space should be given to the more important ideas, since readers often assign importance on the basis of the number of words and sentences used. Do not expand insignificant ideas or underdevelop significant ones.

In a longer composition, a mixture of short and long paragraphs is usually most effective, but make sure the length of each is appropriate for the topic being covered.

2. Attain good proportion through careful planning.

Consider each idea in relation to the whole composition. Begin by thinking about the subject as a whole before writing individual paragraphs.

Think about the reader more than your own interests. Decide what central purpose each paragraph will have in communicating the topic to your reader. You may find a particular point to be personally interesting, but make sure it is given only the attention that the topic deserves in order to communicate the overall idea to the intended reader.

After writing, review sentences and paragraphs for correct proportion. Shorten those which are expanded beyond the significance of their topic; lengthen those which underdevelop the main idea.

3. Your composition usually should NOT consist only of a series of short, choppy, bullet-like paragraphs.

News stories often use this approach for various reasons that are peculiar to newspaper makeup and style. A creative composition, however, in which all or most of the paragraphs consist of one or two sentences, is usually not effective. Ideas cannot be properly developed if paragraphs are consistently too short.

Choppiness can usually be avoided when the writer adequately considers the inter-relatedness of the various ideas he is discussing. Clearly related ideas should be kept together and developed together within a well-proportioned paragraph.

Exception: This approach may be used in an expository composition in which step-by-step instructions are being offered, such as the instructional nature of this workbook. Short paragraphs can also be used for special emphasis.

---

4. Your composition usually should NOT consist only of very long, ponderous paragraphs.

Overly long paragraphs, especially if one such paragraph follows another, may strain the reader's attention. Give the reader a mental break occasionally.

Often, when paragraphs get extremely long, they contain material that does not properly belong there. Check to see how the material in a very long paragraph might be rearranged and broken into two better proportioned paragraphs without harming overall unity.

The tendency in modern writing is toward shorter paragraphs. However, in technical or scholarly writing, or fiction, longer paragraphs are still common.

✎ **EXERCISE** Below are three groups of sentences.[6] Arrange each group in meaningful order to form a paragraph. In each of your newly-arranged paragraphs, underline the topic sentence.

1. a.   If you don't eat the right spiritual food, you will starve to death or you will seek any nourishment that promises to satisfy your hunger.

    b.   Just as there are all types of food for the body, there is food for the soul or spirit, "spiritual food" (1 Corinthians 10:3).

    c.   You must nourish the part of you that the Bible describes as your "spirit."

    d.   Keep in mind that you are a spiritual creation.

    e.   Just as there is "junk food" that can rob your body of essential nutrients and can turn a healthy body into an anemic one, there are all types of "spiritual junk food" that can wreck your spiritual health.

    f.   But not just any food will meet the nutritional demands required by your spirit.

6.   These paragraphs are taken from Gary DeMar's *War of the Worldviews* (Atlanta, GA: American Vision, 1994).

2.   a.   Christians are told, "You can develop your own *personal religious* convictions, but you cannot bring these *personal religious* convictions to the classroom. You must be neutral like your professor."

      b.   Unfortunately, many Christians have fallen in the trap by assuming that a subject can be studied without any reference to religious presuppositions.

      c.   The neutrality myth has been used by secularists to keep a Christian perspective of the world out of the arena of intellectual thought.

3.   a.   Throughout all ages and into eternity, man's deepest yearnings will only be filled in Christ.

      b.   As man seeks consistency in his anarchy, he will watch his futile autonomy trickle from his clutches into a pile of dust at his feet.

      c.   It is the church's duty now to answer the world's wail of despair.

      d.   Postmodernism has broken the stiff neck of humanistic modernism.

LESSON 9: TRANSITIONAL MATERIAL

BRIDGING ONE IDEA TO ANOTHER

Transition means passage from one *place, condition, stage of development, type,* or *period of time* to another. In writing, the term **transition** applies to material which leads the reader from one idea or unit of composition to another. Transitional words, phrases, clauses, sentences, and paragraphs are "bridges" or "links" between separate but related elements. Proper transition is very important in maintaining unity and progress in a composition.

Use *transitional devices* to show the relationship between sentences within a paragraph and between paragraphs in a larger composition. Changes in thoughts may confuse a reader unless you can carefully guide him from one thought to the next. Transitional devices in writing have been compared to road signs along a highway, warning the driver what to expect next.

While transitions are one of the most important elements in good writing, they should be relatively brief so as not to detract from the central ideas they are seeking to connect. Just as a road sign should not obscure a hazard to which it is calling a driver's attention, transitional devices should not call attention to themselves but should, rather, reveal the relationships of ideas to which the writer is seeking to draw attention.

■ *Transitional Words or Phrases*

Transitional words or phrases placed at or near the beginning of a paragraph will often suffice to guide the reader. Some of the more common ones are:

TRANSITIONAL WORDS AND PHRASES			
accordingly	by way of comparison	in like manner	on the other hand
after	consequently	in short	otherwise
again	during	in the first place	second
and	finally	let us compare	similarly
another reason	for	likewise	since
as	for example	meanwhile	then
as an illustration	for instance	moreover	therefore
as a result	furthermore	neither	thus
as I said	hence	nevertheless	to summarize
because	however	nor	whereas
besides	in conclusion	not only	yet
but	in contrast	on the contrary	

■ *Transitional Phrases or Sentences*

Longer phrases or sentences may also be used as transitions.

☞**EXAMPLES:**

> But first let us consider....   We have seen how...; let us now consider....

■ *Transitional Paragraphs*

Transitional paragraphs may be used to show the relationship between a preceding paragraph and a following paragraph.

✎ **EXERCISE A** Read the paragraphs below and answer the following questions.

At the age of twenty-five, after conducting a successful caravan trade to Syria for a wealthy widow by the name of Khadija, Muhammad accepted Khadija's offer to marry her. Despite the fact that she was fifteen years his senior, the marriage proved to be a happy one for both. The couple had two sons who died in infancy, and four daughters. Almost nothing is known about this stage of Muhammad's adult life except that it seems his good reputation and respect constantly grew among his people.

It is during this time period that many have speculated Muhammad grew more and more discontent with the paganism and idolatry of his society. This was not unique since several other prominent citizens of Mecca denounced the paganism of their homeland and declared their faith in the one true God, including Jews and Christians. In accordance with the customs of the pious souls, Muhammad began the practice of devoting "a period of each year to a retreat of worship, asceticism, and prayer." Some say he would spend the whole month of Ramadan in a cave on Mount Hira two miles north of the city of Mecca, living on meager rations and meditating in peace and solitude.[7]

1. Underline words and phrases in the paragraphs above which serve as transitional devices.

2. Which type of order is used primarily in the first paragraph above? _____

✎ **EXERCISE B** Place an "X" where you think the following sentence would best be placed: It made relatively little headway in some of the churches and met with great opposition in others.

Even in view of this assault of liberalism on the educational institutions of the church, the progress of modernism was uneven and was not obtained without great struggles. It gained greater strength in those churches that were Armenian in their theology, or which had no creeds of any consequence to guide their theological development. Although heresy made itself felt in the Presbyterian Church USA in the closing years of the nineteenth century, this church, with a group of stalwarts for the faith at Princeton Seminary, continued its testimony for the historic faith until well into the twentieth century; it was not until the appearance of the Auburn Affirmation in 1923, and the ensuing reconstruction of Princeton Seminary at the close of the decade, that liberals could be said to have officially taken over this once great church. It met even greater resistance in the Southern Presbyterian Church, and in some branches of the Lutheran Church in this country. The conquest of Princeton Seminary by the forces of liberalism was a strategic victory, and of great consequence for the evangelical church in the nation, for this school had given forth a scholarly defense of the Gospel for over a century....[8]

7. Geisler, Norman L., and Abdul Saleeb, *Answering Islam: The Crescent in the Light of the Gospel* (Grand Rapids, MI: Baker Books, 1993), pp. 69, 70.

8. C. Gregg Singer, *A Theological Interpretation of American History* (Greenville, SC: A Press, 1964), pp. 180, 181.

LESSON 10: RESOURCES AND WRITING

Writing grammatically correct sentences is important, but it is not enough. A good writer needs to know *how* and *why* one flawless grammatical expression is more favorable, or less favorable, than another that is equally impeccable. He needs to know *how* certain words, phrases, clauses, and sentences function in a given paragraph or composition, and *why* they would change the meaning of what is being communicated in another context. In essence, **the writer needs to learn to control his resources**—not just possess them.

TWO KINDS OF RESOURCES

Every good writer must possess and control two kinds of resources, namely, those that belong to him personally and those that belong to people in general. *Personal resources* consist of the writer's faith, personality, family background, gifts, talents, education, weaknesses and strengths; *public resources*, on the other hand, consist of the vast body of experience and knowledge that has been amassed over the centuries.

In this lesson, you will learn to draw on the **public resources** which make up our rich literary heritage—past and present. It would be deplorable if we only had our personal resources upon which to rely. Imagine what the world would be like without dictionaries, grammars, or libraries filled with the great treasures of ancient and modern authors, not to mention the unimaginable thought of life without God's Word. One of the benefits of this course will be your increased awareness and appreciation of this great heritage.

WRITING USING PUBLIC RESOURCES

■ *Put Your Mind in Motion*

Having covered the *thinking process* and developed a sound **writing strategy**, you will now have the opportunity to put what you have learned into practice. An essay of about 750 words, using public resources, is a good place to begin. First, you will answer the five questions related to the thinking process, and second, you will implement the five steps of the writing process.

What is my goal?

The first question you must answer is: "What is my goal in writing?" Is it *narrative, expository, descriptive, or argumentative*? Narrative and argumentative writing may be used if you want to tell a story or argue a point. In expository and descriptive writing, however, you are concerned with explaining a process or idea, or revealing an in-depth portrayal of the person, place, or thing. Which of these goals, though, is appropriate for writing an essay using public resources? Expository would probably be your choice, since **expository writing**—*giving reasons for something happening, presenting facts on how something works, explaining an idea*, or *giving a definition* in a detailed manner—is the best approach for such an assignment. Granted you will want to use descriptive language in your writing, but exposition would be your main goal. Nevertheless, you may want to venture using one of the other goals for this exercise.

Answering this first question is relatively straightforward; however, as you move along in the thinking process, you will need to use your mental abilities more acutely. Approach each question with the same critical thinking. Analyzing every possible answer will help you focus your thoughts. As you answer the next four questions, keep in mind your main goal—*expository*, if that is your choice. To keep track of your progress, write the following outline on a separate piece of paper and fill in the appropriate information as you go:

Your Goal:	*Expository*—topic of your choice
Your Audience:	Who are your readers?
	What do they know?
	What don't they know?
	What kind of language do they use?
	What biases or convictions do they hold?
Your Main Idea:	Subject—
	Topic—
Your Stance:	Worldview—
	Tone—
Your Raw Material:	Gathering Information—
	Classifying Information—
	Arranging Information—

Who is my audience?

This step may not be as obvious as you might think. For whom are you writing this essay? Close friends? Relatives? Church newsletter? Community bulletin? Local Newspaper? *WORLD* magazine? You need to decide how narrow or how broad your audience is going to be. This will affect the rest of the issues related to your audience.

To help you decide which audience you want to target, analyze various viewpoints. The following chart will assist you in organizing your thoughts. Begin by choosing several different audiences and then filling in the appropriate information. After you have done your analysis, choose an audience.

AUDIENCES ⟹	FRIENDS	RELATIVES	NEWSLETTER	NEWSPAPER	(your choice)
What They Know	know quite a bit about your topic	know general things about your topic	readers know some information		
What They Don't Know	don't know a few things	don't know specific things			
Kind of Language They Use	use informal language				
Biases or Convictions					

What is my topic?

You have selected the *subject* you are going to tackle in this assignment. The challenge now is deciding what you want to say about your subject. The subject is quite broad and the thoughts you do have may be vague and shapeless. Your goal is to give your collection of ideas a significant form. You cannot say everything. Therefore, select what will best represent your subject— those ideas that actually go together to make a unified whole.

You need to focus your subject enough to come up with a *workable topic*. Remember that the *main idea* is the conscious determination of the writer to make every part of his writing move in *one* direction and conform to *one* clear intention.

What facts, information, and concepts will you highlight? What is it that you want people to know about your topic that they never knew before? After you make your decision, **write a clear topic statement** on your paper. Now you are ready for the next question.

What is my stance toward the topic?

As a Christian, your **worldview** most certainly will have an impact on what you write and how you write about your topic. Perhaps you will choose the topic of "embryonic stem-cell research." As a Christian, you would undoubtedly hold the conviction that the practice of "harvesting" stem cells from embryos is immoral. Such research destroys the very essence of life, which is embodied in the embryo. So you would advocate ceasing all such research.

On the other hand, if spiritual matters are foreign to your thinking, the point of view which you have acquired over the years will be reflected in your experiences and ideas. Perhaps you believe in fate, human ingenuity, or the random chance of evolutionary thought. Whatever your worldview, it will be reflected in how you approach life in general and what you write about in particular.

The **tone** of your essay is another matter to decide before you begin to write. If you *explain an idea* you may choose to give your writing a lighter touch by bringing out some humorous incidents that would bare on your topic. A more somber note might be struck if you write about the seriousness of a moral dilemma—e.g., the destruction of embryos through the "harvesting" of stem cells, which scientists say *could possibly* be used to "save" the lives of those with incurable diseases. Remember that tone will affect the details you include and the language you use.

How am I going to support my topic?

The next question in the thinking process involves selecting the details that will support your topic. The best method of gathering this data is **brainstorming**. Find a secluded place where you can quietly list possible ideas about your topic. Perhaps you will need to do some library research to obtain a better grasp on the topic you want to develop. At this point, do not be worried about classifying or arranging your raw material, just write whatever comes to mind.

As your ideas begin to flow, **you may see a pattern developing** that suddenly comes to the fore. If you have written down all you know or have discovered about your topic, start selecting various details that would reveal more about your topic. *Eliminate any extraneous information* and try to *make a general outline* of the material you have collected. Now you are ready to arrange your raw material into some kind of order.

"Where do I begin? Where do I end? What do I do in between?" These questions may be answered in various ways. If you are *explaining an idea*, you could begin with a definition of this concept, and then you could show how that idea unfolds in a more detailed way. If you are *giving reasons for something happening*, chronological order may be used to reveal why the event took place as it did.

If you are *presenting facts on how something works*, you could begin by discussing the individual functions or parts of the "whole." An alternate approach would be to reverse the order: you could give an overview of how the "whole" works and then give details of its individual functions or parts. Allow your details to lead to a clear, defined appraisal of what the "whole" is.

PUT YOUR PLAN INTO ACTION

Now you are ready to put your plan into action, but first a few last minute instructions are in order. Keep your *progress outline* and *raw material* close at hand. Also use simple and direct language as you write, since writing in a bombastic or ostentatious manner will lose the impact of plain, straightforward speech. Last but not least, do not forget your audience.

If your goal is **expository**, do not attempt a complex or technical topic for the first theme of this type. Choose instead a simple *process* (i.e., how something works) in which you define your terms and explain each step of the process clearly. Above all, make your explanation interesting, but not with stylistic flourishes, clever remarks, or pretentious language. If the process is prone to mistakes, interest can be kindled by highlighting those mistakes and warning the reader against them; also, interest can be intensified by introducing a human element into your essay.

Step 1: Writing Your First Draft

You are now ready to **write your first draft**. Don't be worried about grammar, spelling, or technical matters at this point; just let your ideas flow—keeping in mind your goal, topic, and audience. Later on you will be able to appraise, rework, and proofread your essay. Write your first draft and lay it aside for two days.

Step 2: Appraising Your First Draft

The process by which you initially judge the content of your essay is called **appraising your first draft**. As you have been writing, you probably have been making changes as you go along, but now that you have completed your first draft, you must appraise it as a whole. Approach it as if you were looking at it for the first time.

Since you have laid your draft aside for a couple of days, you will have a fresh perspective on it. **Read your essay out loud**. With a critical ear, listen for words, phrases, clauses, or sentences that are pointless, inappropriate, or inconsistent with your worldview or the tone of your paper. **Mark any changes or corrections** on your first draft. You may also wish to have someone else read your work and give you some constructive criticism. The following questions will help in your appraisal:

1. Does the information you included support your goal?

2. Do you think that your proposed audience will find your essay interesting?

3. Does your audience need more background data or explanation of terms?

4. Is the topic developed well enough for your audience to grasp your message?

5. Is your writing coherent or will the reader need to jump around to put your ideas together?

6. Does the logical order of your details and ideas make your main idea clear?

7. Do you make smooth transitions between your sentences and paragraphs?

8. Does your choice of words and thoughts clearly convey the *tone* you desire to impart?

9. Does your writing effectively and consistently communicate your *worldview*?

10. Have you varied the length and structure of your sentences to avoid "reader boredom"?

11. Are the words you have chosen precise and concrete or indefinite and ambiguous?

12. Are the descriptive terms you use vivid or colorless, graphic or dull?

Step 3: Writing Your Second Draft

Your appraisal of your essay will no doubt reveal some problems in your work. When reworking your first draft, you need to find specific ways to correct the problems that have arisen. This can be accomplished in the following ways: (1) by adding new ideas or details, (2) by removing extraneous information, (3) by replacing material with information that is more relevant or suitable, and (4) by rearranging ideas and details in a more logical way. **Write your second draft** using these techniques. The following set of problems and solutions will assist you in writing your second draft:

Problem	Solution
1. Your ideas and details do not help explain your topic.	You can remove irrelevant or unnecessary information and add narrative detail.
2. What you have written seems monotonous and may lose the interest of your readers.	You can replace details that your audience is not interested in with a human element.
3. You have inadvertently inserted words that are unknown to your audience.	You can replace these terms with more familiar ones or add further explanation to your essay.
4. You have not provided enough data for your readers to understand the topic.	You can add facts and examples, or highlight mistakes and give warnings, for clarity.
5. Some ideas do not support your topic and may confuse or distract your audience.	Remove all phrases, clauses, and sentences that do not relate directly to your topic.
6. The order of ideas may cause your readers to lose the thrust of your topic.	Check the original order of your paper and reorder your ideas to clarify your message.
7. The connection between your thoughts may not be clear to your audience.	You can add such transitional words as *this, when, then, first, in addition, as a result*, etc.
8. Your attitude toward the topic may be inappropriate for your goal or audience.	Lighten or subdue the tone by replacing formal with casual words or vice versa.
9. Your writing does not communicate the tone you desire to project.	You can add words or details that befit the tone or replace ones that are unsatisfactory.
10. Your point of view toward the topic may be inconsistent or lacking in emphasis.	Remove information that does not reflect your worldview, or add words and ideas that do.
11. Your sentences are so dull or uninteresting that they provoke boredom or tedium.	You can combine sentences, subordinate one to another, or vary sentence structure.
12. Your words may be dull or ambiguous, so that their meanings become obscure.	Replace dull or ambiguous words with terms that are graphic and concrete, respectively.

Step 4: Proofreading Your Second Draft

Now that you have written your second draft, you need to find and correct possible errors in grammar, usage, punctuation, capitalization, spelling, etc. This step in the writing process is called **proofreading**. The reading and marking of corrections on your second draft demand special attention to details, which you cultivate with practice.

The best way to approach this step is to put your paper aside for another day or two. When you pick it up again, you will be able to catch errors more readily. One technique you may employ is placing a piece of paper below the line that you are proofreading. This will force your eye to not skip ahead and miss an error. Read your second draft more than once in this fashion, and you will be surprised at how many mistakes you come across.

Learn to approach proofreading with a critical eye. Question everything that you have put on paper. Answering the following questions will help you in the proofreading process:

1. Is every sentence written as a complete thought?

2. Are all punctuation marks correct, including end-of-sentence punctuation?

3. Are all appropriate words (*proper nouns, first words in sentences, etc.*) capitalized?

4. Do all subjects and verbs agree in number?

5. Are all verb forms and tenses correct?

6. Are all personal pronouns in both nominative and objective cases correct?

7. Does every pronoun agree with its antecedent in number and gender?

8. Are frequently misused words, such as *lie* and *lay*, used correctly?

9. Are all words spelled correctly according to standard (*American, British, etc.*) usage?

10. Is your paper clean, neat, and free of any markings or erasures?

Step 5: Writing Your Final Draft

The remaining step in the writing process is to prepare the final draft. This version should reflect all the revisions and corrections that you have made to the text. There are many ways in which to ready your final draft, but for our purposes the following guidelines will serve as the standard by which your essay should be written.

Guidelines for Writing the Final Draft
1. If you are writing your essay by hand, use standard lined composition paper. If you are using a word processor or computer, use 8 1/2 by 11-inch white paper.
2. Write, type, or print on only one side of each sheet of paper.
3. Write in black or blue ink. If typing or printing, use black ink and double-space each line.
4. Your margins should be about one inch from each side of the paper, and the text should be aligned along the left-hand side of the paper.
5. The first line of every paragraph should be indented about one-half inch.
6. Your name should be aligned to the left, one inch from the top of the first page; then your teacher's name, course title, and date appear—each on a separate line, double-spaced; below this, center the title, which is also double-spaced. The text follows immediately.
7. Each page should be numbered in the upper right-hand corner, one-half inch from the top.
8. You should write as clearly and neatly as possible. If you are typing, do not type or strike over letters or words. If you are using a word processor or computer, finalize all changes and corrections before printing.
9. Your final draft needs to be proofread carefully to make sure no errors have crept in as you hand-copied, typed, or electronically changed your manuscript.
10. If necessary, rewrite or retype your paper without any mistakes.

LESSON 11: UNIT REVIEW

✎ **EXERCISE** Fill in the blanks.

1. The _____ process precedes the _____ process.

2. The key to effective writing is _____.

3. Writing involves an _____ process which includes using your mind, making

    decisions, and organizing your thoughts _____ you write them down in a
    meaningful and orderly way.

4. What are the five ways in which your raw material may be arranged?

    a. _____   d. _____

    b. _____   e. _____

    c. _____

5. List the four basic writing goals.

    a. _____   c. _____

    b. _____   d. _____

6. Expository writing explains an idea, gives a definition, _____

    _____, or _____ in a detailed manner.

7. Descriptive writing describes a _____, _____, or _____.

8. _____ writing tries to persuade or convince.

9. List the four stages of argumentative writing.

    a. _____   c. _____

    b. _____   d. _____

10. When considering your audience, what four questions must you answer?

    a. _____   c. _____

    b. _____   d. _____

11. A _____ is an unrestricted, familiar area of knowledge.

12. A limited subject is called the _____.

13. The point of view that you bring to your writing is called your _____.

14. The attitude that you bring to your writing is called _____.

15. The most basic means of gathering raw material for a topic is through _____.

16. Name three ways in which you may generate specific details to support your topic:

   a. _____   b. _____

   c. _____

17. Raw material may be classified in what four ways?

   a. _____   c. _____

   b. _____   d. _____

18. What are the five questions that must be answered during the *thinking process?*

   a. _____   d. _____

   b. _____   e. _____

   c. _____   _____

19. A paragraph is defined as the _____ _____ of the main idea.

20. Name the four parts of an effective paragraph.

   a. _____   c. _____

   b. _____   d. _____

21. The _____ _____ is the conscious determination of the writer to make every part of his writing move in *one* direction and conform to *one* clear intention.

22. A topic _____ is an expression or mental construction of the main idea.

23. The _____ sentence creates *unity* within the paragraph because it expresses the central thought among the sentences of the paragraph.

24. _____ sentences develop or expand the main idea of the paragraph.

25. The _____ sentence rounds off the discussion of the paragraph's topic, giving the reader a sense of completeness and closure.

26. List the nine ways in which a paragraph's topic may be developed.

   a. _____   f. _____

   b. _____   g. _____

   c. _____   h. _____

   d. _____   i. _____

   e. _____

27. What is meant by *paragraph unity*? What is one thing unity does *not* mean?

    _____

    _____

    _____

28. Name three main kinds of progression that show orderly sentence arrangement in a paragraph.

    a. _____   c. _____

    b. _____

29. Explain the difference between *inductive* and *deductive* logical order.

    _____

    _____

    _____

    _____

30. Normally, what is the most effective position for the most important sentence in a paragraph?

    _____

31. What is meant by *proportion* in paragraph and composition writing?

    _____

    _____

    _____

    _____

32. What is meant by the term *transition* in paragraph and composition writing?

    _____

    _____

    _____

33. What are the two kinds of resources that the writer needs to control?

    a. _____   b. _____

34. What are the five steps in writing a composition?

    a. _____   d. _____

    b. _____   e. _____

    c. _____

Unit 2
Writing a
Research Paper

INTRODUCTION

Now that you have examined the *thinking process* and developed a sound *writing strategy*, you will have the opportunity to apply these principles to composing a research paper. The goal of writing a research paper is **expository**, because it reveals information or explains. As stated in Unit 1, this kind of writing *gives reasons for something happening, presents facts on how something works, explains an idea,* or *gives a definition* in a detailed manner. This writing project is basically different from the first essay you wrote in length and depth. In this unit, you will learn how to **research** and **write** your paper. First we will look at what a research paper *is* and *is not.*[9]

LESSON 12: WHAT IS A RESEARCH PAPER?

■ *What a Research Paper Is*

It has been said that writing a research paper is much like the task of a sculptor who takes a massive block of stone and chisels it into a work of art. As the writer gathers information and begins to chip away extraneous data, he begins to sculpt his large block of research into a **creative composition**. A research paper is *creative* because it is the student's own thoughts presented in written form; it is a *composition* because a research paper deals with a limited topic that is based on information gathered from documents, books, periodicals, interviews with experts, as well as various electronic resources.

Donald Davidson defines a **research paper** as follows:

> The research paper ... is a long expository essay or article which represents the results of systematic inquiry into the facts.... The research paper is an answer to two questions: (1) What are the facts? (2) What do the facts mean? These two questions, when properly understood, fuse into one question: **What is the truth?** [*Bold italics added for emphasis.*] For facts rightly interpreted are the truth.... The research paper demands of [the student], first, careful and diligent inquiry into the facts; second, accurate recording and reporting of the facts; third, inclusion of enough facts to make the discussion complete within its limits; fourth, honesty and clarity in interpretation of the facts.[10]

Therefore, a research paper is basically **an in-depth expository essay** in which you investigate a specific issue or problem, analyze what the experts have to say on the topic, and then make an evaluation of your findings. The problem or issue you choose to focus on is usually related to a broader historical, political, social, literary, or scientific context. Your task is to write an expanded expository essay that informs or explains.

---

9. This unit has been adapted from the booklet *Writing a Research Paper* (Arlington Heights, IL: Christian Liberty Press, 1998). The library research section from the booklet has been included in the teacher's manual.

10. Donald Davidson, *American Composition and Rhetoric* (Chicago: Charles Scribner's Sons, 1939) 454–456.

■ *What a Research Paper Is Not*

Keep in mind that a research paper is a *creative composition*. It is a **composition** in that it requires *communicating information about a limited topic*; that is, information gathered from documents, books, periodicals, interviews with experts, as well as various electronic resources. It is **creative** in that it requires the student *to convey this information in his or her own thoughts or words*.

Some students, however, miss the point and freely copy the words of others and present them as their own! This is called *plagiarism*—not creative composition.

Students have also been known to copy complete articles from encyclopedias, to copy extended sections of books, and even download entire papers from the Internet and submit them as if these papers were their own. Sometimes, parents have been known to "help" their children to the point of writing papers for them. This does not aid students in mastering the research process or in learning the skill of writing their own papers. *Research and writing are learned through personal experience and honest labor*—not by plagiarizing or letting someone else do the work for you.

One student submitted a paper that was nothing more than a series of paragraphs copied from a single book. The student rearranged a few words in each paragraph and cited the source, believing that such an action was the same as *paraphrasing*. Not a single paragraph in the paper represented the student's own thinking, and the student never used quotation marks at any time. Was this a research paper? No! This was **plagiarism**.

To make matters worse, the student falsely cited some of the paragraphs as coming from other sources, intending to deceive the reader into believing that the "research" covered more sources than it actually did. Such dishonest behavior is unacceptable for anyone, but especially Christians.

What is Plagiarism?

Plagiarism and *documentation* are related issues in that the former has to do with honesty in presenting your findings, and the latter has to do with how to honestly give credit to those you have cited. *Plagiarism* is the act of taking the ideas of someone else and passing them off as your own. Even if you paraphrase or summarize the words of an author, you have to cite your source to avoid plagiarism. Plagiarism is a serious offense, which most educators and institutions have recognized—but few speak about why it is blatantly wrong.

As a Christian, you should uphold the highest standard. The eighth commandment explicitly declares that stealing is sin; accordingly, *plagiarism is the sin of stealing the ideas of another person and presenting them as one's own*. In other words, if you plagiarize, you are lying about the source of your information and deceiving your readers into believing that the ideas you present are your own. When you plagiarize, you sin first against God and second against others—thus breaking the two greatest commandments (Mark 12:30–31), the sum of the Law.[11]

To Paraphrase or Not To Paraphrase?

As mentioned above, a student thought that copying an entire paper from one book, citing the source, and changing a few words in each paragraph was not plagiarizing. This student, however, missed the whole point of the research and writing process. First of all, submitting an entire paper that "paraphrases" the ideas of another is not a research paper—it is plagiarism. *Writing a research paper should be the creative work of the student*, presenting *his* thoughts on a limited topic about which *he* has studied and drawn *his own* conclusions.

Second, changing a few words in a paragraph is not paraphrasing—this is plagiarism. *Paraphrasing*, by definition, is restating the ideas of another *in your own words* for the sake of clarity. This method of supporting a topic should be used **sparingly**, not throughout the whole paper.

---

11. For more information on plagiarism and how to avoid it, visit Indiana University's Web page on this topic at <http://www.indiana.edu/~wts/wts/plagiarism.html>.

For what is the purpose of merely repeating the ideas of others? You should simply tell your audience to read these authors for themselves—not just rephrase their ideas. In other words, you are not adding anything new to a particular topic; you are only being repetitious.

✎ **EXERCISE A** Write a paragraph on what a research paper *is* and *is not*. Be sure to include some of the pitfalls students should avoid when writing a research paper.

_____

_____

_____

_____

_____

_____

_____

_____

_____

_____

_____

_____

_____

_____

_____

_____

_____

_____

_____

HOW TO AVOID PLAGIARISM

We dare not fall into the trap of plagiarism, but should always give credit where credit is due, which brings us to the second issue—*documentation*. Whether you are making a direct quotation, paraphrasing, or simply reiterating someone else's thoughts, you must cite the source of that information. The question arises, though, "Should I use footnotes, endnotes, or parenthetical notes?" Obviously, your course requirements should be followed explicitly; however, the standard which is now widely accepted is *parenthetical documentation*.

■ *Parenthetical Documentation*

What is *parenthetical documentation*? It is the means of citing a source in the body of a paper, as opposed to placing notes at the bottom of the page (footnotes) or at the end of the paper (endnotes). For example, if I were citing Ron Fry's delightful book *Improve Your Writing*, I would simply put his last name followed by the appropriate page numbers of the citation in parentheses: (Fry 82–90). If you wanted to know more about the source, you could turn to the "Works Cited" page at the end of the paper for full bibliographical information on Fry's book.

Parenthetical documentation will be covered in detail later, but it has been introduced here for three reasons: (1) when doing your research, you should obtain the proper information for citing your sources as you go along; (2) if you are having someone else type your paper, you need to find a typist who knows this style of documentation, and you should make plans to do so now; and (3) when you begin to write your paper, you should immediately begin to document your paper accordingly.

The Modern Language Association (MLA) style is more or less the standard for documenting research papers at most undergraduate institutions today. The MLA style uses parenthetical notes for documentation and "Works Cited" pages for bibliographical information. If you have any questions regarding this style, be sure to consult a research manual that teaches the MLA style of documentation.[12]

✎ **EXERCISE B** From your local library, check out a manual that teaches the MLA style of documentation and start reading through it. You may want to purchase a copy for future reference.

LESSON 13: WHERE DO I BEGIN?

Your mind may be flooded with many questions: How do I start? What topic should I pick? Where am I going to find information to support my topic? How do I analyze the information I find? How am I going to arrange my material and write this paper? How should I cite my sources in the paper? These and other questions may seem overwhelming, but there is hope. If you have a plan, you will be able to conquer not only your fears or questions but your assignment as well. The following steps will help you in reaching your objective.

TWELVE STEPS TO WRITING A RESEARCH PAPER

1. **Select** and **limit your topic.**

2. Carry out your **initial library research.** Gather your resources and prepare a "Works Cited" page.

3. Determine what your **thesis statement, limiting ideas,** and **audience** are going to be.

4. Write out your **thesis statement** and **general outline.**

5. Do **detailed library research** by reading and taking notes. (If necessary, revise your initial thesis statement and outline.)

6. Prepare a **detailed outline** from your note cards.

---

12. The standard for this style is based on Joseph Gibaldi's *The MLA Style Manual and Guide to Scholarly Publishing* (2nd., 1998) and his *MLA Handbook for Writers of Research Papers* (5th ed., 1999), which has been adapted for high school and college students. Other useful manuals that use the MLA style are Jeannette A. Woodward's *Writing Research Papers: Investigating Resources in Cyberspace* (1997) and James D. Lester's *Writing Research Papers: A Complete Guide, Eighth Edition* (1996).

7.   Write your **first draft**.

8.   Do **additional research** if necessary.

9.   Edit and write your **second draft**.

10. **Type the paper**, including parenthetical notes.

11. Check spelling and **proofread** your work. (Have someone else proofread your paper, if at all possible.)

12. Produce the **final draft**.

These twelve steps will be covered in this unit; however, when you research a topic and publish your findings, you will not necessarily follow the exact steps outlined above. Most likely, you will not follow each step in sequence either; rather, you will move ahead and then return to a former step and then move forward again. Often a looping pattern develops, where latter steps may be launched before certain previous steps, and former steps are revisited. The key is to *be flexible as your research proceeds*.

Since some papers do not require the same amount of attention as others, you must learn to *prioritize your writing assignments*—giving the most important ones the greatest effort. The length of your assigned papers will also determine which ones you tackle first. BEWARE: A five-page project on some obscure topic may take as much time to write as a twenty-page paper on a more familiar one. In either case, you need to *schedule your time to meet the deadline*. If you miss the deadline, your grade will be affected accordingly.

Usually your instructor or the instructions for the course will give you a list of requirements[13] for writing your paper:

➤   Choice of topics

➤   Length of the report

➤   Style of documentation to be used

➤   Requisites for doing a "Works Cited" page

➤   How the paper is to be presented

➤   Whether the topic has to be approved, an outline needs to be submitted, or note cards are required to be handed in

➤   If there is any penalty for submitting a late paper

AN EIGHT-WEEK PLAN

Let's say your research paper is due eight weeks from now; then *you should establish goals for each week*. Set aside the first week to select and limit a topic. During the second week, find various sources and prepare a functional "Works Cited" page. Reserve the third and fourth weeks for preparing the preliminary outline, reading your sources, and taking notes. Block out two or more hours at set times to do this library research.

During the fifth and sixth weeks, finish gathering sources and taking notes, detail your outline, and write the first draft. Schedule week seven for editing and rewriting your work, and preparing your final "Works Cited" page. When all is said and done, proofread and type the final copy in the eighth week. Typing the paper yourself will save time.

The following *eight-week plan* will help you in mapping out what you have to do and when you have to do it. This plan may also be adapted as you see fit. Using your time wisely is the key to success. REMEMBER: Writing a good paper takes time, so plan ahead.

---

13.   For specific requirements for submitting a research paper, consult page 6 of the teacher's manual.

✎ **EXERCISE** Photocopy the *eight-week plan* below. Get out your calendar and fill in the projected dates for each step of the process. As a rule of thumb, plan to spend half of your time on **research** and the other half on **writing**.

Weeks One and Two

➢ Contact a typist by _____. (Do not wait until the last minute or you may not find someone available. Be sure that your typist knows the MLA style sheet.)

➢ Select your general topic by _____.

➢ Complete your initial research by _____.

➢ Prepare a functional "Works Cited" page by _____.

Weeks Three and Four

➢ Finalize a workable topic by _____.

➢ Write your thesis statement by _____. (Include this statement in your paper.)

➢ Develop your general outline by _____.

➢ Gather the majority of your research material by _____.

Weeks Five and Six

➢ Finish gathering your research material by _____.

➢ Compose your final outline by _____. (Include this outline in your paper.)

➢ Write your first draft by _____.

➢ Lay aside your work for a couple of days.

➢ Reread your first draft, making any notes on the draft in regard to additions or deletions, by _____. (Save this marked-up draft. You may have to submit it with your paper.)

➢ Write your second draft by _____.

➢ Lay your paper aside for another two days.

➢ Read your second draft out loud or have a relative or friend do so for you by _____.

➢ Make any final changes. Check sentences for clearness, transitions for effectiveness, mechanics, and spelling by _____.

Weeks Seven and Eight

➢ Compose the final draft by _____.

➢ Proofread by _____.

➢ Type the final draft by _____. (Be sure your typist has plenty of time to type your paper, including the "Works Cited" page, and knows the required style.)

➢ Proofread by _____. (This is your responsibility. Do not depend on your typist to do this for you—*you will be sorry*.)

➢ Type the "Works Cited" page by _____.

➢ Submit your paper by _____.

LESSON 14: SELECTING AND LIMITING YOUR TOPIC

STEP ONE

The first step in writing a research paper answers the following questions: "What is my goal in writing?" "What is my topic?" and "What is my stance toward the topic?" This is the initial part of the **thinking process**. Later, the *topic* will be honed through the development of the *thesis statement* in Steps Three and Four. Step Three will also address "Who is my audience?"

Subsequently, "How am I going to support my topic?" will be answered during the **research process**. This includes the development of the *outline* (Steps Four and Six) for your paper, *detailed library research* (Step Five), and any *additional research* (Step Eight) that is required. In the remaining steps, you will learn how to develop a sensible **writing strategy**.

■ *The Thinking Process*

As you move along in the thinking process, approach each question critically. Analyzing every possible answer will help you focus your thoughts. As you answer the five questions, keep in mind your main goal—*expository writing*. To keep track of your progress, write the following list on a separate piece of paper and fill in the appropriate information as you go:

1.	Your Goal:	*Expository—*
2.	Your Main Idea:	Subject—
		Topic—
3.	Your Stance:	Worldview—
		Tone—
4.	Your Audience:	Who are your readers?
		What do they know?
		What don't they know?
		What kind of language do they use?
		What biases or convictions do they hold?
5.	Your Raw Material:	Gathering Information—
		Classifying Information—
		Arranging Information—

■ *What Is My Goal, Topic, and Stance?*

Question One: What is my goal?

"What is my goal in writing?" is the first question you must answer. This is relatively straightforward, since **expository writing** is the goal of writing a research paper. Granted, you will want to use descriptive language, but exposition is your main goal.

Question Two: What is my topic?

Now, you need to select the **subject** you are going to tackle for this assignment. The challenge, though, is deciding what you want to say about your subject. The subject is quite broad and the thoughts that you have may be vague and shapeless. Therefore, your objective is to give your collection of ideas a significant form. You cannot say everything, so *select ideas that will best represent your subject*—those ideas that actually go together to make a unified whole.

Next, you need to limit your subject to come up with a **workable topic**. Remember that the *main idea* is the conscious determination of the writer to make every part of his writing move in *one* direction and conform to *one* clear intention. What facts, information, and concepts will you highlight? What is it that you want people to know about your topic that they never knew before? After you make your decision, ***write a clear topic statement*** on your paper.[14]

Question Three: What is my stance toward the topic?

As a Christian, your **worldview** most certainly will have an impact on what you write and how you write about your topic. Carefully examine your topic statement and determine how your faith, belief system, or point of view will affect your approach to the topic, the selection of raw material, the classification and arrangement of that material, and the writing process.

The **tone** of your essay is another matter to decide before you begin to write. Depending on your subject material, you may choose to give your writing a lighter touch by bringing out some humorous incidents that would bare on the topic. However, if you are writing about a weighty issue, a more somber approach would be appropriate. REMEMBER: The tone will affect the details you include and the language you use.

✎ **EXERCISE** Write the five questions involved in the *thinking process* on a piece of paper; you may use the list form on the previous page. Begin to fill in the appropriate information as you go along.

LESSON 15: INITIAL LIBRARY RESEARCH

STEP TWO

Now that you have completed the initial thinking process, you are ready to begin the **research process**. As mentioned before, this process takes place over several steps, and you may decide not to follow these steps in the exact order. A looping pattern often develops, where latter steps may be launched before certain previous steps, and former steps are revisited.

Note: The key is to *be flexible* as your research proceeds.

Carrying out your **initial library research** involves going to the library and beginning to locate and evaluate promising sources that will support your topic.[15] As you find sources that are useful, you need to record accurate bibliographical information on each of them. This is accomplished by filling out bibliography cards, as shown by the sample card at the right. Each source will have its own card, numbered in the upper right-hand corner.

	1
Garlock, Frank & Kurt Woetzel
Music in the Balance
Greenville, SC: Majesty Music, Inc., 1992
G GARLOCK, F
City Public Library; non-fiction

Before you set out to the library, be sure to write your **topic statement** on a three-by-five card. Refer to it often as you do your research. Also, bring a pen and several blank cards to record bibliographical information on each source you may want to use in your paper. Use a pen instead of a pencil because ink is less likely to smear as you continually go through the cards. Bring your journal or notebook as well to write down other information that might be helpful.

14. For more specific ideas on selecting and limiting your topic, refer to the teacher's manual, pages 7–8.

15. For information on how to use the library, refer to the teacher's manual, pages 9–12.

■ *Locating Sources*

When you arrive at the library, start at the *reference desk*. The local library staff is very helpful and should be consulted if you have any questions. Next, familiarize yourself with the layout and resources of your library, and begin to look for material that will support your topic. You may want to read a short background article from an encyclopedia about your topic. Often there is a selected bibliography at the end of the article which can help you get started.

Jot down these and other sources that may become part of a *working bibliography*. Skim the card catalog, the *Reader's Guide to Periodical Literature*, or other publication indexes to discover books, magazines, or journal articles that relate to your topic. Likewise, check the *Essay and General Literature Index* to find essays, articles, and speeches contained in collected works. Additional resources may be found in a **bibliography of bibliographies**—a list of source material in all the various fields of knowledge. You may also want to consult the On-line Public Access Catalog (OPAC) for other sources that look promising.

You have now collected several titles of sources that may help you in researching your topic. With your written list or computer printout, go to the section of the library where the sources are located, and review their content by skimming through the books and articles that you have chosen. If you find a source that looks promising, fill out a bibliography card on it.

■ *Evaluating Sources*

After you have selected several promising sources, it is important to evaluate each of them. Remember that your worldview will play an important part in this *evaluation process*. Knowing the backgrounds, qualifications, and worldviews of each author will also help you to determine the value of your prospective sources. Likewise, the date of publication may also indicate the usefulness of a particular source, depending on the focus of your topic.

Use the following steps for your assessment:

a. Determine if the author is well qualified on your topic and note if the publisher is also a reliable source. Check the date of the work to see if there is any significance to it. For instance, a book on world affairs published in 1992 may not have up-to-date information on your topic. In addition, look over the table of contents and skim parts of the text that may be beneficial for your research.

b. You may want to consult an index such as the *Book Review Digest* to help you evaluate the reliability of the author. The *Book Review Digest* lists book reviews which are contained in a variety of periodicals and journals. Each entry holds excerpts from several reviews to give readers a balance of opinions.

c. At the bottom of each bibliography card, jot down a reminder so you will be able to recall the value of that particular source. Note the library or location in the library where you found the source as well.

d. Review all the sources you have gathered, evaluating their usefulness. Remove any sources that are definitely inferior or unrelated to your topic. Well-chosen sources will be used in limiting your thesis statement, which will control your research and writing.

■ *Preparing a "Works Cited" Page*

Now that you have located and evaluated your sources, they need to be recorded for your "Works Cited" page. This is accomplished by writing **bibliography cards**, which are simply three-by-five inch cards that contain basic bibliographical information on each source. When writing out bibliography cards, you need to follow some basic guidelines. You need to include the following information on each new source:

1. Author's full name
2. Title of your source
3. Publication information
4. Call number
5. Notation of where you acquired the source

In the upper right corner, start numbering your bibliography cards beginning with the Arabic numeral one (1), like on the sample card on page 44. This will allow you to cross-reference your *note cards* to their source information. In this way, you will not have to rewrite the same information every time you fill out a note card. If you decide you do not need a particular source, simply discard that bibliography card and any corresponding note cards.[16]

Completely and accurately fill out a three-by-five card on each source. If you do this right the first time, you will not waste time retracing your steps. REMEMBER: Include the author's name, title of the source, publication information, call number, and any notation that would be helpful. Do not forget to number each source card in the upper right-hand corner sequentially.

With these bibliography cards, you are ready to create a *functional "Works Cited" page*. If you have properly gathered all the necessary information, this task will be straightforward. On a separate piece of paper, list the authors in alphabetical order according to their last names. Next, the titles of the sources are designated. Finally, the publication information is given, including the city, publisher, and date.[17] Study the sample "Works Cited" page below.

Works Cited

American Diabetes Association. Diabetes Factsheet. Alexandria: ADA, 1998.

- - - . Medical Management of Non-Insulin Dependent (Type II) Diabetes. 3rd ed. Alexandria: ADA, 1994.

Center for Disease Control and Prevention. National Diabetes Fact Sheet. Atlanta: CDC, 1998.

Goodyear, L. J., and R. J. Smith. "Exercise and Diabetes." Joslin's Diabetes Mellitus. Ed. C. R. Kahn and G. C. Weir. 13th ed. Philadelphia: Lea & Febinger, 1994. 451–459.

Quickel, Jr., K. E. "Economic and Social Costs of Diabetes." Joslin's Diabetes Mellitus. Ed. C. R. Kahn and G. C. Weir. 13th ed. Philadelphia: Lea & Febinger, 1994. 568–604.

"Diabetes." Taber's Cyclopedic Medical Dictionary. 13th ed. 1981.

Valentine, V. "Nursing Role in Management: Patient with Diabetes." Medical-Surgical Nursing: Assessment and Management of Clinical Problems. Ed. S. M. Lewis, I. C. Collier, and M. M. Heitkemper. 4th ed. St. Louis: Mosby Yearbook, 1996. 1438–1475.

✎ **EXERCISE** Do your *initial library research*. Evaluate each source you find and record any that look promising on three-by-five bibliography cards. Then create a functional "Works Cited" page.

---

16. Do not renumber your *bibliography cards*, otherwise you will have to renumber your *note cards*.

17. NOTE: *Periods* are used after each part of the bibliographic information—author, title, publication data, and page numbers. *Commas* are used after the first author's last name, between subsequent authors of the same source, and between the publisher's name and the year of publication. *Colons* are used after the city of publication only. Additionally, the titles of the sources are either underlined or italicized, depending on the equipment you use to type your work.

LESSON 16: FOCUS YOUR THOUGHTS

STEP THREE

Now that you have done your initial library research, it's time to *focus your thoughts* by writing a *thesis statement*, developing your *limiting questions*, and considering your *audience*. These factors will help guide you as you research and write your paper. Under "Developing Your Limiting Questions," you will begin to organize your thoughts by answering *"the five W's and the H."* In addition, the **fourth question** in the thinking process will be addressed—*Who is my audience?*

■ *Writing Your Thesis Statement*

First, you should develop a tentative **thesis statement**—a sentence, or paragraph, stating the central idea of your research paper. This statement is tentative because it may not be your final topic sentence. As your research proceeds, you will be able to write a more accurate statement. Submit your thesis statement to your teacher, or a qualified person, who will give you the kind of feedback you need. *Your thesis statement is the most important tool in writing a research paper.*

State your thesis in a single, precise sentence. Remember, this statement has three important functions: (1) to express the main point of the report, (2) to explain to your reader your stance toward the topic, and (3) to propose the path that your paper will follow. This statement will help you focus on your topic, locate appropriate materials, and guide your reading. Your thesis statement needs to be included at the beginning of your paper under the outline title.[18]

✎ **EXERCISE A** Write out your *thesis statement* as directed above. Consult your instructor, or someone who is qualified, for any help you may need.

■ *Developing Your Limiting Questions*

Writing **limiting questions** is an often overlooked aspect that is crucial to the research process. To formulate a good research plan, ask yourself, "What questions would I like to have answered about my topic?" Start with "the five W's and the H": *Who? What? Where? When? Why?* and *How?* These questions will lead you to the main points you will cover in your paper.

☞**EXAMPLE:**

Suppose your topic is "Ways to Use the Sun Rather Than Conventional Fuels." The following questions might be used as a guide to your research: What scientific principles does a solar house use? What is the best design which applies these principles? What other designs are possible? Where is the use of a solar house most practical? How efficient is a solar house?

After preparing your questions, examine them to be sure that they ask the things you want to explore in your paper. Do not worry if you have too many questions. Some questions may be combined into one, and others may be eliminated altogether. REMEMBER: Your questions are a starting point in your research—not simply questions that could be answered *yes* or *no*.

These questions form a **working plan** that will guide your research. As you progress, though, you may come up with new questions which should also be covered in your paper. Be flexible and change your plan. But do not work without a plan, or you will find out too late that you wasted valuable time gathering information that may be useless or answers the wrong questions.

✎ **EXERCISE B** Write out your *limiting questions* as directed above. Consult your instructor, or someone who is qualified, for any help you may need.

---

18. For more information on writing a thesis statement, visit <http://www.indiana.edu/~wts/wts/thesis.html>.

■ *Determining Your Audience*

After you have formulated your thesis statement and limiting questions, you should determine what *audience* you want to address. It is important to identify your readers, since they are going to be the recipients of your findings, analysis, and conclusions.

Question Four: Who is my audience?

Here, the fourth question in the *thinking process* is addressed. The answer to this question, however, may not be as obvious as you might think. First, you need to ask who your audience is going to be: A group of peers? Your teacher or mentor? Your 4-H Club? Your science class? You also need to realize that, for a research paper, the language you use should be more formal than that used for other compositions. Moreover, *all terms must be defined*, since no prior knowledge of the subject can be assumed. Your wording and content will be affected, as well.

You need to consider the following factors:

➢ What they know or do not know

➢ Background information they need to learn

➢ Terms or technical data they need to have explained

➢ Complexity of language they can handle

➢ Biases or convictions they may hold

All these factors determine *what* you present and *how* you present it.

✎ **EXERCISE C** Determine who your readers are going to be and the type of language and content you will need to use in your paper. Refer back to Unit 1, page 6, for more information.

LESSON 17: PREPARE A GENERAL OUTLINE

STEP FOUR

Step four involves preparing a *general outline*. Begin by jotting down various ideas you plan to investigate about your topic. You should use your limiting questions to guide you in this process. *Brainstorming* and *clustering* are two other ways of organizing these thoughts. After listing your thoughts, eliminate any ideas that are not related to your thesis statement.

Next, group the subordinate ideas under several main headings and make the preliminary outline. While you are taking notes, make as many changes as necessary to this general outline by inserting new ideas and removing nonessential ones. This outline will require considerable modification before you will be able to base your paper on it.

■ *Crafting an Outline*

First, however, we will look at *how to craft an outline*. As a blueprint is needed for a builder to construct a house, so an outline is needed for a writer to craft a composition. No writer can hold an audience's attention unless he knows what he is talking about, so be sure that you make an outline whenever you sit down to write.

Use the following rules to make your outline. Notice that rules 1–3 have already been discussed. They are included here, though, to show the overall process involved in creating an outline:

1. **Select a topic.** Choose one that is not too broad to be adequately covered in the allotted space or time. Narrow the topic to a manageable size.

2. **Write out a thesis statement** explaining how you are going to tackle your topic.

3. **Make a list of ideas that support your topic.** Compare each idea with your thesis statement, and cross off any unrelated or dubious thoughts.

4. **Choose the main headings** from your list or your creative thought processes. Refer to your thesis statement as your guide. *Group the subordinate ideas under the main headings.* Determine what the subheadings and supporting details are going to be, then arrange them in some kind of order.

5. **Use Roman numerals** (I, II, III, etc.) *to highlight main ideas*, which are written in a similar way. The best approach is to compose a complete sentence, or a concise phrase. Capitalize the first letter at the beginning of each sentence or phrase.

6. **Use capital letters** (A, B, C, etc.) *to indicate each of the subtopics*, which are indented under the Roman numerals. Normally, there should be at least two subheadings under each main idea. The introduction and conclusion, however, may or may not have subtopics listed.

7. **Use Arabic numerals** (1, 2, 3, etc.) *to mark off the details under each subtopic*, which are indented under the capital letters. Often, there should be at least two supporting details for every subheading. Many subtopics, though, do not need to have any details listed.

8. **Arrange the main ideas in a logical order** (chronologically, spatially, or in the order of their importance). Your outline needs to reflect a unified and coherent plan of execution.

Your outline serves as a ***road map*** for getting you to your desired destination. It is a logical exercise toward that end—cutting through your own confusion about the topic. Your "road map" will also vary depending on your subject matter. Your itinerary may follow an historical progression, a comparative analysis, or a thematic development.

In any case, your outline will always cover three main sections: the **introduction**, the **body**, and the **conclusion**. Save the introduction and conclusion for last, and concentrate on the body of your paper, using your outline as a tool to get you where you want to go. Hopefully, you will lead your audience to the same destination. (*For a sample outline, see page 64.*)

Question Five: How am I going to support my topic?

The fifth question in the ***thinking process*** involves selecting the details that will support your topic. The best method of gathering this data is by *brainstorming*, which will help you list possible ideas about your topic. Before you begin, you may need to do some library research to obtain a better grasp on the topic. At this point, do not be worried about classifying or arranging your raw material, just write whatever comes to mind.

As your ideas begin to flow, you may see a pattern developing that suddenly comes to the fore. If you have written down all you know or have discovered about your topic, start selecting various details that reveal more about your topic. As you go along, eliminate any extraneous information and try to make a general outline of the material you have collected. After that, you will be ready to arrange your raw material into some kind of order.

■ *Brainstorming*

The best method of organizing your thoughts for developing your general outline is *brainstorming*—the free flow of ideas that may be used as the specific details which support your topic. In this method of gathering raw material, write down every word, phrase, or concept that comes to mind as you focus your thoughts on your topic. Let your imagination "run wild," jotting down every idea that crosses your mind. Do not stop until you have exhausted all possibilities. By the time you are finished, you will have a long list of words or phrases.

After generating your list, evaluate the items you have written down. Begin by circling or marking those items which seem to best support your topic. You may see certain patterns or related ideas coming together. Note any such developments next to the list.

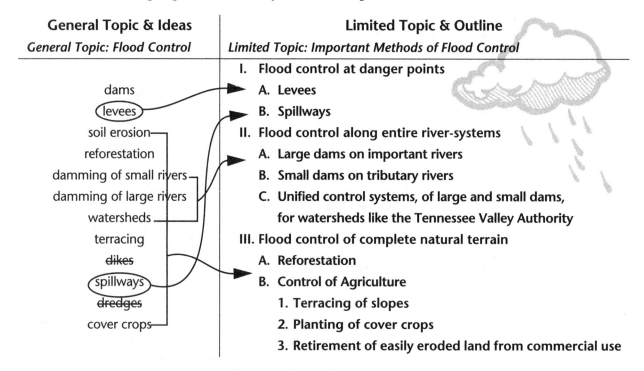

General Topic & Ideas	**Limited Topic & Outline**
General Topic: Flood Control	*Limited Topic: Important Methods of Flood Control*

I.   Flood control at danger points
    A. Levees
    B. Spillways

II. Flood control along entire river-systems
    A. Large dams on important rivers
    B. Small dams on tributary rivers
    C. Unified control systems, of large and small dams,
        for watersheds like the Tennessee Valley Authority

III. Flood control of complete natural terrain
    A. Reforestation
    B. Control of Agriculture
        1. Terracing of slopes
        2. Planting of cover crops
        3. Retirement of easily eroded land from commercial use

General Topic ideas list: dams, levees, soil erosion, reforestation, damming of small rivers, damming of large rivers, watersheds, terracing, dikes, spillways, dredges, cover crops

Diagram 1 — Brainstorming

Brainstorming will help you generate a list of ideas which may be used to support your topic. Observe that the broad area of interest (i.e., "flood control") was narrowed down to a manageable topic—"important methods of flood control." Then certain ideas were grouped together or eliminated completely. The grouped ideas were then put into outline form.

■ *Clustering*

Another method of organizing your thoughts is *clustering*, which is similar to brainstorming, except that the free flow of ideas is placed in a diagram instead of a list. This is called clustering because certain specific ideas "cluster" around more general items called *controlling ideas*, which then "cluster" around the *limited topic*, or thesis statement.

First the *limited topic* is written in the center of a paper and a circle drawn around it. As new ideas come to mind, they are added and circled; then connecting lines are drawn from them to the topic or other related ideas on the diagram. As new ideas are added, certain *controlling ideas* will emerge having various subordinate ideas connected to them.

The following diagram uses the information from the previous brainstorming section to show how clustering these ideas would look in a diagram.

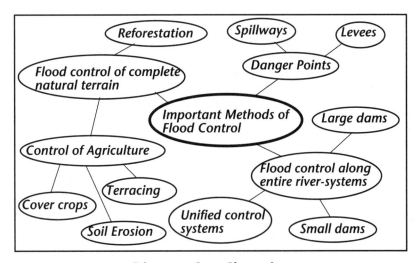

Diagram 2 — Clustering

In the diagram above, the topic was placed in the center of the diagram so the other ideas could easily be connected to it. Notice that the controlling ideas are connected directly to the topic and all subordinating ideas are connected to them. The "clustering" of ideas gives you a definite picture of how your specific ideas relate to your topic and how they may fit into your writing.

✎ **EXERCISE** Craft a *general outline* using the brainstorming or clustering method. Be sure to follow the eight rules for making an outline on page 49.

LESSON 18: IN-DEPTH RESEARCH

STEP FIVE

Step five tackles your ***detailed library research***—reading and taking notes. This is where you will spend the bulk of your research time, using blank index cards. Four-by-six cards should be used to write out *one* idea, quote, or fact per card. This way, your three-by-five bibliography cards will not be confused with your larger note cards. This step also involves the revision of your initial *thesis statement* and *general outline*, if your research leads you to do so.

■ *Writing Note Cards*

The mechanics of note taking is simple but crucial to understand before you start your detailed library research. You should begin by using ***note cards***, each of which should contain one note that corresponds to only one outline heading. If you are going to use the same information for another heading, write out a duplicate card.

When writing note cards, the outline heading should be placed in the upper left corner of the card for easy reading. Below the heading, write if it is a quote, paraphrase, etc. In the upper right corner, record the source and page number(s) where you found the information. Use a separate card for each note, and try not to carry over a note onto a second card. If you do, staple them together. Also, do not write on the back of cards; if you must, write "OVER" in bold letters.

Contemporary "Christian" Music	Garlock 1
(quote)	p. 75

"Note the trend. Today the melody (spiritual part) and harmony (the emotional-intellectual part) is not only overshadowed, but nearly smothered out of existence by the overpowering, pulsating rhythm (physical part). We have become obsessed with the physical; and our music, secular and even sacred, reflects that obsession."

Notice the number 1 in the upper right corner. It corresponds to the number 1 on the bibliography card prepared for the source of this quotation (*See page 44*). "Garlock" refers to the author, and should always be placed before the number of the corresponding bibliography card.

■ *Beginning Detailed Library Research*

With this background in note taking, you are ready to begin your ***detailed library research***. You should read and comprehend your source material *before* you start taking notes. You need to begin by doing a lot of reading in several sources. Choose as many different kinds of sources as possible. The more you know, the easier it will be to formulate your thoughts and take notes.

Becoming Familiar with Your Source Material

At this point, reading and ***grasping the "big-picture"*** of each source is your main objective. Check the title page, the table of contents, and the basic structure of the source. Look for the hints the author(s) gives along the way—chapter headings, subheadings, pictures, and sections that are set apart. Bibliographies may also be helpful in finding other source material.

Going over the basic outline of a book and skimming over promising portions can go a long way in developing an overall perspective of what the author is trying to say. If your source has any charts, tables, diagrams, maps, or illustrations, use them to increase your understanding of the material. They often clarify difficult concepts that cannot be easily depicted in words.

Reading Your Source Material

Upon completing these preliminary steps, the actual ***reading of the source material*** will move along quickly. Now you should begin to carefully read portions that relate to your topic. Do not try to read an entire book on your topic, but only those sections that are relevant. Use small Post-it notes to mark places where you may want to take notes.

While you are doing your research, you should constantly be on guard about what you are reading. First, be aware of the *presuppositions* (or underlying belief systems) of your sources. Many writers and publishers do not view the Bible as authoritative, so you must continually ask yourself, "Is this in line with God's Word?" (Proverbs 3:5–7, Psalm 119:128).

Second, be cautious of writers who mix biblical truth with man's reasoning. Such authors accept human ideas uncritically. The Bible may even be used as a basis for their arguments, but their underlying presuppositions are worldly. For example, "progressive creationists" claim to have a high view of God's Word, but they essentially hold to a "threshold evolutionary" worldview.

Third, be wary of certain studies by writers who state findings based on quasi research which supposedly supports their arguments. Do not be misled—such studies frequently are erroneous, misleading, or interpreted incorrectly. Above all, remember that everything you read must pass through the "filter" of God's Word. Pray that the Holy Spirit will guide you to the truth.

As you read source material for your paper, you should keep in mind the following guidelines:

➢ Initially, read general background material that is easily understood.

➢ Do not accept or believe everything you find. Learn to read critically.

➢ Gradually work your way up to more scholarly works.

➢ Check the credentials and reliability of your various sources.

➢ Look for evidence or justification for the author's ideas.

✎ **EXERCISE A** Become familiar with your source material. Then begin to read it carefully, marking promising passages for taking notes.

■ *Note Taking on Research Material*

Careful reading and ***note taking*** are crucial in gathering good research data. Taking good notes does take effort, but not necessarily much time. The goal here is to organize the important points from a particular source in such a way that you can easily understand the material at a glance, increase your retention of its content, and think clearly about your topic.

Taking Concise, Useful Notes

It is better not to write in complete sentences when you take notes, unless you are quoting or paraphrasing an author. Simply capture the principal ideas in key words or phrases, then place the most important supporting details under them. Remember that you only want to write one note per card for each outline heading.

To make ***concise, useful notes***, ask the following questions:

➤ What are the most important points that have emerged while I was reading?

➤ What information must I look for that will support my thesis statement?

➤ What are the important theories or concepts from other sources that are explained or expanded on in this source?

Summarizing, Paraphrasing, or Quoting

As you take notes you should either ***summarize, paraphrase***, or ***quote*** directly from your sources. Any and all of these ideas must be documented when they appear in your paper. Remember, failure to give credit where credit is due is called *plagiarism*—the act of taking ideas or writings of someone else and passing them off as your own.

If you choose to summarize or paraphrase most of your notes, your paper will flow easily, but direct quotes will take a little more effort. If you decide to use quotations, limit them to three or four. Enclose these excerpts within quotations marks, if they are within the body of the text. If the quote is more than forty words, put it in a block quote and indent one half inch from the left margin. Make sure that you copy the quotation accurately, following all punctuation, capitalization, and exact spelling as it appears in your source.

Omitting Certain Words in a Quotation

At times you may want to omit certain words from a quotation which do not bear directly on your thesis statement. Use dots or ***ellipsis points*** to indicate that these words have been omitted. Three dots with a space before and after each period are used within a sentence to show an omission, while four spaced dots are used for the last part of a sentence, the first part of the next sentence, or a whole sentence or paragraph which has been deleted.

Note: As you take notes and become more familiar with your topic, you may want to incorporate or delete certain ideas on your *general outline* or make changes to your *thesis statement*. Occasionally, sort through your *note cards*, placing each note under its proper outline heading so you will be able to determine areas you may have neglected or overemphasized; again, make the proper adjustments.

✎ **EXERCISE B** Begin your detailed library research, starting with your reading first. After you have a good grasp of your material, start taking notes.

LESSON 19: PREPARE A DETAILED OUTLINE

STEP SIX

By Step Six you will be ready to prepare a ***detailed outline*** from your note cards. After you have established the accuracy of your preliminary or general outline, make sure that the points are in the best order. Since you want your work to flow logically, orderliness becomes a vital aspect of the research process. This will pay dividends in the writing phase of your project.

Place your note cards in the right sequence under their appropriate outline headings, and take a few moments to read through them from front to back. This will become the approximate draft of your paper. Now you are ready to create your detailed outline—written in precise, logical order. If necessary, refer back to Step Four to review the eight rules of making an outline.

✎ **EXERCISE** Prepare your detailed outline from the information you have gathered in the notes you have taken during your library research.

LESSON 20: WRITE YOUR FIRST DRAFT

STEP SEVEN

The next major phase of writing a research paper begins with Step Seven—writing the ***first draft*** of your paper. This step may be easier than you might think. If you have taken good notes, organized them properly, and developed a well-organized outline, then your first draft will flow quite easily. Find a quiet spot where you can begin to write.

Use a large work space that is free of all distractions. Your desk or table should be well lit, so you can easily read your note cards and write your rough draft. If at all possible, use a computer or word processor. This will aid you when you reach Step Nine—the revision and editing stage. Remember, write fast and furiously. Get your thoughts down on paper, and do not forget to identify your sources. Do not worry about finding the right word, using the correct grammar, or placing the proper punctuation. All those concerns will come later.

✎ **EXERCISE** Organize your note cards according to your detailed outline, then begin to write!

LESSON 21: DO ADDITIONAL RESEARCH

STEP EIGHT

Step Eight involves ***additional research***. After the first draft is completed, you may realize that some points do not quite fit, or information is lacking under a certain heading. Here you must return to the library or your sources at hand. You will have to return to Step Five and follow the guidelines on reading and note-taking. Be sure to carefully examine your outline to see where any changes should be made so your research will not be in vain. Go over your limiting questions as well, making sure that this additional research fits into your overall research plan.

✎ **EXERCISE** Examine what you have written in light of your thesis statement, limiting questions, audience, and detailed outline. If necessary, do additional research.

LESSON 22: EDIT THE FIRST DRAFT AND WRITE THE SECOND

STEP NINE

Step Nine will take some time because you are ready to edit the first draft and write the **second draft**. First, you improve the flow of your paper by organizing your thoughts better, clarifying foggy concepts, and strengthening weak arguments. After that, you proofread your paper.

■ *Improving the Flow of Your Paper*

Initially, you need to focus on any problem areas, and make editorial changes as you deem necessary. Ask yourself, "Is my paper complete and in good order?" You should also check for *oneness, cohesion*, and the proper *stress*. As you **rewrite your composition**, determine whether the work is complete or not. As you take on the role of *editor*, ask yourself these five questions:

➤ Is everything I need included?

➤ Are all the parts in the proper order?

➤ Is the paper unified, with all extraneous details removed?

➤ Do the thoughts flow smoothly from one paragraph to the next?

➤ Has each part been developed at an appropriate length in proportion to its importance?

You should continue to rewrite your paper until you have complied with the above five questions. When you are completely satisfied with the second draft, assume the role of *proofreader*.

■ *Proofreading Your Paper*

Here, you will tackle each sentence for **correctness**, **grammar**, and **mechanics**. The phrases also need to be examined for the proper figure of speech and expression of idiom. Eliminate inappropriate jargon, trite phrases, and wordiness or redundancies. In formal writing, you should eliminate any use of the first person and any use of contractions. Check to see that your verbs are bright and alive, and that your nouns are specific and direct. Above all, see that your words are used in an appropriate way—*particularly in regard to your audience*.

Make sure all words are spelled correctly, as well. If you are using a computer or word processor, you may use the spell check function to correct your work. BEWARE: This feature is limited in scope and cannot tell the difference between such words as "by" and "buy." After all the changes have been made, you will be ready for the next step.

✎ **EXERCISE** Carefully go over your paper to improve its flow and clarity. When you have answered the five questions positively, begin to edit and rewrite your work. Next, proofread your paper.

LESSON 23: TYPING YOUR FINAL DRAFT

STEP TEN

Step Ten is **typing** your final draft. If you are not typing the paper yourself, now is the time to submit your paper to a typist. In either case, you should use white, twenty-pound, 8 1/2-by-11-inch paper. (NOTE: Erasable bond is not acceptable.) Standard pica is preferable, but elite is also accepted. Do not use any "script" or fancy type styles which are hard to read and inappropriate for this kind of work. A fresh black ribbon in your typewriter, or a good cartridge in your printer, goes a long way in producing a sharp, clean paper.

Any inserted lines, strikethroughs, or crossed-out letters should be completely eliminated. Corrections should be made properly with liquid paper or some kind of self-correcting device on your typewriter. Obviously, corrections done on a word processor or personal computer can easily be made prior to your paper being printed. You may also check to see if photocopies are acceptable, because these are often better than the original—especially if the copier is of the highest quality, such as those found at a printer or professional copy shop.

■ *Laying Out Your Research Paper*

The *layout of your paper* can get quite involved, but refer to the *MLA Handbook for Writers of Research Papers* (5th Edition, 1999) or visit the MLA Web site at <http://www.mla.org/style/ style_index.htm> for any questions that might arise. This style has become the standard for many colleges and universities. Therefore, **the MLA style is required for your paper.**[19]

Since the *The MLA Handbook* does not require a title page, you must type your name, your teacher's name, the course title, and the date (day, month, year) in the upper left corner of the first page of your paper. Your name should be one inch from the top of the page, and the rest of the information double-spaced. Below this, center the title of your paper, which also should be double-spaced. Your last name and the page number is placed in the upper right corner of each page—one-half inch from the top of the page and one inch from the right. (*See page 65.*)

The text of your paper should be double-spaced and have one inch margins on the top, bottom, and right and left sides of your paper. Refer to the *MLA Handbook* for any additional parts that may be required or for additional documentation questions that are not covered in the next section.

■ *Documenting Your Sources*

Parenthetical notes are an important aspect of a well-documented paper. When citing a particular source in your paper, put in parentheses the author's last name and the page number(s) from the source where the information was taken. This parenthetical note is placed after the material that has been cited.

Likewise, when quoting an author directly, use quotation marks before and after the direct quote but before the parenthetical note. If you use the author's name in the text of your paper, then simply put the page number(s) in parentheses after the quote or paraphrase. Be sure to document each quote, paraphrase, or summary in your paper, without exception.

Citing material from Vic Lockman's *The Dietary Laws of the Bible* would appear as follows:

☞**EXAMPLES:**

> Romans 14 infers that "all things" are edible. Biblically, "all" refers to things that are *clean*, for *unclean* things never are edible (Leviticus 11). Compare "all things are lawful." Paul obviously means all *lawful* things, for *unlawful* things never are lawful (Lockman 71–82).
>
> "… God's laws of health and morality … have always been universal in scope and they continue so (Jer. 50:14; I Tim. 1:8–10). To flaunt them is to despise God's righteous reign and governance of our lives" (Lockman 70).
>
> Lockman vividly reveals why pork is prohibited by God for human consumption (52–54).

Note: The parenthetical information comes *before* the end punctuation.

---

19. This does not mean that other styles of documentation are specious, but the MLA style is mandatory.

Citing Multiple Works by the Same Author

What do you do, however, when you need to cite more than one work by the same author? Let's say you are citing material on the killing of unborn children from Harold O. J. Brown's two works entitled *The Reconstruction of the Republic* and *Death before Birth*. In this case, your documentation would include the author's last name, a comma, a truncated version of the title, and the page number(s) placed in parentheses: (Brown, Reconstruction 122–123).

Whenever you are referencing material and mentioning the author's name in the same sentence or paragraph of your paper, put only the truncated title and page number(s) in parentheses: (Reconstruction 122–123). If both the author and the title of the source are named in the text, simply put the page number(s) in parentheses: (122–123).

Citing Sources with Two or More Authors

If your source has two authors, put both last names joined by *and*, followed by the page number(s), in parentheses. For example, if you were quoting from *Fearfully and Wonderfully Made* by Dr. Paul Brand and Philip Yancey, cite it as follows: (Brand and Yancey 125). If there are three authors, cite it like this: (Smith, Wilson, and Jones 537). If there are four or more authors, only the first author's name appears plus *et al.*, and the page number(s): (Wilson et al. 777).

At times, you may have two or more sources by authors with the same last name. If this is the case, cite each source with the author's first initial and last name: (A. Smith 179). If two different authors have the same last name and first initial, then include both the author's first and last names: (Adam Smith 57).

Citing Sources without an Author's Name

Some sources may not have an author named. If it has a "group" author such as an association, corporation, or government agency, use the complete name or a shortened form: (INTELSAT 45). Observe that in this parenthetical note the term "INTELSAT" stands for the International Communications Satellite Organization. If only the title of a source is available, use the full title or a shortened version and be sure to underline the title: (King and Country 57).

When citing other print or non-print sources, these basic patterns apply to your parenthetical notes. The bibliographical entries on the "Works Cited" page is where you will find variations. If you come across an unusual or complicated citation, however, refer to the latest edition of the *MLA Handbook for Writers of Research Papers* or an up-to-date manual that uses the MLA style.

✎ **EXERCISE A** Type your paper using the guidelines above. If someone else is typing your paper, make sure your typist is familiar with the MLA style. This step may take several days.

■ *Creating the "Works Cited" Page*

The *Works Cited* page, which lists only the sources referenced in the paper, appears at the end of your paper and begins on a new page. As in the rest of the paper, type your last name followed by the page number in the upper right corner. The margins also conform to the general guidelines used in the body of the text. Next, center the title "Works Cited" one inch from the top of the page. Between the title and first line of the entries you should double-space.

Next, arrange your bibliography cards in alphabetical order. The first word that appears on each card will be the author's last name or the first word in the title of the source, except for *a, an,* and *the.* Single-space each entry; between entries use double-spacing. The first line of each entry is flush with the left margin, and subsequent lines are indented five spaces, or one-half inch.

You should make your ***bibliographical data*** as brief as possible, without neglecting any important information your reader might need to locate the source. The following two sections cover the basic MLA formats used for *books, periodicals, non-print material,* and *Internet sources.*

Basic MLA Format for Listing Books and Other Non-periodical Publications

➢ Name of the author(s)

➢ Title of a part of a source (chapter, article, etc.), if any

➢ Title of the source

➢ Names of the editor(s), translator(s), or compiler(s), if any

➢ Edition used

➢ Number of the volume(s) used, if from a series

➢ Name of the series, if any

➢ City of publication (use the first city, if several are listed)

➢ Name of Publisher(s)

➢ Year of publication

➢ Page number(s)[20]

➢ Additional information (e.g., internet documentation)

➢ Annotations

If there is ***one author***, list his name in inverted order with a period after his name; then list the title of the source followed by a period, and then the publication information.

MODEL:

Elton, G. R. <u>The Tudor Constitution</u>. Cambridge: Cambridge UP, 1962.

If there are ***two authors***, place the first author's name in inverted order, followed by a comma and the conjunction *and,* then the second name in normal order followed by a period; then add the underlined title, followed by a period, and the publication information.

MODEL:

Ponicke, Sir F. Murice, and E. B. Fryde. <u>Handbook of British Chronology</u>. 2nd ed. London: Royal Historical Society, 1961.

If there are ***three authors***, list their names as with two authors joining the last two with *and.* If there are ***four or more authors*** or ***editors***, list the first one, inverted, followed by *et al.* Place a period after the complete author information has been given.

In the title, only the main words are capitalized, except when *a, an,* or *the* comes at the beginning of the title or subtitle. Underline the title and add a period.[21] This is followed by the publication information, which includes the city of publication,[22] a colon, the publisher's name (which may be shortened, if identifiable), a comma, the year of publication, and then a period.

---

20. Use only if citing an article, essay, poem, etc. from an anthology or some other collection; give the page numbers of the entire piece being cited.

21. The underlining of book titles is preferred by the MLA guidelines; however, you may choose to italicize them instead.

22. For cities outside the United States, add an abbreviation of the country, or the province of Canada, when the cities are unfamiliar or ambiguous.

If you are citing *two or more books by the same author*, list his name in the first entry only. After that, in place of the name, type three hyphens, with spaces after each hyphen, followed by a period. Then add the title of the book and the publication information.

MODEL:

Bainton, Roland H. <u>Here I Stand</u>. Nashville: Abingdon, 1950.

- - - . <u>The Reformation of the Sixteenth Century</u>. Boston: Beacon, 1952.

If you are citing a *compilation or anthology*, list the name of the compiler and/or editor in inverted order, followed by a comma and *comp.* or *ed.* where applicable; then list the title of the source, and then the publication information.

MODEL:

Clouse, Robert G., ed. <u>The Meaning of the Millennium: Four Views</u>. Downers Grove: InterVarsity, 1977.

If there is a *corporate author*, such as the Center for Disease Control and Prevention, list it followed by a period; then list the title of the source and the publication information.

MODEL:

Center for Disease Control and Prevention. <u>National Diabetes Fact Sheet</u>. Atlanta: CDC, 1998.

If you are citing an *article or entry from a reference book*, such as an encyclopedia or dictionary, first list the author of the article in inverted order; then give the title of the entry being cited, which is usually enclosed with quotation marks; and then add the title of the source, the edition (if given), and the year of publication. If no author is given, first list the entry being cited (with quotation marks); then the title of the source, the edition (if given), and the year of publication.[23]

MODELS:

"Diabetes." <u>Taber's Cyclopedic Medical Dictionary</u>. 13th ed. 1981.

Rookmaaker, H. R. "Art and the Spirit." <u>Eerdmans' Handbook to the History of Christianity</u>. 1977.

If you are citing *two or more volumes of a multivolume work*, list the author (or editor), the title of the work, the editor (if not mentioned before), and the edition (if given); then add the *total* number of volumes ("10 vols.") in the work, followed by a period; finally, add the publication information.[24] If you are citing only one volume of a multivolume work, only list the number of the volume ("Vol. 3") and the publication information for that volume.

MODELS:

Paton, John G. <u>John G. Paton, Missionary to the New Hebrides: An Autobiography</u>. Ed. James Paton. 2 vols. New York, 1889.[25]

Hodge, Charles. <u>Systematic Theology</u>. Vol. 3. New York, 1872.

Calvin, John. <u>Calvin: Institutes of the Christian Religion In Two Volumes</u>. Ed. John T. McNeill. Trans. Ford Lewis Battles. Philadelphia: Westminster, 1960.

23. If entries are listed alphabetically in the encyclopedia or dictionary, the volume and page numbers are not needed. Note that full publication information is also not necessary, if the reference work is well-known.

24. Note that the specific volume and page numbers of a multivolume work are cited in the text, not on the "Works Cited" page.

25. Note that if a book was published before 1900, simply list the city of publication, add a comma instead of a colon, then list the publication year.

MLA Format for Periodicals

➤ Name of the author(s)

➤ Title of the article

➤ Name of the periodical

➤ Number or name of the series, if any

➤ Number of the volume

➤ Number of the issue, if necessary (*See footnote 12.*)

➤ Year of publication (in parentheses): page number(s)[26]

➤ Additional information (e.g., *late ed.: C+*, for a newspaper)

MODELS:

Fleming, Kenneth C. "The Gospel to the Urban Zulu: Three Cultures in Conflict." Evangelical Missions
    Quarterly. *22 (1986): 24–31.*

Packer, J. R. "Children of a Larger God." Leadership: A Practical Journal for Church Leaders. *19.3 (1998): 108–*
    113.[27]

Dreazen, Yochi J. "Job Losses Suggest Economy May be Slowing." Wall Street Journal 5 June 2000: A2.[28]

MLA Format for Non-Print Sources

➤ An interview:

Lindstrom, Dr. Paul. Personal interview. 4 April 1998.

➤ A film or video:

Attenborough, Richard, dir. Gandhi. Perf. Ben Kinsley. Columbia Pictures, 1982.

➤ A radio or television program:

Oregon: A House Divided. Narr. and prod. Jim Leinfelder. OPB. KOPB, Portland, OR. 25 Sept. 1994.

➤ A CD-ROM:

Williams, T. Harry. The Military Leadership of the North and South. U.S. History on CD-ROM. Parsippany, NJ:
    Bureau Development, 1990.

➤ An audio recording:

Frost, Robert. "The Road Not Taken." Robert Frost Reads His Poetry. Caedmon, TC 1060, 1956.

---

26. Pagination is normally continuous in an annual volume of a journal.

27. If the pages are numbered separately in each issue, then add the issue number as follows: 19.3 (meaning volume and
    then the issue number).

28. Note that newspapers require full date.

MLA Format for Internet Sources

Guidelines for documenting Internet sources are plentiful, but Janice Walker laid the groundwork in 1994 with her *Walker/ACW Style Sheet*, which was endorsed by the Alliance for Computers and Writing. Later Walker and Todd Taylor expanded the original style sheet into a comprehensive guide called *The Columbia Guide to Online Style*. Visit their Web site at <http://www.columbia.edu/cu/cup/cgos/idx_basic.html>.

Andrew Harnack and Gene Kleppinger have improved on Walker's style sheet in their exceptional book *Online! A Reference Guide to Using Internet Sources*. Visit their Web site (<http://www.bedfordstmartins.com/online/cite5.html>), or MLA's Web site (<http://www.mla.org/www_mla_org/style/style_index.asp?mode=section> and click on "Frequently Asked Questions," then click on "How do I document sources from the World Wide Web in my works-cited list?") for specific models of various Internet citations.

Various Internet Sources

1. Web sites

2. E-mail messages

3. Web discussion forum postings

4. Listserv messages

5. Newsgroup messages

6. Real-time/synchronous communications

7. Telnet Sites

8. FTP (File Transfer Protocol) sites

9. Gopher sites

10. Linkage data

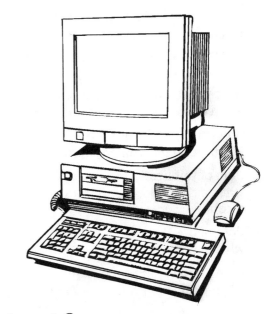

Basic Referencing for Internet Sources

Referencing Internet documents, messages, or communications can be very complex, but you can simplify your work by using the following checklist. Include only the documentation that applies to the particular Internet source you are citing. Below each item, an indented paragraph specifies which Internet source(s) requires that piece of information.

➤ name of author, editor (*ed.*), etc. (if known), last name first
  when citing any of the Internet sources listed above, except **real-time/synchronous** [MOOs, MUDs, ICR, etc.] communications

➤ name of speaker(s) (if known), or name of site
  when citing a **real-time/synchronous** communication

➤ the author's e-mail address, enclosed in angle brackets (< >) [NOTE: do not underline][29]
  when citing an **e-mail**, **listserv**, or **newsgroup** message; or a posting to a **Web discussion forum**

---

29. An underlined e-mail address or URL on the Web means that it is an active hypertext link. Therefore, do not underline it on your "Works Cited" page.

➤ various source titles

   ✦ full title of document, in quotation marks (" ")
     when citing a document from a **Web, telnet, FTP,** or **gopher** site; or when citing a specific **linkage data** file or data found in a **"frame"** in a sizable Web document

   ✦ title of complete work (if applicable), in *italics* or <u>underlined</u>
     when citing a book or magazine from a **Web** or **telnet** site

   ✦ the subject line or title of posting, in quotation marks (" ")
     when citing an **e-mail, listserv,** or **newsgroup** message; or a posting to a **Web discussion forum**

   ✦ type of message (if appropriate)
     when citing a posting to a **Web discussion forum**

   ✦ title of event (if applicable), in quotation marks (" ")
     when citing a **real-time/synchronous** communication

   ✦ type of communication, if not stated elsewhere in entry
     when citing an **e-mail** message (e.g., personal e-mail, distribution list, or office communication) or a **real-time/synchronous** communication (e.g., group discussion or personal interview)

➤ name of editor, compiler, or translator (if applicable and not cited earlier), preceded by *Ed., Comp.,* or *Trans.,* respectively

➤ site description (if applicable)
  when citing a document from a **Web** site

➤ "lkd." (i.e, "linked from") and the title of the document to which the file is linked, in *italics* or <u>underlined</u>, and any additional linkage information (if applicable), precede by "at"
  when citing a specific **linkage data** file or data found in a **"frame"** in a sizable Web document

➤ any print publication information, *italicized* or <u>underlined</u> where appropriate
  when citing a document from an **FTP** or **gopher** site

➤ date of publication or last revision (if known)
  when citing a document from any Internet source, except for a **real-time/synchronous** communication

➤ date of event
  when citing a **real-time/synchronous** communication

➤ date of access in parentheses
  when citing a document from any Internet source

➤ URL, in angle brackets (< >) [NOTE: do not underline][29]
  when citing a document from a **Web** or **gopher** site, or a posting to a **Web discussion forum**; or listing a source document for a specific **linkage data** file

For documenting address information for **listserv** and **newsgroup** messages, **real-time/synchronous** communications, and **telnet** and **FTP** sites consult *Online! A Reference Guide to Using Internet Sources* by Andrew Harnack and Eugene Kleppinger (Bedford/St. Martin's, 1998). This book gives models for documenting such sources using the MLA style sheet. For more information you may visit their *Online!* site at <http://www.bedfordstmartins.com/online/cite5.html>.

Two other helpful reference works are *The Columbia Guide to Online Style* (Columbia UP, 1998), by Janice Walker and Todd Taylor, and *Electronic Styles: A Handbook for Citing Electronic Information* (Information Today, Inc., 1996), by Xai Li and Nancy Crane. The standard, of course, is Modern Language Association's style manual entitled *MLA Handbook for Writers of Research Papers* (5th Edition, MLA, 1999). Visit their site at <http://www.mla.org/style/style_index.htm>.

✎ **EXERCISE B** Carefully prepare your bibliographical information and type your "Works Cited" page following the MLA style. If you are using a typist, be sure he follows these guidelines.

LESSON 24: PROOFREAD YOUR PAPER

STEP ELEVEN

Step Eleven covers **proofreading** of your work. Do not carelessly skip this important step. Glaring mistakes in spelling, grammar, or punctuation do not reflect well on your abilities, nor do they benefit your final grade. Consult your dictionary, thesaurus, grammar handbook, or any other reference that will help in the process of checking for errors.

Carefully examine each typed page with your original manuscript to see if any portion was overlooked. Proofread every word, phrase, sentence, and paragraph for proper usage: spelling, clarity, oneness, cohesion, stress, order, grammar, and mechanics. REMEMBER: *You* will be held accountable for the final product, not your typist.

You may use the spell check function on your word processor or computer to check your spelling, but do not rely completely on this program feature. The dictionaries used in these programs are not exhaustive and will not differentiate between words such as "there" and "their," or any time that the typographical error forms a real word, such as "from" versus "form."

You must take the proper measures to scrutinize every letter, mark, and word so no errors will slip by. It is best to *seek out a good proofreader* such as a parent, relative, or friend who can go over your paper. Another set of eyes can easily spot certain things you may have missed. The fact is, you are so close to the report that you cannot see these inaccuracies.

✎ **EXERCISE** Proofread your paper carefully, checking for any kind of spelling, grammar, or punctuation errors. Proofread every word, phrase, sentence, and paragraph for proper usage.

LESSON 25: PRODUCE THE FINAL DRAFT

STEP TWELVE

The twelfth step involves incorporating any changes your proofreader has suggested. After this, you will be able to **produce the final draft**. Go over your report one more time—carefully! This is sometimes referred to as the *publication stage*, because you are in essence offering your work to the public. Proofread your final draft at least twice for any errors and make the necessary changes. Perhaps, you may want to go to a local copy shop or printer to have your paper finalized. **It always pays to have some kind of backup copy in case the original is lost or damaged.** Now you are ready to submit your manuscript!

✎ **EXERCISE** Make any necessary changes that you or your proofreader have found. Type your final draft. Submit your paper!

A Sample Research Paper

The following paper was written by Jill Eisnaugle, who fulfilled the requirements of writing a research paper for the Christian Liberty Academy homeschooling program.[30] As you carefully read over Jill's paper, examine her *thesis statement* and determine if she accomplished what she set out to do. Notice that Jill used various sources to support her points and properly employed the MLA style to document her paper.

---

30. This is an example of a good research paper. The content, however, does not necessarily represent the views or the official position of Christian Liberty Academy School System.

Understanding Diabetes and Its Complications

Thesis: Education about diabetes is essential to understanding the disease and preventing its complications.

I. The disease diabetes mellitus

   A. Definition of diabetes

   B. Role of metabolism

      1. Cells

      2. Glucose

   C. Role of insulin

      1. Actions on blood sugar

      2. Production by pancreas

      3. Other related factors

II. Classifications of diabetes

   A. Categories

      1. Type 1

      2. Type 2

   B. Risk factors

   C. Symptoms

III. Components of treatment of diabetes

   A. Nutrition

   B. Exercise

IV. Complications of diabetes

   A. Short term

   B. Long term

V. Importance of education about diabetes

Jill Eisnaugle

Mr. and Mrs. Al Eisnaugle

Senior Research Project

28 December 1998

Understanding Diabetes and Its Complications

An estimated 16 million people in the United States have diabetes—more than one third are not aware they have the disease. This year alone, more than 798,000 cases will be diagnosed. Diabetes is the seventh leading cause of death by disease in the United States; this year alone, more than 187,000 Americans will die from this disease and its complications (CDC). Education about diabetes is essential to understanding the disease and preventing its complications.

Diabetes mellitus is a chronic, systemic disturbance in the metabolism of carbohydrates, protein, and fat (ADA, Medical Management 3). The term *diabetes* derives from the Greek word which means "to go through a siphon." Thus diabetes refers to the overproduction of urine known as polyuria. *Mellitus* comes from the Latin word *mel* (honey) and describes the sweet odor of the urine (Taber's 396). Diabetes occurs when the beta cells of the pancreas fail to produce or secrete an adequate amount of insulin. Diabetes also affects the vascular and nervous systems.

In order to understand diabetes, it is important to understand how we normally metabolize food. Our bodies are composed of millions of cells, and in order to function, these cells must create energy. This energy comes from glucose. Glucose is mainly obtained from food.

When we eat, food enters the digestive system and is broken down into glucose. The three components from which glucose is made are carbohydrates, proteins, and fats. Carbohydrates convert 100% into glucose; protein converts 50–60%; and fat converts 10% (ADA, Medical Management 12).

Eisnaugle 2

Once food is broken down into glucose, it can be absorbed in the blood and carried to the cells of the body. However, for glucose to enter the cells, insulin must be present.

Insulin is a hormone that regulates the entire absorption process. It acts like a key that can unlock the doors of the cells. Cells have receptor sites, like keyholes, that receive insulin. When insulin attaches to a receptor site, a passageway is created that enables glucose to enter the cell. Once glucose is absorbed in this manner, it can be immediately used for the release of energy or it can be stored as glycogen in the liver and muscle cells for future use. Excess glucose is converted into fat. The normal fasting glucose level is 70–100 mg/dl; after meals it is 70–140 mg/dl (ADA, Factsheet).

Diabetes can be the result of several conditions: a complete absence of insulin; an insufficient amount of insulin; and/or a diminished sensitivity of the cells to insulin, called insulin resistance (Valentine 1440). Under any of these conditions, when a meal is eaten there is a less than normal glucose uptake by the tissues. With less glucose entering the cells, less glucose is converted into glycogen.

Insulin keeps the blood glucose levels normal after a meal. When blood glucose levels go up, insulin is released from the pancreas, allowing the cells to absorb more glucose and remove glucose from the bloodstream. To provide the body with glucose during a fasting state, insulin secretion is decreased—forcing cells to break down the stored glycogen into glucose or acquire glucose from non-carbohydrate sources such as amino acids and fats. Breakdown of fats produce the by-product known as ketones (CDC).

Insulin is produced in the pancreas, a vital organ situated behind and below the stomach and weighing about one-half of a pound. Within the pancreas are the Islets of Langerhans which contain three important types of cells: beta cells for producing insulin to lower blood sugar, alpha cells for producing glucagon to raise blood sugar, and delta cells for producing somatastatin that regulates the balance of insulin and glucagon (Valentine 1452). In response to glucose, the normally functioning pancreas can produce unlimited amounts of insulin in 60-90 seconds (Valentine 1454). The action of insulin is also affected by other hormones such as epinephrine, cortisol, and growth hormone. These hormones are typically released for energy during times of stress; they raise blood sugar levels by stimulating the liver to produce glucose and to break down fat. These hormones can also make the body cells resistant to insulin, thus rendering insulin in the bloodstream less effective (Valentine 1454).

If there is an extreme lack of insulin, lipolysis will occur. During lipolysis, fat stores are broken down to provide energy. The by-products of this process are ketone bodies, acids which are poisonous. When ketones build up in the bloodstream, they cause an imbalance in the system which causes ketoacidosis. The build-up of glucose and ketones causes the kidneys to increase filtering in an attempt to rid them from the system. This causes increased thirst and frequent urination commonly experienced by diabetics (CDC).

There are two classifications of diabetes. These are Type 1 and Type 2. In Type 1 diabetes, individuals have no insulin secretion. Therefore they are prone to breaking down fat and having high ketone levels, which requires insulin injections to maintain life. In Type 1 diabetes, the body's immune system destroys the insulin-producing beta cells of the pancreas. Symptoms develop when most of the beta cells are destroyed. It is believed that there is a genetic link to Type 1 diabetes, but there is also some debate as to viruses and environment playing a significant role in the development of this type of diabetes.

Type 2 diabetes occurs when insufficient amounts of insulin are produced. Type 2 diabetics secrete some insulin, but not enough to maintain normal blood glucose levels. Typically, this type of diabetes

Eisnaugle 4

occurs after the age of 45, and there is a family history of diabetes; also, 85% of these diabetics are overweight (Goodyear 452). Type 2 diabetes is treated by diet, exercise, weight loss, and oral medications to lower blood glucose levels. There has been debate as to how Type 2 diabetes begins. It seems unclear whether decreased tissue sensitivity to insulin or impaired beta cell function occurs first. Regardless of which actually comes first, both occur over time in Type 2 diabetes.

The identifying risk factors and high risk groups for developing diabetes include being over 45 years of age; having a parent or sibling with diabetes; having a body weight of more than 20% above ideal; being a Native American, Hispanic, African-American, Asian, or Pacific Islander; having high levels of physical or emotional stress; using certain medications, such as steroids, estrogen, and nicotine; having a history of childbirth producing babies weighing more than 9 pounds; having an elevated blood pressure (greater than 140/90) and elevated serum lipids or triglycerides—HDL less than 35 mg/dl and/or triglycerides greater than 250 mg/dl (CDC).

Because so many people have diabetes and are undiagnosed, it is important not only to identify risk factors, but also become familiar with the symptoms of this disease. The symptoms of Type 1 diabetes usually occur more rapidly and are more noticeable than the symptoms of Type 2 diabetes. In fact, Type 2 diabetics may not experience any typical symptoms because their disease is so slow to develop. The symptoms of diabetes are directly related to the elevated blood glucose and its effects. Symptoms of diabetes include increased thirst; increased frequency and volume of urination; fatigue; increased and/or decreased appetite; rapid unexplained weight loss; abnormal healing of cuts and sores; frequent infections; blurred vision; numbness; and tingling in hands, toes, and feet. There may also be headaches, light-headedness, dizziness, loss of balance; irritability, mood swings, and personality changes; nausea, vomiting, and abdominal pain often with the presence of ketones in the urine; and a fruity odor to the breath from ketones (ADA Factsheet). There is evidence that individuals

can have diabetes seven to eight years before ever being diagnosed with the disease. This allows

retinopathy, circulatory, and renal complications to occur before treatment of the disease is begun.

People with undiagnosed Type 2 diabetes are at higher risk for heart disease, stroke, vascular disease

in the legs, elevations in lipid levels, high blood pressure, and obesity.

Diet plays a key role in managing diabetes. The American Dietary Association recommends that

total calories from carbohydrates be 45–55% of the total diet; about 12–20% should come from

protein. Fat should be individually adjusted. No more than 300 milligrams of cholesterol should be

consumed daily. Fiber should be 25–30 grams daily. No more than 2400–3000 milligrams of sodium

should be ingested daily (ADA, Medical Management 22). Each diabetic should have his diet plan

regulated by a physician or diabetic nutritionist. Most diets are based upon an exchange list plan.

Understanding and following a diabetic diet is central to maintaining control over the disease.

Exercise is also an important part of diabetes management. Regular exercise and physical fitness

can decrease the cardiovascular disease that diabetics and the general population are prone to

developing (Goodyear 454). Exercise can improve insulin sensitivity, resulting in greater glucose usage

and better blood glucose control. It also helps in maintaining a desired body weight, and can improve

the quality of life by decreasing stress levels and improving individual self-esteem. Diabetics should

select an exercise that can be done regularly and is enjoyable. One should start slowly, and gradually

increase the length of exercise. Aerobic exercise provides the greatest benefit to the diabetic by

increasing blood flow, strengthening the heart, and improving blood glucose utilization. Anaerobic

exercise is of little benefit to the diabetic, other than strengthening, because it does not decrease blood

glucose levels. Because aerobic exercise causes blood glucose levels to drop, the diabetic should wait at least one hour after eating before beginning to exercise in order to prevent the symptoms of hypoglycemia (Goodyear 618). Extra food should be eaten before extra activity. Other precautions the diabetic should take when exercising include the following: avoiding vigorous activity when the weather is very hot or very cold; using proper equipment; being sure shoes are well-fitting and examining feet after exercise; maintaining hydration while exercising; and stopping exercise if you feel faint, have pain, or become increasingly short of breath.

There are many complications of diabetes. These include hypoglycemia, retinopathy, nephropathy, and neuropathy. "Hypoglycemia is by far the most common and easily treated complication of diabetes" (CDC). Hypoglycemia occurs when the blood glucose level becomes too low, usually below 70 mg/dl. The actual level where symptoms begin varies from person to person. It can be caused by too much medication, inadequate calorie intake, or in response to exercise. Common early warning symptoms, related to the release of adrenaline in response to the drop in blood sugar, are shakiness, sweating, increased heart rate, pallor, and excessive hunger. At this stage, the diabetic is usually alert and can eat to relieve the symptoms. If the blood glucose level continues to drop, the central nervous system is affected. At this level, there is a decreased level of concentration, confusion, slurred speech, blurred or double vision, a staggering gait and extreme fatigue. At this level, someone might mistake this behavior for someone who is intoxicated. The diabetic at this point may or may not be able to seek help. By the time the hypoglycemia becomes severe, the person experiences loss of consciousness, seizures, and/or the inability to be aroused from sleep and requires another's assistance to seek help.

Retinopathy, nephropathy, and neuropathy are long term complications of untreated or poorly controlled diabetes (ADA, Medical Management 62). The first of these complications is retinopathy.

Among adults, diabetes is the leading cause of new blindness. Persons with poorly controlled diabetes, high blood pressure, or diabetic nephropathy are at an increased risk for developing retinopathy.

Destructive effects are caused by changes in the small vessels of the retina. Damage begins in the capillary walls and the vessels become permeable to some of the blood components. At this point there are no symptoms, but small hemorrhages in the retina can occur. Later, there is further destruction of retinal capillaries and blood flow is decreased. Often even at this point there are no symptoms. In the final stages, retinal vessels become thin and easily bleed. Blood leaks into the vitreous and causes blurring, seeing spots and cobwebs in the field of vision. Early treatment, annual dilated eye exams, control of blood pressure, and stable glucose levels are vital to protecting the diabetic from this complication. Diabetics are also at greater risk for developing cataracts and glaucoma. "After 10–15 years of diabetes, 50–80% of individuals have retinal disease" (Valentine 1471).

Nephropathy is a complication of diabetes that involves the kidney. It is characterized by albumin (protein) in the urine, high blood pressure, and progressive renal insufficiency. "It is the most common cause of new cases of end-stage renal disease" (ADA, Medical Management 65). Within three years of developing Type 1 diabetes, there is an increase in kidney size, weight, and filtration rate. Mild presence of albumin in the urine, and slight elevations in the serum BUN (blood, urea, nitrogen) levels and creatinine are present if the blood glucose level is poorly controlled. After 10 to 15 years, the first laboratory evidence of renal impairment may be present. The prevalence of hypertension greatly increases the progression to nephropathy.

Renal failure occurs in 40% of Type 1 diabetics on the average of about 20 years after diagnosis. For Type 2 diabetes, it is more difficult to select an onset because many other conditions exist concurrently. However, 20% of Type 2 diabetics develop nephropathy (Valentine 1471).

The remaining long term complication of diabetes is diabetic neuropathy. It is extremely common and affects almost half of all individuals who have diabetes. Neuropathy involves abnormalities in the nerve fibers that result in chronic nerve atrophy, injury and blunted nerve regeneration. These conditions are all the result of an elevated blood glucose level's effect upon peripheral nerve tissue, its connective tissue, and vascular components.

The nervous system is divided into the central nervous system and the peripheral nervous system. The peripheral nervous system includes the autonomic and sensorimotor nerves (Valentine 1474). Frequently, sensorimotor neuropathy occurs first in the hands and feet, and then moves upward. Small fiber neuropathy can occur after only a short time, and results in varying degrees of pain and sensory loss, especially loss of temperature and pressure sensation. Large fiber neuropathy often occurs at the same time as small fiber neuropathy, resulting in loss of position sense.

When painful neuropathy develops, the severe pain in the extremities often worsens at night. Treatment is aimed at relieving symptoms. Foot care is important, because there is a lack of feeling in the feet. Problems can develop without the individual being aware of an injury. Daily foot inspection is important to maintain skin integrity (ADA, Medical Management 68).

Diabetes mellitus is a devastating disease that costs nearly $138 billion annually (ADA, Medical Management 91). The staggering statistics make the impact of diabetes clearly evident. On the average, a diabetic's life span is decreased by one third. Even when diabetes, the seventh leading cause of death in the United States, fails to kill, it remains the major cause of new blindness, limb amputations, and frequent hospital stays averaging six weeks/year (Quickel 586). Gaining a better understanding of this disease, its progression, complications, and treatment will help the individual become better able to face this disease with a realistic outlook for the future. Since the initial discovery of insulin, much has changed in the management of diabetes. As research continues, methods of management and monitoring this disease continue to improve. Knowledge about diabetes, its treatment, and research help provide the newly diagnosed and existing diabetics an improved outlook for their future. Because of the complexity and chronic nature of diabetes, it demands daily attention from the individual with the disease. Fortunately, many resources are now available in the community. These may include local hospitals, pharmacies, and the American Diabetes Association. Through support groups, literature, and education, it is estimated that approximately one third of major diabetes complications—such as blindness, kidney disease, and limb amputations—could be prevented by removing avoidable risk factors. Since individuals who seek follow-up care and education about diabetes are four times less likely to develop a major complication, diabetes education remains the most effective way to avoid the serious complications of this disease. The ultimate result of better education about diabetes is an improved quality of life for those individuals with the disease. The key to successfully managing diabetes and its complications lies in gaining a better understanding of this silent killer.

Eisnaugle 10

WORKS CITED

American Diabetes Association. <u>Diabetes Factsheet</u>. Alexandria: American Diabetes Association, 1998.

- - - . <u>Medical Management of Non-Insulin Dependent (Type II) Diabetes</u>. 3rd ed. Alexandria: American Diabetes Association, 1994.

Center for Disease Control and Prevention. <u>National Diabetes Fact Sheet</u>. Atlanta: Center for Disease Control, 1998.

Goodyear, L. J., and R. J. Smith. "Exercise and Diabetes." <u>Joslin's Diabetes Mellitus</u>. Ed. C. R. Kahn and G. C. Weir. 13th ed. Philadelphia: Lea & Febinger, 1994. 451–459.

Quickel, Jr., K. E. "Economic and Social Costs of Diabetes." <u>Joslin's Diabetes Mellitus</u>. Ed. C. R. Kahn and G. C. Weir. 13th ed. Philadelphia: Lea & Febinger, 1994. 568–604.

"Diabetes." <u>Taber's Cyclopedic Medical Dictionary</u>. 13th ed. 1981.

Valentine, V. "Nursing Role in Management: Patient with Diabetes." <u>Medical-Surgical Nursing: Assessment and Management of Clinical Problems</u>. Ed. S. M. Lewis, I. C. Collier, and M. M. Heitkemper. 4th ed. St. Louis: Mosby Yearbook, 1996. 1438–1475.

Unit 3
Writing an
Article of Opinion

INTRODUCTION

Years ago, students prided themselves on speaking well. They studied *rhetoric*—a term which is derived from the Greek word for "orator"; that is, they studied *oratory* or composition that imitated oratory. Today, however, many have dismissed the standards that emphasized *oral* rather than *written* proficiency. In some grammar courses, rhetoric has been abandoned altogether.

At the beginning of the twentieth century, we at least spoke of "composition and rhetoric"—now we merely talk of "composition and grammar." In our study of composition, however, we seek to bring rhetoric back into its rightful position. The basics of logic are introduced in this unit, and informal logic has been interjected throughout. This study will emphasize how composition and rhetoric may be used to express thought persuasively and effectively.

> … We may say that *composition* refers chiefly to structural arrangement, organization, the putting together of parts to make a whole; and that *rhetoric* refers to the skill or artifice used in making composition persuasive and effective. The study of these closely allied subjects rests upon a knowledge of grammar and usage; it must also make full use of the resources of logic.[31]

LESSON 26: THE ARTICLE OF OPINION

Although we still have debating clubs, symposiums, round-table discussions, and town meetings, we rarely have the rhetorical debate that our forefathers relished. Our public discourse is too limited for formal logical development. We hear only news sound bites, 60-second issue ads, or political speeches that have been edited for fast-paced radio or television programs.

Instead of rhetorical debate, though, we do have the ***article of opinion***. It is found in newspapers, magazines, journals, and on the Internet. Over time, we have come to prefer the printed word over the spoken word. This preference is so prevalent that even many speeches resemble the structure of magazine articles; and these speeches are frequently *read* rather than *delivered*. Consequently, this unit will apply the basics of logic as they relate to the article of opinion.

■ *What is an Article of Opinion?*

One of the four basic writing goals is to persuade or convince, that is, ***argumentative writing***. This type of writing *influences, reasons,* or *gives opinions*. If you desire to persuade someone you must take him through the specific steps which you have taken to reach your conclusion. In essence, you are engaging your reader with reasoned arguments that you set forth in writing.

---

31. Davidson, *American Composition and Rhetoric*, 2. Much of the material for Unit 3 has been adapted from Davidson's chapter on "The Article of Opinion" (512–555). These basic principles of writing opinion articles are widely recognized and commonly applied in "composition and grammar" courses. However, they may be arranged in various ways.

An *article of opinion* falls into this category because it expresses the opinion of the author and gives reasons and evidence in support of his opinion. It is a formal essay that deals with a debatable issue in a serious and definitive manner. An article of opinion not only

> deals with facts and with the interpretation of facts, but [also] with the purpose of arguing an issue and expressing an opinion. It hopes to persuade the reader to accept, or at least entertain, the opinion which it expresses. It seeks to convince rather than merely inform.[32]

An article of opinion follows the four stages of argumentative communication. In the *opening stage* the approach is clarified and the "rules of argumentation" agreed upon. The approach is **persuasion** (*see page 4*) and the rules are the **informal guidelines** of customary, polite discussion and of sound logic. In the *confrontation stage*, the debatable issue is clarified. Then the *argumentation stage* gives the reasons and evidence that support the opinion and prove the argument. Finally, the *closing stage* is the point where you achieve your goal.

✎ **EXERCISE** Editorials are brief articles of opinion. Analyze three editorials from newspapers or magazines to find how journalists defend their opinions. Mark the four stages of argumentation.

LESSON 27: SOUNDNESS OF ARGUMENT—PART 1

At the heart of writing an article of opinion are the following two questions: "What is a sound argument?" and "How is a sound argument presented well?" The answers to these questions will be developed in this and subsequent lessons. First, we will look at the *soundness* of an argument; then we will consider the *presentation* (*page 95*) of that argument.

WHAT IS A SOUND ARGUMENT?

A *sound argument* is based on three factors. First, a sound argument needs to have a clear, precise proposition of what you are trying to prove—in essence, a *thesis statement*. Second, a sound argument must be grounded on solid, established facts—that is, *evidence*. Third, a sound argument must be ordered by the laws of thought—in other words, the *rules of logic*. This lesson introduces the first factor of a sound argument.

■ *Writing a Thesis Statement*

As with all compositions, you first need to limit your *subject* to come up with a **workable topic**. The conscious decision of the writer is to make every part of his writing move in *one* direction and conform to *one* clear intention; this is called the *main idea*. When you choose the main idea, or topic, for your article of opinion, you will be ready to formulate your **thesis statement**.

Determining Your Topic

In formal argumentation, a thesis statement is called the **proposition**, or question. It should be a **debatable issue** that allows a reasoned *affirmative* and *negative*—arguments that can be made for and against a topic. Do not choose a topic that is a recognized fact, personal preference, or vague opinion; it must be a clear, precise proposition that is debatable.

Your thesis statement also needs to *express an opinion*—not a fact. A *fact* cannot be debated, because a fact can be verified. An *opinion*, though, is an inference or conviction that can be debated, because it cannot be proved, or tested, like a fact. An opinion is the basis of a reasoned argument that needs to be supported with evidence.

---

32. Ibid., 512–513.

☞**EXAMPLE**

> Abortion should be outlawed because it is the killing of unborn children, who have no choice in the matter—and no legal recourse.

Moreover, your thesis statement, or proposition, may have words that are misunderstood, so these *terms should be defined*. Unless your readers know what is being debated, the argument cannot proceed in a rational manner. In the above example, "abortion," "unborn," and "choice" are three such terms that need to be defined. Note that this proposition also assumes that life begins at conception; this assumption, therefore, has to be verified with evidence, as well.

Why is it important that the terms you use in your thesis statement be understood? If you do not define these terms, your readers may attack the premises of your argument. In addition, they may hold different definitions for these terms, which may create confusion or hinder your argumentation. As a result, you may find that your reasoning is not swaying your audience.

Finally, a thesis statement, or proposition, *needs to be precise*—that is, accurate in grasping and expressing the issues which are to be debated. "[These] issues are the essential points which have to be proved if the question as a whole is to be upheld. It requires some skill to distinguish true issues from false issues." The following exercise will help you discern the issues.[33]

✎ **EXERCISE A** Review the following list of possible issues related to the proposition of whether or not movies should be censored. Check off which questions are *relevant*, *irrelevant*, or may be *combined*. Then list the four main issues which form the basis of the argument.

	Issues Stated in the Form of Questions	Relevant	Irrelevant	Combine
1.	Do the movies need reform?	✔		
2.	Has censorship succeeded or failed in the past?			
3.	Will censorship impair the artistic quality of the movies?			
4.	Will censorship spoil their entertainment value?			
5.	Will it curtail movie admissions and thus harm business?			
6.	Who will do the censoring?			
7.	How will Hollywood react?			
8.	Why don't the movie studios censor themselves?			
9.	Doesn't the public prefer uncensored pictures?			
10.	Is censorship practical?			
11.	Is censorship legal?			
12.	Will it result in social good to the people as a whole?			
13.	Why not wait and see what will happen?			
14.	Will it increase taxes?		✔	

Note: You will win your argument, if you can prove that the movies need reform; that censorship is a practical means of reform; that it will not harm the artistic quality of movies; and that it will result in the social good. You will lose the argument, however, if the opposition can prove these issues are invalid.

---

33. Ibid., 516–517. **Exercise A** is also based on the example from these pages.

✎ **EXERCISE B** Examine the following list of possible thesis statements. Write an *F* if the statement is a fact, *O* if it is an opinion, or *P* if it is a preference. If the statement is an opinion, then underline any terms that need to be defined to make the proposition clear and definite.

1. ___*P*___ The study of art is more interesting than learning about computers.
2. ___*O*___ The <u>government</u> should not fund <u>euthanasia</u> through any <u>entitlement</u> programs.
3. ___*F*___ Homosexuality is condemned in the Bible as sexually deviant behavior.
4. _____ States' Rights was a key factor in the South ceding from the Union.
5. _____ The school year should follow a four-month pattern—three months of study and one month off—repeating the pattern to cover the twelve months of the year.
6. _____ Most doctors in Europe integrate both traditional and alternative medicine, whereas most doctors in the United States still frown upon alternative medical practices.
7. _____ By the age of twenty-six, Tiger Woods had won forty-three tournaments, thirty-one of which were achieved on the PGA Tour.
8. _____ Money spent on entitlements should be used for what government was designed to do—to uphold the Constitution, to maintain civil order, to defend the nation, etc.
9. _____ The Department of Education should be abolished because the federal government has gained excessive control over these state institutions.
10. _____ More students are preferring soccer—i.e., international "football"—over American football since the U.S. team placed in the World Cup.
11. _____ Traveling in the Middle East is more adventuresome than driving in the Indy 500.
12. _____ Followers of Christ should learn to defend their beliefs in the secular arena.
13. _____ C. S. Lewis was one of the most lucid Christian writers of the last century.
14. _____ Christian students should attempt to emulate Lewis's engaging writing style.
15. _____ The dictionary is a "friend" that you should keep close by whenever you write.

Stating Your Topic

Once you have determined what your topic is going to be, then you are ready to **write your thesis statement**. Remember that your proposition must be a *debatable issue*, express an *opinion*, use clearly *defined terms*, and have a *precise understanding of the issues* which are to be debated. Your thesis ought to be stated in a declarative sentence, which generally uses the word *should*.

At times, you may choose a topic that is so complex that you do not know what you believe about it. To gain insight into the issues involved, **do research** at the library or on the Internet to become more familiar with your topic. Current editorials or articles found in newspapers, magazines, or journals are a good place to start. Talking with a knowledgeable person may also help.

After you have formulated your opinion, write an **initial thesis statement** on paper or in your journal. At this point, you will begin to ask yourself: "Is this a debatable issue? Is this an opinion?" If you answer "yes" to these questions, go on and analyze the terms you used. You should ask: "Do any terms need to be defined? Is there a better way of wording my proposition?"

Finally, your thesis statement should reflect an accurate understanding of the issues. You should ask: "Is my proposition precise? How can I make it more specific?" Your topic should also have **a plan of action**: "What do I want my readers to do? Do I want them merely to change their opinion, or should I challenge them to modify their behavior?" Examine the following examples.

☞**EXAMPLES**

1. Our church should do something about reaching out to the community.

2. Our outreach programs should be expanded to meet people's needs in the community.

3. The members of our church should build friendships with their neighbors, plan activities at the Community Center for unchurched kids, and help at the local food pantry.

Which of the above propositions is the most specific? Obviously, the third statement is the most precise—clarifying *what* should be done, *who* should do it, and *where* the outreach should take place. The first two statements are too ambiguous to qualify for a well-written proposition. The following exercises will help to hone your skill at writing a thesis statement.

✎ **EXERCISE C** Write *thesis statements* for the following topics, making them clear and precise. Be sure to include a *plan of action* in each proposition.

1. High school students choosing their own curricula and textbooks

    _____

    _____

2. Capital punishment reform at the federal and state levels

    _____

    _____

3. The abuse of the over-the-counter supplement ephedrine by athletes

    _____

    _____

4. Raising the age limit to eighteen for students who want to obtain driving permits

    _____

    _____

5. Teaching creationism or intelligent design alongside evolution in the public schools

    _____

    _____

6. Federal judges taking a more proactive role in making laws and regulations

    _____

    _____

7. Increasing taxes on cigarettes, alcohol, and gambling to pay for state budget shortfalls

    _____

    _____

8. Tougher screening standards for foreigners who want to travel or study in this country

    _____

    _____

9. Requiring businesses to offer health care and other benefits to same-sex partners

    _____

    _____

✎ **EXERCISE D** Consider the following news items and formulate your own opinions. Then write a thesis statement for each item, making it clear and precise and including a plan of action.

1. The idea that people may worship as their consciences dictate does not negate the fact that some rule of morality must judge the actions of men. Is it right for one to steal from his neighbor? Is it moral to kill another person, except in self-defense or protecting one's family?[34]

    For example, homosexuality is a hotly debated political issue which has to do with "values"—what people *do*; it is not an issue of religious liberty—how people *worship*. Furthermore, sodomy cannot be compared to race and gender—what people *are*.

    Colin Powell, former chairman of the Joint Chiefs of Staff and Secretary of State under the George W. Bush administration, wrote concerning the inappropriate association of homosexual *behavior* with the civil rights movement:

    > Skin color is a benign, non-behavioral characteristic. Sexual orientation is perhaps the most profound of human behavioral characteristics. Comparison of the two is a convenient but invalid argument (*WORLD* [September 26, 1992], 5).

    _____

    _____

    _____

    _____

    _____

2. "We have a crisis in our country of language and truth. While there has always been the cosmic struggle between truth and falsehood, between good and evil, between the authority of God and the claims of the Devil, between the best laid plans of man (e.g., tower of Babel) and the plans of God, this conflict of truth and language (word) has been intensified into an outright cultural war by the secular (Melvin Mencher's introductory journalism text) or mass media. Carl Henry has argued, 'never in the past have the role of words and the nature of truth been as misty and undefined as now.' In previous ages, concepts of truth and discourse communicated through words were the accepted medium of human intercourse. Today, however, the nature of truth and the role of words are in dispute. We are witnessing a massive breakdown of confidence in verbal communication. Marshall McLuhan is right; words have become obsolescent. In our post-modern world, language is used not to reveal and enlighten but to conceal, deceive, and obfuscate. Symbols are more important than words" (Dr. Robert Case II, from the "Mission Statement" for the World Journalism Institute).

    _____

    _____

    _____

    _____

    _____

---

34. This news item was adapted from Gary DeMar's book entitled *America's Christian History: The Untold Story* (Atlanta, GA: American Vision, Inc.), 168.

3. "Take the case of Donald Thornton. He was demoted for refusing to work on the Lord's Day. Since Connecticut law required that employers give workers one day a week off to practice their religion, Thornton figured the law had been violated and his rights had been stomped on. He filed a law suit against his employers. The United States Supreme Court disagreed with Thornton; it held that the Connecticut law was unconstitutional. The ACLU [American Civil Liberties Union] and the Americans for Separation of Church and State cheered the decision" (Rus Walton, "Justice and the Courts," *Biblical Solutions to Contemporary Problems* [Arlington Heights, IL: Christian Liberty Press, 1988], 169).

_____

_____

_____

_____

_____

LESSON 28: SOUNDNESS OF ARGUMENT—PART 2

As mentioned in the previous lesson, a **sound argument** is based on three factors: (1) to have a clear, precise proposition of what you are trying to prove—in essence, a *thesis statement*; (2) to be grounded on solid, established facts—that is, *evidence*; and (3) to be ordered by the laws of thought—in other words, the *rules of logic*. Here we will look at the second factor.

UPON WHAT DOES A SOUND ARGUMENT REST?

A sound argument cannot rest on its own merits. It needs to be grounded on solid, established facts. In other words, the issues surrounding your thesis statement, or proposition, need to rest upon conclusive **evidence**. Otherwise, the opposition will be able to demonstrate that the issues that you have raised cannot be supported, and your argument will be lost.

If your goal is to gather solid facts that constitute evidence, then emotional responses, nostalgic notions, "earwitness" accounts, and "brainwashing" techniques need to be eliminated. Moreover, if you *express* your opinion with bombastic claims or acrimonious approval—or disapproval, for that matter—you will not make your argument **plausible** to others.

The evidence that you gather must be based on solid, established facts. Consequently, this evidence must meet **three requirements**: The evidence must (1) relate directly to the issues; (2) be trustworthy, fair, and current; and (3) be presented in such a way that it defends the argument effectively. As a result, your evidence will impart conviction.

■ Gathering Evidence

At this point, you will be **gathering raw material** that supports your topic. The first four steps in the *thinking process* have been completed—your goal (*argumentation*) has been predetermined, your topic (*thesis statement*, or *proposition*) has been limited, your stance (*worldview* and *tone*) has been established, and your audience (*readers*) has been defined.

Now you must answer the question, "How am I going to support my topic?" The **three requirements**, mentioned above, apply to the evidence that is chosen in this step of gathering raw material. First, we will consider how the *explanations, definitions, analyses, reasons, distinctions,* or *facts* that you select must relate to the issues surrounding your argument.

Direct Relationship to the Issues

A paragraph, essay, or paper needs to be *unified*. Likewise, an article of opinion must have evidence—*explanations, definitions, analyses, reasons, distinctions,* or *facts*—that **unifies** the argument. At times, you may be tempted to include extraneous evidence that only relates indirectly to your argument, but such evidence will weaken your argument and confuse your readers.

Further, humorous anecdotes, personal recollections, or words that lack moral restraint may amuse your readers but do little to reinforce your argument. You may charm them with such informal language, but if it does not clarify an issue by means of analogy or example, then it is not considered evidence. You must ask: "Does the evidence relate directly to the issues?"

☞**PROPOSITION:**

> War inevitably devastates the lives of children, but not a single child should be engaged in the fighting. Children who become combatants before they gain emotional maturity suffer physically, mentally, and emotionally from military life and the horrors of war.

✎ **EXERCISE A** Review the following evidence which relates either *directly* or *indirectly* to the issues surrounding the proposition stated above. Check off the correct column for each item.

	Evidence Related to the Issues Surrounding the Proposition	Directly	Indirectly
1.	Casualty rates among child soldiers are generally high because of their lack of training.	✔	
2.	More than 300,000 children under the age of 18 are fighting in conflicts around the world.		✔
3.	Many children have felt they had no choice but to "volunteer" for armed service; others have joined up voluntarily.		
4.	Due to inexperience, many child soldiers have died in action.		
5.	Most of the children fighting with rebel forces in Sierra Leone have been abducted from their homes and families and forced to fight.		
6.	Child soldiers have lower recovery rates from battlefield injuries than adult soldiers.		
7.	An Ethiopian high school student disclosed, "Everyone was dying. You saw the legs or hands of your friends lying in front of you. It was so horrifying, you couldn't make sense of it. It was hell!"		
8.	Child soldiers are considered as especially useful because their size and agility means that they may be sent on hazardous assignments.		
9.	Many girl soldiers are expected to provide sexual services as well as fight.		
10.	Peter, a 12-year-old, said: "When I was killing, I felt like it wasn't me doing these things. I had to because the rebels threatened to kill me."		
11.	The majority of Afghan children have been witness to acts of violence and destruction which have destroyed the social fabric of their society.		
12.	Children suffer more than adults from the rigors of military life, especially in the bush, and are particularly vulnerable to disease and malnutrition.		
13.	To cope with combat, many former child soldiers with rebel forces were forced to drink alcohol and take drugs, or be beaten or killed.		
14.	Young Ethiopian recruits tell harrowing stories of being marched over minefields to clear a path for the regular army.		

Trustworthy, Fair, and Current

After evidence has been gathered, you must determine if it is ***trustworthy***, ***fair***, and ***current***. Evidence—gleaned from personal experience, news stories, articles, and books—ought to be examined to verify if it meets the criteria of being credible, impartial, and up-to-the-minute. First, we consider **personal experience**.

> In some instances, personal experience may furnish reliable evidence, but it should be considered carefully to see whether it *offers grounds for making a generalization* [italics added]. If it comes from wide observation, done close at hand, it may be valuable. If it comes from a narrow or isolated experience, or an experience colored by strong personal feeling, it may not be trustworthy.[35]

For example, a tourist to the Middle East may acquire particular convictions about the Arab-Israeli conflict, but he would not have the same credibility that a *New York Times* correspondent posted in Jerusalem would have. Yet that correspondent may not have the breadth of knowledge that a diplomat who has been stationed in several countries in the region would have.

Second, we consider **news stories**. Many newspapers are known for their particular viewpoint, such as the *New York Times* (liberal) or the *Washington Times* (conservative). However, if the reporter is well-trained, experienced, and unbiased, then his writings may offer reliable evidence. Due to the nature of such daily publications, you should beware of any hidden agendas.

Third, we consider **articles** and **books**. Magazine articles provide more competent, developed exposes, yet you should be on the lookout for any bias or hairsplitting. Books, however, are generally the most dependable sources for evidence; for only they provide thoughtful, mature deliberations of distinguished experts. Nevertheless, you should be cautious.

It is always wise to consult several sources rather than one. In addition, you will probably find that your sources disagree; if that is the case, you should consider how each author arrived at his conclusions and what biases or viewpoints he may hold. Finally, be sure your facts are current. REMEMBER: Evidence may be easy to garner, but gathering ***reliable evidence*** is hard work.

✎ **EXERCISE B** Review the following evidence and determine if it is *trustworthy*, *fair*, and *current*. Check off the correct column for each item; place an ✗ if the evidence does not meet the criteria.

	Evaluate the following statements based on Exercise A.	Trustworthy	Fair	Current
1.	Amnesty International calls for the end of child soldiery.	✔	✔	✔
2.	Tens of thousands of children partake in armed conflicts.	✔	✔	✗
3.	Children who join voluntarily should be allowed to fight.			
4.	Young girls are often exploited when inducted into the army.			
5.	Children suffer more than adults from the rigors of military life.			
6.	Child combatants were forced to take drugs for the fun of it.			
7.	Child soldiers suffer physically, emotionally, and mentally.			
8.	Most Afghan children have witnessed acts of violence.			
9.	Young Ethiopian recruits cleared minefields for regular army.			
10.	Child soldiers recover faster from battlefield injuries.			
11.	Many children have been forcibly recruited into rebel armies.			
12.	Due to inexperience, many child soldiers have died in action.			

---

35. Davidson, *American Composition and Rhetoric*, 518.

Defending the Argument Effectively

As mentioned above, the evidence that you gather must be based on solid, established facts. Consequently, this evidence must (1) relate directly to the issues; (2) be trustworthy, fair, and current; and (3) be presented in such a way that it defends the argument effectively. Here, we will examine the third requirement of **defending the argument effectively**.

If you are going to defend your argument effectively, you must offer **enough evidence**. Otherwise, your readers will not be satisfied. If you have a paltry amount of evidence, your argumentation will be hollow, because readers may conclude that your premises are implausible or, worse yet, indefensible. Conversely, too much evidence may weaken your argument.

The amount of evidence that should be offered is a matter of **judgment** and **proportion**. You should carefully *appraise* the amount of evidence you have gathered and *determine* if that evidence is arranged proportionally with respect to the article as a whole. REMEMBER: A few small "gems" of solid evidence are better than a massive "boulder" of flimsy evidence.

✎ **EXERCISE C** Analyze three articles of opinion from magazines or journals to find how the authors defended their opinions. Write a short paragraph for each article verifying if the evidence meets the three requirements mentioned above. Each paragraph should answer the following three questions:

1.   How does the evidence relate directly to the issues?

2.   Why is the evidence trustworthy, fair, and current?

3.   How does the evidence defend the argument effectively?

LESSON 29: SOUNDNESS OF ARGUMENT—PART 3

As mentioned in the previous two lessons, a **sound argument** is based on three factors: (1) to have a clear, precise proposition of what you are trying to prove—in essence, a *thesis statement*; (2) to be grounded on solid, established facts—that is, *evidence*; and (3) to be ordered by the laws of thought—in other words, the *rules of logic*. Here we will look at the third factor.

HOW IS A SOUND ARGUMENT ORDERED?

Since this study of composition and grammar seeks to raise rhetoric back to its rightful position, the basics of logic will be introduced presently. In this context, though, it is not practical to spell out the laws of thought in their totality, because this falls under the domain of formal logic. Yet, **sound logic** will be emphasized by studying **inductive** and **deductive** reasoning.

■ *Inductive Reasoning*

Reasoning from the particular to the general is called the **inductive method**. As Davidson asserts, "When a large number of *particulars* are accepted as pointing toward a *generalization* as being true or probably true, an induction has been made [italics added]."[36] This means, the writer first presents particular points and then draws a general conclusion from them.

The writer, therefore, *infers* that the various particulars produce a valid generalization. Consequently, a **logical inference** is made, based on the truth of the respective bits of evidence that have been presented. When using this method of sound logic, avoid any erroneous or misleading inferences. This is achieved by **induction**—the same logical process used in the *scientific method*.

---

36. Ibid., 520.

For example, Galileo postulated that all objects—regardless of their size or weight—fall at the same rate within a vacuum. This generalization became his initial *working hypothesis*; he then had to prove it through **extensive experimentation and observation**. Based on many, meticulous experiments, Galileo was able to infer from the particulars that his *generalization* was true.

Arguing by the Use of Statistics

You should always try to imitate the thorough, unbiased induction of the scientific method, even though you may not be able test and observe your "hypothesis" as a scientist would. However, you will be able to approximate the scientific method through **arguing by the use of statistics** to support your argument. This approximation is used in the following example.

☞**EXAMPLE:**

> One may infer from much observation that home school students, who are self-motivated and take full advantage of their opportunity, advance academically at a faster pace, with higher scores, and greater aspirations than their counterparts in the public schools.

✎ **EXERCISE A** Consider the following items that use *arguing by statistics*. Write a short paragraph on how each author used statistics to support his argument. Are there any weaknesses in their use? Be sure to include each author's thesis statement, and determine if its *generalization* is upheld.

1. The "war on poverty" is a dismal failure.… Presidents like Bill Clinton have had to admit that big government welfare programs have created a permanent underclass of hopeless Americans.

    Poverty is actually increasing. In 1950, one-in-twelve Americans (about 21 million) lived below the poverty line. In 1979, that figure had risen to one-in-nine (about 26 million). Today, one-in-seven (36.5 million) fall below the line.

    More than twenty percent of all American children live in poverty (up from 9.3% in 1950 and 14.9% in 1970). And for black children under the age of six, the figures are even more dismal: a record 51.2%.

    Today, 24.3% of elderly women living alone live in poverty, all too often in abject poverty, up from a mere 7% in 1954.

    As many as three million Americans are homeless, living out of the backs of their cars, under bridges, in abandoned warehouses, atop street side heating gates, or in lice-infested public shelters. Even at the height of the depression, … there have never been so many dispossessed wanderers. (George Grant, *In the Shadow of Plenty* [Arlington Heights, IL: Christian Liberty Press, 1998], 4).

    _____

    _____

    _____

    _____

    _____

    _____

2. During the past 45 years, the student-teacher ratio in public elementary and secondary schools in the United States has dropped by one third, from 26.9 students per teacher in 1955 to an estimated 17.2 in 1998.

    Despite this dramatic decline, class sizes reported by the U.S. Department of Education remain persistently high, around 24 students to a class....[37]

    Concerned that too many federal education dollars are being dissipated in bureaucratic overhead, Congressional Republicans have focused on trying to get more education dollars to flow into the classroom. That concern seems well-placed. U.S. Department of Education statistics reveal that just 52.2 percent of the staff involved in elementary and secondary public education are actually teachers. ("Public School Spending: Where Does the Money Go?" George A. Clowes, ed., *School Reform News* [February 2000], cited from the Web site of The Heartland Institute).

    _____

    _____

    _____

    _____

    _____

3. Researchers at the University of Michigan compared graduates of Catholic single-sex [boys only, or girls only] high schools with graduates of Catholic coeducational private schools. Boys in the single-sex high schools scored better in reading, writing, and math than did boys at coed high schools. Girls at the single-sex schools did better in science and reading than girls in coed schools. In fact, these researchers found that students at single-sex schools had not only superior academic achievement, but also had higher educational aspirations, more confidence in their abilities, and a more positive attitude toward academics, than did students at coed high schools....

    In one remarkable study of 2,777 English high school students, girls at coed schools were found to lose ground to boys in science and vocabulary as they progressed through high school. Exactly the opposite occurred at single-sex schools: the girls at single-sex schools outperformed both the boys at single-sex schools and the boys at coed schools. Again, this study reported the familiar pattern: girls at single-sex schools on top, followed by boys at single-sex schools, then boys at coed schools, with girls at coed schools doing the worst. (Leonard Sax, "What's the evidence? What have researchers found when they compare single-sex education with coeducation?" cited from the Web site of the National Association for Single Sex Public Education).

    _____

    _____

    _____

    _____

    _____

---

37. According to the article, this is probably due to the fact that many of the extra staff are music or reading teachers, who do not have their own classrooms.

Arguing by Analogy

A simpler, more compelling use of the inductive method is **arguing by analogy**. In inductive reasoning, an analogy is actually a *parallel*—that is, an inference made by a generalization that closely corresponds to a particular issue. In other words, you may choose to clarify an issue by showing how it is like something that may be more familiar to your readers, as follows:

☞**EXAMPLE:**

> What is apparent from the inspired record is that Peter had a truly biblically sound [method of interpretation]. He believed that scripture interprets scripture, i.e., GOD interprets his own word. In this regard, *Peter is much like Joseph in Egypt who also waited for God to interpret symbolic dreams involving food that meant something else* [italics added]. By Peter's inaction at the command to kill and eat in the vision, he assented with Joseph that interpretations belong to God ... NOT MEN (Genesis 40:8)! ... Peter showed that he understood the imagery of his vision when he declared, "But God has shown me that I should not call any man common or unclean" (Acts 10:28)! (Vic Lockman, *The Dietary Laws of the Bible* [Lafayette, IN: Sovereign Grace Publishers, 1997], 30–31).

Obvious pitfalls should be avoided when reasoning by analogy. The analogue has to be a **true parallel** for it to be logically accepted. For example, if the differences between Joseph and Peter are greater than their similarities, then it will not necessarily be true that Peter's vision symbolically refers to the salvation of Gentile sinners (Acts 10:1–48, 11:1–18), instead of the literal consumption of unclean food. Yet, if the parallel is sound, then the generalization will stand.

Of course, an analogy that *appears* persuasive, even containing some striking similarities, may not be **logically sound**. Thus the analogy's incongruity will become easy prey for an opponent. Also, the expository element in an analogy, which may not be strictly logical, demands that you carefully select a "parallel" that is truly typical or **plausible** so your argument will stand.

☞**EXAMPLE:**

> The ... *ten* members of the Politburo elected Mikhail S. Gorbachev as Secretary General of the Communist Party. Ten members, kings who have no kingdoms of their own [Revelation 17:12] but who serve by the consent of the leader of the Soviet Union, appointed the General Secretary of the Communist Party.
>
> Revelation 17:13 tells us about these men, "These have one mind, and shall give their power and strength to the beast." ...
>
> This portion of the antichrist prophecy has been filled in double measure. There are ten nations[38] under the direct control of the Soviet Union. These are led by Soviet puppets who are of one mind, to serve the leader of the Soviet Union.
>
> The ten members of the Politburo give their power and strength to Gorbachev. Our candidate for the antichrist can certainly claim ten crowns, just as the Revelation prophecy has told us. (Robert W. Faid, *Gorbachev! Has the Real Antichrist Come?* [Tulsa, OK: Victory House Publishers, 1988], 35).

Although this apocalyptic analogy *seems* persuasive and has some remarkable parallelism, it is false, as history always proves such analogies to be. In 1991, the above argument began to

---

38. The ten nations, according to the author, refer to the former Soviet bloc countries of Latvia, Estonia, Lithuania, Poland, Czechoslovakia (now two separate nations, the Czech Republic and Slovakia, gaining their independence in 1993), Hungary, Romania, East Germany (reunited with West Germany in 1990, forming the Federal Republic of Germany), Bulgaria, and Afghanistan—all of which are now independent nations.

unravel with the demise of the Soviet Union, the end of Gorbachev's presidency, and the break-up of the Soviet bloc—from which the "ten nations" became eleven independent ones.

In regard to the ***expository element*** in an analogy, this apocalyptic argument also falls short. The explanation that the ten members of the Politburo had "no kingdoms of their own" was not accurate, since each member did represent a particular political entity. In addition, no proof was given that these "Soviet puppets" were of "one mind" and gave "their power and strength to the beast"—i.e., Gorbachev. Therefore, this argument stands on shaky ground.

✎ **EXERCISE B** Consider the following items that use *arguing by analogy*. Write a paragraph on how each author used analogy to support his argument. Are the analogies *logically sound* and the parallels *plausible*? Be sure to include each thesis statement and determine if its *generalization* is upheld.

1. In schools, the antireligion campaign is often hysterical. When schoolchildren are invited to write about any historical figure, this usually means they can pick Stalin or Jeffrey Dahmer but not Jesus or Martin Luther, because religion is reflexively considered dangerous in schools and loathsome historical villains aren't. Similarly, a moment of silence in the schools is wildly controversial because some children might use it to pray, silently, on public property. Oh, the horror. The overall message is that religion is backward, dangerous, and toxic.... (John Leo, "Folly 'round the flag," *U.S. News and World Report* [July 8/July 15, 2002], 4).

    _____

    _____

    _____

    _____

2. The following quote is a graphic portrayal of the true nature of the Abolitionist movement:

    "[M]ighty questions … are shaking thrones to their center—upheaving the masses like an earthquake, and rocking the solid pillars of the Union. The parties in this conflict are not merely abolitionists and slave-holders—they are atheists, socialists, communists, red republicans, Jacobins[39] on the one side and the friends of order and regulated freedom on the other. In one word, the world is the battleground—Christianity and atheism the combatants.... One party seems to regard society with all its complicated interests, its divisions and subdivisions, as *the machinery of man*—which, as it had been invented and arranged by his ingenuity and skill, may be taken to pieces, reconstructed, or repaired as experience shall indicate defects or confusions in the original plan. The other party beholds it as *the ordinance of God* [italics added]." (J. H. Thornwell, *Collected Writings*, vol. 4 [Carlisle, PA: Banner of Truth, 1973 (1850)], 405–406; cited in C. Gregg Singer's *A Theological Interpretation of American History* [Greenville, SC: A Press, 1964], 84–85).

    _____

    _____

    _____

    _____

    _____

---

39. Members of a radical political club that instituted the Reign of Terror during the French Revolution.

3. We have copies [of the New Testament] commencing within a couple of generations from the originals, whereas in the case of other ancient texts, maybe five, eight, or ten centuries elapsed between the original and the earliest surviving copy....

Consider Tacitus, the Roman historian who wrote his *Annuls of Imperial Rome* in about A.D. 116. His first six books exist today in only one manuscript, and it was copied about A.D. 850. Books eleven through sixteen are in another manuscript dating from the eleventh century. Books seven through ten are lost. So there is a long gap between the time that Tacitus sought his information and wrote it down, and the only existing copies.

With regard to the first-century historian Josephus, we have nine Greek manuscripts of his work *The Jewish War*, and these copies were written in the tenth, eleventh, and twelfth centuries....

More than five thousand [New Testament Greek manuscripts] have been cataloged....

The quantity of New Testament material [5,000+ Greek manuscripts] is almost embarrassing in comparison with other works of antiquity. Next to the New Testament, the greatest amount of manuscript testimony is of Homer's *Iliad*, which was the bible of the ancient Greeks. There are fewer than 650 Greek manuscripts of it today. Some are quite fragmentary. They come down to us from the second and third century A.D. and following. When you consider that Homer composed his epic about 800 B.C., you can see there's a very lengthy gap. (Bruce M. Metzger, Ph. D., cited from an interview in Lee Srobel's *The Case for Christ: A Journalist's Personal Investigation of the Evidence for Jesus* [Grand Rapids, MI: Zondervan Publishing House, 1998], 59–60).

_____

_____

_____

_____

_____

_____

■ *Deductive Reasoning*

Reasoning from the general to the particular is called the ***deductive method***. In deductive reasoning, a principle or assumption is established and then applied to a set of particulars. As Davidson claims, "The principle may be a *generalization* that has been reached by a process of induction; or it may be some *general truth* which is assumed as a matter of course to be accepted to all concerned in the argument [italics added]."[40] The latter is used in the following example.

☞**EXAMPLE**

We cannot do without discipline. It is never a question of "discipline or no discipline." It is always a question of *whose* discipline. Will we be disciplined by ourselves, as individuals under God's law? Will we be disciplined by God directly...? Or will we be disciplined by the State? In our day, State tyranny is the most common alternative to self-discipline.[41]

40. Davidson, *American Composition and Rhetoric*, 522.

41. Gary North, *Honest Money: Biblical Principles of Money and Banking* (Arlington Heights, IL: CL Press, 1986), 29–30.

In this example, the "necessity of discipline" is a *general truth* which all concerned can accept. This truth is then applied to *particular* sources of discipline—self-discipline, divine reproof, or State tyranny. Of course, you might insist that there are other overlooked forms of discipline, such as parental or ecclesiastical; but, from the immediate context, they may not apply.

Nevertheless, deductive reasoning is used in the above argument, where the general truth of *being disciplined* is taken for granted and then is applied to the particulars of *which entity will be doing the disciplining*. Having stated this, we still need to take a closer look at the deductive method. We must explore what is behind all deductive reasoning—namely, the *syllogism*.

Syllogism

The deductive method is based on what logicians call a **syllogism**—a term which is derived from the verb *to syllogize*, that is "to reckon or infer" by the means of "discourse." Accordingly, a *syllogism* is the form of an argument that has a *major premise* and a *minor premise* connected with a *middle term* and a *conclusion*. Study the following formula and example of a syllogism.

Syllogistic Formula: If all A is C, and all B is A, then all B is C.

☞**EXAMPLE:**

> *Major Premise*:   All humans [A] have souls [C].
>
> *Minor Premise*:   You [B] are a human [A].
>
> *Conclusion*:   You [B] have a soul [C].

In this example, the **major premise** states a *generalization*—"All humans have souls."—which is assumed or verified to be true. The **minor premise** states a *particular*—"You are a human."—which is a point that comes under the generalization. Then, the **conclusion**—"You have a soul."—draws a *logical connection* that is obvious between the major and minor premises.

The *logical accuracy* of a syllogism like the one above depends upon the accuracy of the major and minor premises. As Davidson infers, "If each of these is necessarily and invariably true, as stated, then the conclusion must necessarily be true."[42] The only flawless syllogisms, however, may be gleaned from the study of pure logic or mathematics, where syllogistic formulations can be hypothetical and absolute. Consider the following example from plane geometry.

☞**EXAMPLE:**

> *Major Premise*:   A straight line is the shortest distance between two points. (*axiom*)
>
> *Minor Premise*:   The line XY, between the points X and Y, is a straight line. (*particular*)
>
> *Conclusion*:   Therefore, the line XY is the shortest distance between X and Y.

Nevertheless, there is a close association between pure logic and persuasive writing. The difference is that, in an article of opinion, the main premise normally is not an *axiom* or *theorem* but an **expressed opinion**. Consequently, such informal syllogisms may include some ambiguous elements, where the conclusions drawn from the premises are not entirely logical.

Although persuasive writing cannot always be strictly logical, the basic structure of your arguments should always follow the *syllogistic formula*. Use this formula to test your arguments. If they do not pass the test, then your arguments are unsound and will mislead—or, worse, deceive—your audience, though your arguments may *seem* plausible, even ingenious.

---

42. Davidson, *American Composition and Rhetoric*, 522.

✎ **EXERCISE C** Determine whether the following *syllogisms* are true or false. If the syllogism is false, explain why the particular syllogism is false.

	Syllogisms	True	False
1.	All two-legged creatures are human beings. An ostrich is a two-legged creature. An ostrich is a human being.		✔
	The major premise is false because there are many kinds of two-legged creatures besides human beings. Therefore, the conclusion is false even though the minor premise is true and the syllogistic formula was followed.		
2.	All people need love. Mary is a person. Mary needs love.		
3.	Many seniors applied to college. Bill is a senior. Bill applied to college.		
4.	Communists believe in state ownership of natural resources. Ruby believes in state ownership of oil reserves. Ruby is a communist.		
5.	All butterflies are insects. A monarch is a butterfly. A monarch is an insect.		
6.	It is the duty of every American citizen eighteen and older to vote in every election. Renée is an eighteen-year-old American citizen. For this reason, it is Renée's duty to vote in every election.		
7.	All birds have feathers. A gamin is a bird. A gamin has feathers.		
8.	The Denver Zephyr is the only nonstop train between Denver and Chicago. Cousin Fran, who lives just outside Denver, said she was coming to visit us via a nonstop train, so she must be traveling on the Zephyr.		
9.	A gas-guzzler gets relatively few miles to the gallon. Since my van gets about fifteen miles to the gallon, it must be a gas-guzzler.		
10.	The cost for educating public high school students is greater than elementary students. Since more students will be attending high school in the future, the cost of public education will most certainly rise.		

Common Fallacies

Since persuasive writing cannot always be strictly logical, there are certain **common fallacies**—that is, errors, or failures, of logic—that may creep into your composition. As Davidson points out, "Some of [these errors] have Latin names which come down to us from the Middle Ages, when both logic and Latin were the first necessities of education."[43]

These flaws in reasoning generate illogical statements that distort or misrepresent the truth, thus undermining rather than enhancing your argument. Most of these fallacies disguise themselves as being logical; they actually try, however, to manipulate readers by appealing to their emotions rather than their intellects, reaching their hearts rather than their heads.

The most common fallacies of logic are enumerated below. REMEMBER: Do not use these errors and be aware when others fall into the trap of using them. The first four groups of fallacies listed arise out of **false inference**.

1. **BEGGING THE QUESTION or ARGUING IN A CIRCLE** [*Petitio principi*]

    When someone **begs the question**, he assumes the truth of a premise that is supposed to be proven in the argument:

    > Mr. Bush was the best choice for President because there's just no one else who's better.

    When someone **argues in a circle**, he also assumes the truth of a premise, draws a conclusion from the premise, and then uses the conclusion to prove the initial premise:

    > Being a foreign correspondent is a dangerous job because it is unsafe.

    "Unsafe" conveys the same idea as "dangerous," so the speaker has not proven that danger exists.

2. **NON-SEQUITUR or FALSE CAUSE** [*Post hoc*] **or BANDWAGON**

    False Logic: A preceded B, therefore A caused B.

    A **non-sequitur** ("it does not follow") argument provides evidence which does not really prove the point:

    > Oprah Winfrey is a dynamic speaker, so she would make a great mayor for Chicago.

    A **post hoc ergo proper hoc** ("after this, therefore because of this") argument confuses chronology with a cause-effect relationship:

    > At 9:43 in the morning, Lucy bolted into the office. Rather than quietly sitting down at her desk, she blurted out, "I got caught in rush hour traffic. That's why I am late." Seeing the indignant expression on her boss's face, she whined, "Sorry, Mr. Mooney."

    Should Lucy's statement be accepted as logical? No.

    This is an example of a **causal fallacy** of logic. Lucy blamed the heavy traffic for her tardiness. Obviously she was aware of the morning rush and could have listened to the radio for traffic updates, but Lucy failed to admit that she did not leave home on time.

    A **bandwagon** argument, likewise, implies something is right because everyone is doing it:

    > Smoking must not be bad for people. Millions of people smoke.

---

43. Ibid., 524.

3. **IGNORING THE QUESTION or ARGUING AGAINST THE PERSON** [*argumentum ad hominem*]

When someone *ignores the question*, he diverts the ground of argument from the real issues to false ones by presenting a totally unrelated issue:

> Why worry about world hunger when we should be worried about the needy in our country?

This is also called a *red herring*, because a writer who introduces an irrelevant issue (i.e., "needy in our country") hopes to mislead his audience in the same way a criminal would try to distract bloodhounds from his scent by "dragging a red herring across the trail."[44]

Likewise, when someone *argues against the person* (argumentum ad hominem)—another form of "ignoring the question"—he focuses attention on the person advocating an opposing opinion, usually with derogatory comments, instead of dealing with the real issues:

> Reform of labor unions sounds great—until you realize that the one advocating it is a former member of the Communist Party.

Communism is a despicable ideology, but having been a member of the Communist Party does not necessarily mean that the person still promotes such a philosophy or that his ideas of reform are not genuine and helpful.

4. **FALSE DILEMMA or EITHER-OR FALLACY**

When someone *creates a false dilemma*, he gives only two alternatives when more exist, which means that he is oversimplifying the issue:

> Either go to college or forget about getting a job.

The "two horns"[45] of this kind of dilemma do not advance all the viable alternatives. For example, many educate themselves by using books, correspondence courses, computer programs, or the Internet. Others who have never darkened the door of a university go into business for themselves. In other words, all jobs do not require a college degree.

✎ **EXERCISE D** Review the following arguments and determine if it is *arguing in a circle* (**AC**), *arguing against the person* (**AP**), *begging the question* (**BQ**), *bandwagon* (**BW**), *false cause* (**FC**), *false dilemma* (**FD**), *non-sequitur* (**NS**), or *red herring* (**RH**).

	False Arguments	*Fallacy*
1.	Ann argued, "Mom, I should be allowed to wear make-up. All the other girls are."	*BW*
2.	The Republicans passed a tax rebate for all taxpayers; however, an economic downturn followed the passing of the new law. The Democrats claimed that the tax rebate caused the recession and they pushed to repeal it.	
3.	There is some merit in the Republicans' tax cut plan. Therefore, if Democrats are going to survive as a party, they should come up with something like it. They have got to be as tough-minded as the Republicans, since that is what the public wants.	
4.	You must resolve that you can afford this Bose Wave® Radio/CD, or you will be choosing to do without music for a while.	

---

44. This deception was used by fugitives during the nineteenth century in Great Britain, until bloodhounds were trained to know the difference.

45. The original *dilemma* in rhetoric was a device by which an orator offered his opponent two alternatives; it did not matter which one his opponent chose to answer—either way he lost the argument. In that case, the orator was said to present his opponent with "two horns," as that of a bull, on either of which he might be impaled.

	False Arguments	Fallacy
5.	If euthanasia was legal, then it would not be prohibited by the law.	
6.	You believe that abortion is morally wrong because you're a priest. Moreover, you are just a lackey to the Pope, so I can't believe what you say.	
7.	The vast majority of people in this country believe that abortion is a right of every woman. To suggest that it isn't in the face of so much evidence is ridiculous.	
8.	A communist must not be allowed to hold government office and, if discovered, will lose his job. Consequently, a communist will do anything to hide his secret and will be open to blackmail, so he cannot be allowed to hold government office.	
9.	Jay bought a new computer and it worked fine for months. He then installed a new software program. The next time he started up his computer, it froze up. Jay deduced that the program must have caused the problem.	
10.	The belief in God is universal. After all, everyone believes in God.	

The following seven fallacies represent other common errors of logic to which some fall prey.

1. **CARD STACKING**—states only those facts that support the point being made and ignores all other important evidence:

   A person argues for term limits but only presents the failures of those who have served more than three terms.

2. **FALSE ANALOGY**—a comparison in which the differences outweigh the similarities or an assumption that if two things are alike in one or a few ways, they are alike in all ways:

   Old Joe Smith would never make a good President because an old dog cannot learn new tricks.

   Homespun analogies like this often seem wise, but just as often they fall apart when examined. Learning the role of President does not compare to a dog learning new tricks.

3. **FALSE or IRRELEVANT AUTHORITY**—cites an authority or "expert" who has no claim to expertise about the subject. This fallacy attempts to transfer prestige from one area to another:

   Trusty Pharmaceutical (TP) employs an actor to portray a doctor in a television commercial that touts TP's drug XYZ.

4. **HASTY GENERALIZATION**—draws a broad conclusion from inadequate evidence. Stereotyping is a form of hasty generalization:

   Everything made in China is manufactured by prison labor.

5. **SLIPPERY SLOPE or DOMINO THEORY**—uses one weakness in a position to assume that the whole is doomed to failure. The sheer negativity of the possible effects is supposed to persuade:

   The federal government has to regulate big business or all of corporate America will become like Enron.

6. **STRAW MAN**—oversimplifies to make a choice seem obvious or relies on the creation of a false image of someone else's statements, ideas, beliefs:

   My opponent believes that higher taxes are the only way to pay for needed improvements. She has never met a tax she didn't like.

7. **SWEEPING GENERALIZATION**—overly general statement which needs to be qualified by words or phrases such as "some," "few," "many," "most," "usually," or "sometimes":

> You will die if that mosquito bites you.

In fact, mosquito-borne diseases—including the West Nile virus—infect up to 700 million people each year, killing more than 2 million. However, in the United States, sophisticated medicine and mosquito-control efforts have made such diseases extremely rare.

✎ **EXERCISE E** Study the seven fallacies listed above. Then write a false argument for each one below.

	Fallacy	Write False Arguments Below
1.	card stacking	
2.	false analogy	
3.	false authority	
4.	hasty generalization	
5.	slippery slope/ domino theory	
6.	straw man	
7.	sweeping generalization	

LESSON 30: PRESENTATION

The final step in the *thinking process* is the actual ***presentation*** of an article of opinion. Granted, a clear, precise proposition (or *thesis statement*); solid, established facts (or *evidence*); and the laws of thought (or *rules of logic*), all of which make persuasive writing effective, are important. However, the *presentation*—that is, the setting forth of your argument—is just as significant as the factors of a *sound argument*.

The presentation of your opinion should seek to cultivate the following elements: (1) a ***spirit of inquiry*** and (2) a ***tone of conciliation***. As you set forth your argument, you do not want to alienate your audience, but to draw them into your line of thinking. You also do not want to antagonize your audience, but to build bridges to their hearts and minds. Consider the following comments by Donald Davidson:

> By approaching the facts in an inquiring spirit rather than in a cocksure, assertive manner, [the writer] sets his readers' minds to working in a similar spirit of inquiry. Whether we fully agree or not, we are set to thinking; we are not antagonized.... His approach is firm, yet it is reassuring, inasmuch as it implies that we too have opinions, which the writer would not lightly disregard but would respect. Yet, in all likelihood, our own thoughts, once started in the direction suggested by [the author], will be decidedly influenced by his reasoned opinions, whether or not we accept them completely.[46]

---

46. Ibid., 514–515.

A SPIRIT OF INQUIRY

When writing an article of opinion, the argument should proceed step by step, where each step is supported by an *explanation, definition, analysis, reason, distinction,* or *fact.* These help by clarifying your position, supporting your argument, and insuring your honest use of the facts. In other words, the facts should be presented in a "spirit of inquiry" rather than a bombastic, know-it-all style. These **facts should lead your readers to further investigation**, not alienation.

This is the proper approach to writing an article of opinion. The goal is to persuade, but it is more important to awaken in your readers a **spirit of inquiry**—thoughtful, open-mined consideration. If an argument is sound and well-presented, your audience should thoughtfully consider the opinion you set forth, even if they are not entirely convinced.

✎ **EXERCISE A** Study the following excerpt. Then, on a separate piece of paper, write a paragraph explaining how the author seeks to create a *spirit of inquiry* in his audience.

> **What is wrong with our world?** [Bold-Italics added.] **Sin.** Mankind is in rebellion against God.
>
> Almost as often, we wonder **what is wrong with the church** [Bold-Italics added]. Why has so much of the church become so ineffective? How can it be that so many Christians in so many churches have such a diminishing effect on the moral climate of society? Can we honestly say that we have been praying and working against evil when we see evil increasing? (Matt 18:18–20; Psalm 94:16). Has the salt of the earth lost its saltiness? Is the light of the world being hidden under a bowl? (Matt 5:13–16).
>
> During the last [sixteen] years of travelling extensively and ministering in [twenty-one] countries, I have had the privilege of witnessing several churches operating as God intended them to—in revival. Since experiencing the powerful presence and blessing of God in the revivals of Romania and KwaSizabantu, it has been very hard to fit back into the shallow and half-hearted state of most churches in our home countries.
>
> From the perspective of the persecuted churches of Pakistan, China, Cuba, Iran and Sudan, and in the light of the revivals in Romania, Sudan and Zululand, it becomes crystal clear what is wrong with the average church in the West. **Our churches are devoid of the fear of the Lord** [Bold-Italics added]. The reverential awe and worship of God is missing. Most congregations lack true spiritual leadership and almost never practise Biblical standards of church discipline. Many church-goers **feel** like Christians, but **think** like humanists. They believe they have Christian hearts, but it's quite clear that most have humanist minds, reading more of the newspapers than they ever do of the Bible and watching TV more than they worship Christ.
>
> Like the church of Laodicea it could be said of most South African, West European or American church-goers: *"I know your deeds, that you are neither cold nor hot. I wish you were either one or the other! So, because you are lukewarm—neither hot nor cold—I am about to spit you out of my mouth…. [Y]ou do not realize that you are wretched, pitiful, poor, blind and naked…. So be earnest, and repent." Rev 3:15-19* [NIV]
>
> The Church is like a rescue boat. The rescue boat must be in the sea rescuing the perishing, but the sea must not be in the boat. In the same way, the church must be in the world rescuing the perishing, but the world must not be in the church.
>
> The tragedy of many modern churches is that: [B]y lowering its standards to allow the unconverted easy access, the church has become flooded and swamped by the world. It is now becoming increasingly difficult to discern any substantial differences between the opinions, moral standards and even conduct of "Christians" and the pagans.
>
> The published statistics of church growth and the vast numbers coming forward at mass crusades are impressive. Yet those of us who deal with the individual in the pews and on the streets are deeply disturbed. The church generally seems to be growing mostly in *quantity.* The *quality* of devotional and spiritual life and moral standards seems to be deteriorating as the church is expanding in numbers. It is as though the churches have become like huge combine harvesters, yet lacking cutting blades: impressive machinery, much noise and activity—but ineffective in dealing with the harvest.
>
> If the Gospel is the cutting blade of the church, then we need to ask: [W]hat could have blunted our Gospel preaching? …[47]

---

47. This excerpt is taken from Peter Hammond's book entitled *Putting Feet to Your Faith* (Newlands, South Africa: Frontline Fellowship), 1 and 2.

A TONE OF CONCILIATION

Secondly, you want to cultivate a *tone of conciliation*. When presenting your article of opinion, you want to build bridges to the hearts and minds of your audience, not to antagonize. If you use a *combative tone*, you will stir up *combativeness* on the part of your readers. Initially, they may be shocked, but they may also be turned off by such an approach.

A *conciliatory approach* would produce a more positive response. When you present your argument in a fair manner, your audience will be more receptive to your perspective. This does not mean that you concede to your opponents, but you must always concede to the truth. A false presentation will not only be dismantled, but also your credibility will be dismissed.

The best way to establish a tone of conciliation is to begin with a *point of agreement*. If you begin with a point of fact or evidence, upon which all can agree, then you can proceed by building your argument on that premise, or point of agreement. This will capture the attention of your readers and possibly gain a moment of receptivity, clearing the way for them to readily follow your argument, step-by-step, and to develop a spirit of inquiry.

✎ **EXERCISE B** Study the following passages. Then, on a separate piece of paper, write a paragraph explaining how each author develops a *tone of conciliation* in argument.

1. For in fact the body is not one member but many. If the foot should say, "Because I am not a hand, I am not of the body," is it therefore not of the body? And if the ear should say, "Because I am not an eye, I am not of the body," is it therefore not of the body? If the whole body were an eye, where would be the hearing? If the whole were hearing, where would be the smelling? But now God has set the members, each one of them, in the body just as He pleased. And if they were all one member, where would the body be? But now indeed there are many members, yet one body. And the eye cannot say to the hand, "I have no need of you"; nor again the head to the feet, "I have no need of you." No, much rather, those members of the body which seem to be weaker are necessary. And those members of the body which we think to be less honorable, on these we bestow greater honor; and our unpresentable parts have greater modesty, but our presentable parts have no need. But God composed the body, having given greater honor to that part which lacks it, that there should be no schism in the body, but that the members should have the same care for one another....

    Now you are the body of Christ, and members individually.[48]

2. I agree with you that there is a natural aristocracy among men. The grounds of this are virtue and talents. Formerly, bodily powers gave place among the *aristoi*. But since the invention of gunpowder has armed the weak as well as the strong with missile death, bodily strength, like beauty, good humor, politeness and other accomplishments, has become but an auxiliary ground for distinction. There is also an artificial aristocracy, founded on wealth and birth, without either virtue or talents; for with these it would belong to the first class. The natural aristocracy I consider as the most precious gift of nature, for the instruction, the trusts, and government of society. And indeed, it would have been inconsistent in creation to have formed man for the social state, and not to have provided virtue and wisdom enough to manage the concerns of the society. May we not even say, that that form of government is the best, which provides the most effectually for a pure selection of these natural *aristoi* into the offices of government?[49]

48. 1 Corinthians 12:14–27
49. Thomas Jefferson, Letter to John Adams, October 28, 1813

LESSON 31: THINK BEFORE YOU WRITE

THE THINKING PROCESS

In this unit, you will again answer the following questions of the **thinking process**: "What is my goal in writing?" "What is my topic?" "What is my stance toward the topic?" "Who is my audience?" and "How am I going to support my topic?" The **writing process** follows; here you will learn how to develop a sensible *writing strategy* for composing an article of opinion.

As you move along in the thinking process, address each question critically. Analyzing every possible answer will help you focus your thoughts. As you answer the five questions, keep in mind your main goal—*argumentative writing*. To keep track of your progress, write the following list on a separate piece of paper and fill in the appropriate information as you go:

1. **Your Goal:** *Argumentation—*
2. **Your Main Idea:** Subject—
   Topic—
3. **Your Stance:** Worldview—
   Tone—
4. **Your Audience:** Who are your readers?
   What do they know?
   What don't they know?
   What kind of language do they use?
   What biases or convictions do they hold?
5. **Your Raw Material:** Gathering Information—
   Classifying Information—
   Arranging Information—

ANSWERING THE FIVE QUESTIONS

Question One: What is my goal?

The first question you must answer is "What is my goal in writing?" This is relatively straight-forward, since **argumentative writing** is the goal of composing an article of opinion. Granted, you will want to use expository language, but argumentation is your main goal.

Question Two: What is my topic?

Now, you need to select the **subject** you are going to tackle for this assignment. The challenge, though, is deciding what you want to say about your subject. The subject is quite broad and the thoughts that you have may be vague and shapeless. Therefore, your objective is to give your collection of ideas a significant form. You cannot say everything, so *select ideas that will best represent your subject*—those ideas that actually go together to make a unified whole.

Next, you need to limit your subject to come up with a **workable topic**. Remember that the *main idea* is the conscious determination of the writer to make every part of his writing move in *one* direction and conform to *one* clear intention. What facts, information, and concepts will you highlight? What is it that you want people to know about your topic that they never knew before? After you make your decision, *write a clear topic statement* on your paper.

Question Three: What is my stance toward the topic?

As a Christian, your *worldview* most certainly will have an impact on what you write and how you write about your topic. Carefully examine your topic statement and determine how your faith, belief system, or point of view will affect your approach to the topic, the selection of raw material, the classification and arrangement of that material, and the writing process.

The *tone* of your essay is another matter to decide before you begin to write. Depending on your subject material, you may choose to give your composition a lighter touch by bringing out some humorous incidents that would bare on the topic. However, if you are writing about a weighty issue, as in an article of opinion, a more somber approach would be appropriate. REMEMBER: The tone will affect the details you include and the language you use.

Question Four: Who is my audience?

The answer to the fourth question in the thinking process may not be as obvious as you might think. You need to *ask who your audience is going to be*: Church newsletter? Community bulletin? Local newspaper? Christian magazine? Political journal? You also need to decide how narrow or how broad your audience will be. This will affect the rest of the issues related to your audience. Your wording and content will be affected, as well.

You need to consider the following factors:

➢ What your readers know or do not know

➢ Background information they need to learn

➢ Terms or technical data they need to have explained

➢ Complexity of language they can handle

➢ Biases or convictions your readers may hold

All these factors determine *what* you present and *how* you present it.

Question Five: How am I going to support my topic?

The fifth question in the thinking process involves selecting the details that will support your argument. The best method of gathering this data is by **brainstorming**, which will help you list possible ideas about your opinion. Before you begin, you may need to do some *library research* to obtain a better grasp on the topic. At this point, do not be worried about classifying or arranging your raw material, just write whatever comes to mind.

As your ideas begin to flow, you may see a pattern developing that suddenly comes to the fore. If you have written down all you know or have discovered about your topic, start **selecting various details** that reveal more about your topic. As you go along, eliminate any extraneous information and try to make a general outline of the material you have collected. After that, you will be ready to arrange your raw material into some kind of order.

✎ **EXERCISE** Write the five questions involved in the *thinking process* on a piece of paper; you may use the list form on the previous page. Begin to fill in the appropriate information as you go along.

LESSON 32: THE WRITING PROCESS

Having completed the *thinking process* and developed a sound *writing strategy*, you now have the opportunity to put what you have developed into writing. An article of opinion should be about 1,000 words. Since you have answered the five questions related to the thinking process, you will now implement **the five steps of the writing process**.

Step 1: Writing Your First Draft

You are now ready to write your first draft. Don't be worried about grammar, spelling, or technical matters at this point; just let your ideas flow—keeping in mind your goal, topic, and audience. Later on you will be able to appraise, rework, and proofread your article of opinion. Write your first draft and lay it aside for two days.

Step 2: Appraising Your First Draft

The process by which you initially judge the content of your sketch is called **appraising your first draft**. As you have been writing, you probably have been making changes as you go along, but now that you have completed your first draft, you must appraise it as a whole. Approach it as if you were looking at it for the first time.

Since you have laid your draft aside for a couple of days, you will have a fresh perspective on it. Read your article out loud. With a critical ear, listen for words, phrases, clauses, or sentences that do not make sense, nor are appropriate, nor fit the worldview or tone of your paper. You may wish to have someone else read your work and give you some constructive criticism. The following questions will help in your appraisal:

1. Does the information you included support your goal of argumentation?

2. Do you think that your proposed audience will find your argument interesting?

3. Does your audience need more background data or explanation of terminology?

4. Is the topic developed well enough for your audience to grasp your message?

5. Is your writing coherent or will the reader need to jump around to put your ideas together?

6. Does the logical order of your details and ideas make your main idea clear?

7. Do you make smooth transitions between your sentences and paragraphs?

8. Does your choice of words and thoughts clearly convey the *tone* you desire to impart?

9. Does your writing effectively and consistently communicate your *worldview*?

10. Have you varied the length and structure of your sentences to avoid reader boredom?

11. Are the words you have chosen precise and concrete or indefinite and ambiguous?

12. Are the descriptive terms you use vivid and graphic or colorless and dull?

Step 3: Writing Your Second Draft

Your appraisal of your article of opinion will no doubt reveal some problems in your work. When reworking your first draft, you need to find specific ways to correct the problems that have arisen. This can be accomplished in the following ways: (1) by adding new ideas or details, (2) by removing extraneous information, (3) by replacing material with information that is more relevant or suitable, and (4) by rearranging ideas and details in a more logical way. Using these techniques, write your second draft. The following set of problems and solutions will assist you in writing your second draft:

Problem	Solution
1. Your ideas and details do not help you set forth your argument.	You can remove irrelevant or unnecessary evidence and add relevant detail.
2. What you have written seems monotonous and may lose the interest of your readers.	You can replace details that your audience is not interested in with anecdotes or analogies.
3. You have inadvertently inserted words that are unknown to your audience.	You can replace these terms with more familiar ones or add further explanation to your sketch.
4. You have not provided enough data for your readers to understand the topic.	You can add reasons, facts, examples, evidence, and analogies to support your topic.
5. Some ideas do not support your topic and may confuse or distract your audience.	Remove all phrases, clauses, and sentences that do not relate directly to your topic.
6. The order of ideas may cause your readers to lose the thrust of your topic.	Check the original order of your paper and reorder your ideas to clarify your message.
7. The connection between your thoughts may not be clear to your audience.	You can add such transitional words as *this, when, then, first, in addition, as a result*, etc.
8. Your attitude toward the topic may be inappropriate for your goal or audience.	Lighten or subdue the tone by replacing formal with casual words or vice versa.
9. Your writing does not communicate the tone you desire to project.	You can add words or details that befit the tone or replace ones that are unsatisfactory.
10. Your point of view toward the topic may be inconsistent or lacking in emphasis.	Remove information that does not reflect your worldview or add words or ideas that do.
11. Your sentences are so dull or uninteresting that they provoke boredom or tedium.	You can combine sentences, subordinate one to another, or vary sentence structure.
12. Your words may be dull or ambiguous, so that their meanings become obscure.	Replace dull or ambiguous words with terms that are graphic and concrete, respectively.

Step 4: Proofreading Your Second Draft

Now that you have written your second draft, you need to find and correct possible errors in grammar, usage, punctuation, capitalization, spelling, etc. This step in the writing process is called **proofreading**. The reading and marking of corrections on your paper demand special attention to details, which you cultivate with practice.

The best way to approach this step is to put your paper aside for another day or two. When you pick it up again, you will be able to catch errors more readily. Place a piece of paper below the line that you are proofreading, to force your eye not to skip ahead and miss an error. Read your paper more than once in this way, and you will be surprised at how many mistakes you find.

Learn to approach proofreading with a critical eye. Question everything that you have put on paper. Answering the following questions will help you in the proofreading process:

1. Is every sentence written as a complete thought?

2. Are all punctuation marks correct, including end-of-sentence punctuation?

3. Are all appropriate words (*proper nouns, first words in sentences, etc.*) capitalized?

4. Do all subjects and verbs agree in number?

5. Are all verb forms and tenses correct?

6. Are all personal pronouns in both nominative and objective cases correct?

7. Does every pronoun agree with its antecedent in number and gender?

8. Are frequently misused words, such as *lie* and *lay*, used correctly?

9. Are all words spelled correctly according to standard (*American, British, etc.*) usage?

10. Is your paper clean, neat, and free of any markings or erasures?

Step 5: Writing Your Final Draft

The remaining step in the writing process is to prepare the final draft. This version should reflect all the revisions and corrections that you have made to the text. There are many ways in which to ready your final draft, but for our purposes the following guidelines will serve as the standard by which your article of opinion should be written.

Guidelines for Writing the Final Draft
1. If you are writing your article of opinion by hand, use standard lined composition paper. If you are using a word processor or computer, use 8 1/2 by 11-inch white paper.
2. Write, type, or print on only one side of each sheet of paper.
3. Write in black or blue ink. If typing or printing, use black ink and double-space each line.
4. Your margins should be about one inch from each side of the paper, and the text should be aligned along the left-hand side of the paper.
5. The first line of every paragraph should be indented about one-half inch.
6. Your name should be aligned to the left, one inch from the top of the first page; then your teacher's name, course title, and date appear each on a separate line, double-spaced; below this, center the title, which is also double-spaced. The text follows immediately.
7. Each page should be numbered in the upper right-hand corner, one-half inch from the top.
8. You should write as clearly and neatly as possible. If you are typing or using a word processor, do not type or strike over letters or words.
9. Your final draft needs to be proofread carefully to make sure no errors have crept in as you copied or typed your manuscript.
10. If necessary, rewrite or retype your paper without any mistakes.

LESSON 33: UNIT REVIEW

✎ **EXERCISE A** Fill in the blanks.

1. _____ refers chiefly to structural arrangement, organization, the putting of parts to make a whole.

2. _____ refers to the skill or artifice used in making composition persuasive and effective.

3. One of the four basic writing goals is to *persuade* or *convince*, that is,_____ writing.

4. This type of writing _____, _____, or _____.

5. A(n) _____ is a formal essay that deals with a debatable issue in a serious and definitive manner.

6. List the four stages of *argumentative communication*.

   a. _____ c. _____

   b. _____ d. _____

7. What are the two questions at the heart of an *article of opinion*?

   _____

   _____

8. What three factors are the basis of a *sound argument*?

   a. _____ c. _____

   b. _____

9. The conscious decision of the writer to make every part of his writing move in *one* direction and conform to *one* clear intention is called the _____.

10. In formal argumentation, a *thesis statement* is called the _____.

11. A *thesis statement* should be a _____ issue that allows reasoned *affirmative* and *negative* arguments.

12. A(n) _____ is an inference or conviction that can be debated, because it cannot be proved, or tested, like a *fact*.

13. A thesis statement, or *proposition*, may have words that are misunderstood, so these terms should be _____.

14. A *proposition* needs to be _____—that is, accurate in grasping and expressing the issues which are to be debated.

15. A proposition should have a _____ of _____.

16. The issues surrounding your thesis statement need to rest upon conclusive _____.

17. What three requirements must the *evidence* you gather meet?

    a. _____   b. _____

    c. _____

18. An article of opinion must have *evidence* that _____ the argument—that is, evidence that relates directly to the debatable issues.

19. After evidence has been gathered, you must determine if it is _____, _____, and _____—that is, if it is *reliable evidence* or not.

20. If you are going to defend your argument effectively, you must offer _____ evidence, so that your readers may conclude that your premises are *plausible* and *defensible*.

21. The amount of evidence that should be offered is a matter of _____ and _____.

22. How is a *sound argument* ordered? _____

23. *Sound logic* is emphasized by studying _____ and _____ reasoning.

24. Define the two types of reasoning mentioned in the previous question.

    a. _____

    b. _____

25. *Logical* _____ is made, based on the truth of the respective bits of evidence that have been presented.

26. _____ is the same logical process used in the *scientific method*.

27. The above inductive method may be approximated through *arguing by the use of* _____ and *arguing by* _____.

28. In _____ reasoning, a principle or assumption is established and then applied to a set of particulars.

29. A(n) _____ is the form of an argument that has a *major premise*, a *minor premise*, and a *conclusion*.

30. The *major premise* states a _____; the *minor premise* states a _____; and the *conclusion* draws a _____ that is obvious between the major and minor premises.

31. The difference between *pure logic* and *persuasive writing* is that the main premise normally is not

    an axiom or theorem but an _____.

32. Write the *syllogistic formula* below.

    _____

✎ **EXERCISE B** Review each of the following arguments and determine if it is *arguing in a circle* (**AC**), *arguing against the person* (**AP**), *begging the question* (**BQ**), *bandwagon* (**BW**), *false cause* (**FC**), *false dilemma* (**FD**), *non-sequitur* (**NS**), or *red herring* (**RH**).

	False Arguments	*Fallacy*
1.	Since I'm not lying, it follows that I'm telling the truth.	
2.	Polls suggest that the Liberals will form a majority government, so you may as well vote for them.	
3.	Smoking is not harmful. Why my grandmother smoked a pack a day and lived to the ripe old age of 92.	
4.	Either you're for me or against me.	
5.	The problem in this community is that it has no library.	
6.	You may argue that God does not exist, but you are just following a fad.	
7.	The sign said "Fine For Parking Here," and since it was fine, I parked there.	
8.	Abortion should remain legal because it is every woman's right to have one.	
9.	**Reporter:** "Senator, what about these allegations of taking campaign money from the Chinese?" **Senator:** "I'm glad you asked me that. This bipartisan bill that I'm introducing will reform campaign finance in this country."	
10.	America: love it or leave it.	

✎ **EXERCISE C** Match the fallacy listed on the left to the false argument or posturing on the right.

Fallacy	False Argument/Posturing
card stacking	Noted psychologist Dr. Frasier Crane recommends that you buy the EZ-Rest Hot Tub.
false analogy	Bill Clinton: "We want to build a bridge to the future. Bob Dole talks about building a bridge to the past."
false authority	The United States is a Christian nation; therefore, each American is Christian.
hasty generalization	A current events program has three liberal panelists, plus a like-minded host, while there is only one conservative guest.
slippery slope/ domino theory	If I make an exception for you then I have to make an exception for everyone.
straw man	Most Democrats promote liberal issues, so voters should not trust their candidates who claim to be pro-life.
sweeping generalization	Employees are like nails. Just as nails must be hit in the head in order to make them work, so must employees.

✎ **EXERCISE D** Fill in the blanks.

1.   The final step in the *thinking process* is the _____ of an article of opinion.

2.   What *two elements* should this final step seek to cultivate?

a. _____   b. _____

3.   The facts presented in your article of opinion should lead your readers to further

_____.

4.   A(n) _____ *approach* produces a more positive response in your audience, if your argument is presented in a fair manner.

5.   The best way to establish a *tone of conciliation* is to begin with a _____.

6.   What are the five questions that need to be answered during the *thinking process*?

a. _____   d. _____

b. _____   e. _____

c. _____

7.   What are the five steps in writing a composition?

a. _____   d. _____

b. _____   e. _____

c. _____

✎ **EXERCISE E** Analyze the article of opinion in the exercise on page 96. State the author's thesis statement, identify his stance toward his topic, define his audience, and list the evidence that the author sets forth to support his topic.

_____

_____

_____

_____

_____

_____

_____

_____

_____

_____

_____

_____

_____

_____

_____

Is the author's argument sound? Explain. Also discuss his presentation.

_____

_____

_____

_____

_____

_____

_____

_____

_____

Unit 4
The Mechanics of Good Writing

This unit examines the **mechanics of good writing**—capitalization, punctuation, and the physical layout of paragraphs. First, the rules of **capitalization** will be covered. Emphasis will be placed on the primary use of capital letters—*proper nouns and adjectives* and *words in titles*. A few miscellaneous uses, which do not fall within these two areas, will also be considered.

Secondly, we will survey the rules of **punctuation**—a system of written marks or symbols designed to make the written word more clear. Punctuation is an important way to make our writing more precise. *Punctuation marks* are like the pauses and changes in one's voice when he speaks. These changes almost always play an important part in expressing our meaning.

Thirdly, the **physical layout of paragraphs** will be analyzed. Obviously, a writer begins with the construction of clear and grammatically correct sentences. Yet, as the writing process becomes more complex, the writer begins to put these sentences together into a meaningful composition. *Indentation, spacing,* and *alignment* become significant at this point.

LESSON 34: PROPER NOUNS AND ADJECTIVES

Proper names of specific geographical locations and features are always capitalized. Likewise, directions found on the compass are capitalized when they refer to political or geographical regions. *Proper adjectives* derived from these regions are also capitalized.

1. **Capitalize the proper names of the following geographical features.**

Cities/Towns	Sydney	Valparaiso	Wittenberg	Singapore
Counties/Parishes/Townships	Cook County	Tangipahoa Parish	Township of Hanover	
States/Provinces	British Columbia	South Dakota	Saskatchewan	New Mexico
Countries/Continents	Australia	Bangladesh	South America	Iraq
Bodies of Water	Lake Victoria	Indian Ocean	Danube River	Hudson Bay
Mountains/Islands	Atlas Mountains	Madagascar	Mount Herman	Line Islands
Streets/Roads	Golf Road	Madison Avenue	Chester Blvd.	First Street
Parks/Monuments	Anacostia Park	Temple of Karnak	Zion Nat'l Park	Eiffel Tower
Recognized Regions	New England	Scandinavia	Indian Subcontinent	
Geographical Features	Lummi River Delta	Belize Barrier Reef	Ohio River Valley	Victoria Falls

2. **Capitalize words like city, street, lake, park, river, mount, mountain, ocean, desert, etc. only when they are part of a proper name.**

Do not capitalize geographical terms when used as common nouns, even when modified by a proper adjective.

>   **Lake** Ontario   Indian **Ocean**   **Mount** Washington   The **river** was bubbling.
>
>   The **expressway** was resurfaced this summer.   Renee visited the French **city** of Versailles.

3. **Capitalize words referring to points of the compass when they are part of a proper name. Do not capitalize them when they merely name directions.**

>   The **West** voted mostly for Democrats, but the **South** went Republican.
>
>   Turn **east** at the next corner, drive two blocks, and turn **north**.

4. **Capitalize proper adjectives derived from proper nouns naming geographical elements.**

>   The **Nigerian** ambassador met with the **American** secretary of state at the **Swiss** city of Geneva. A **Kenyan** delegation also attended.

✎ **EXERCISE** Correct the errors in capitalization below. If a word is improperly capitalized, draw a line (N̶) through the first letter. If a word beginning with a small letter should be capitalized, draw double lines (w̲) under the first letter. The first one is done for you.

1. the I̶slands of the s̲outh Pacific
2. the amazon river
3. an ethiopian village
4. nantahala national forest
5. the italian dolomites
6. DuPage county
7. the chicago expressways
8. the ancient Caspian sea
9. the great basin national park
10. the Nations of Southern Asia
11. the Seaside resort along the mediterranean
12. Village of Radium Hot Springs, BC, Canada
13. province of Prince Edward island
14. the alaskan oil reserves
15. shenandoah national park
16. 1061 e. main st., dundee, illinois
17. a Hotel on the gulf of mexico
18. irving park road runs east and west.
19. the angolan people
20. christmas island in the indian ocean

LESSON 35: GROUPS AND EVENTS

1. **Capitalize names of organizations and political parties.**

>   Berlin Symphony Orchestra   Kovler Transplant Clinic   U.S. Taxpayers party[50]
>   Orthodox Presbyterian Church   Ducks Unlimited   Institute for Creation Research

---

50. Note that the words *party, movement, platform*, etc. are not capitalized for names of organizations, political parties, etc.

2. **Capitalize names of government or international agencies, departments, divisions, etc.**

   International Atomic Energy Agency (IAEA)   Department of Justice   World Bank
   U.S. Senate   the Oregon Court of Appeals   U.S. Army   Interpol (ICPO)

3. **Capitalize the names of businesses, schools, colleges, institutions, museums, churches, etc.**

   Intel Corp.   Whitefield College   Grace Community Bible Church   SBC/Yahoo
   Christian Liberty Academy   the Smithsonian Institution   Natural History Museum

4. **Capitalize names of races, nationalities, and religions, and members of religions.**

   Zoroastrianism   Hispanic   Polynesians   Christianity   Aborigines   Muslims

5. **Capitalize names of specific historical events or periods.**

   Celtic Wars   the Age of Exploration   the Reformation   War on Terrorism
   Russian Revolution   War Between the States   Battle of Britain   Desert Storm

6. **Capitalize the names of days of the week, months, holidays, special events, etc.**

   September   Reformation Day   Harvest Festival   Sydney-Hobart Yacht Race
   Wednesday   Fast of Ramadan   Dominion Day   Chinese New Year

Do not capitalize names of seasons of the year unless they are personified.

   winter, spring, summer, autumn, fall   Old Man Winter covers with a blanket of snow.

✎ **EXERCISE** Write examples of proper names (*real* or *fictitious*) for the following items:

1. winter holiday ***Christmas***

2. military base in your area _____

3. service organization_____

4. your church _____

5. 20th-century war_____

6. your favorite college _____

7. regional museum_____

8. political party of choice _____

9. famous revolution _____

10. main religion of Kenya _____

LESSON 36: OTHER PROPER NAMES

1. **Capitalize the word God when it refers to the deity of religions worshipping one God: Christianity, Judaism, and Islam.**

Capitalize the various *names* given to the God of these religions and *pronouns* referring to God (*He, Him*). Note, however, that *who* and *whom* are rarely capitalized.

> "I am Jehovah, the God of Abraham, Isaac, and Jacob."   Christ, He is God's Son.
>
> Christians confess, "There is but one only, living, and true God...."   I AM WHO I AM[51]
>
> He was baptized in the name of the Father, the Son, and the Holy Spirit.

Do not capitalize the word *god* (or *goddess*) when referring to pagan deities nor the *pronouns* that pertain to them. However, the specific names of pagan deities should be capitalized.

> Pre-Islamic Arabs once worshiped Manat, the ancient goddess of fate and destiny.

2. **Capitalize the names of angels and human beings.**

> Michael, the Archangel   Berta Reyes   Jonathan Edwards   Satan   Karl Marx

Capitalize courtesy titles and their abbreviations.

> **Mr.** Boyle   **Mrs.** Sullivan   William Harrison, **Jr.**   **Dr.** Helen Demetrios

Do not capitalize words referring to family relationships unless the words are used in place of names or when considered to be part of a name. Do not capitalize such words if modified by a possessive pronoun.

> mother, father, sister, uncle   I asked Father how I could help.
>
> cousin, aunt, brother, niece   I invited Cousin Nancy for Thanksgiving.
>
> nephew, grandmother, grandfather   We invited our cousin Freddy to the gathering.

3. **Capitalize names of languages.**

> Assyrian   Hindi   Danish   Amharic   Slavic   Spanish

4. **Capitalize names of ships, aircraft, buildings, bridges, and structures.**

> U.S.S. *Enterprise*   Washington Monument   Hudson Bay Bridge
>
> Sears Tower   Spirit of St. Louis   the Pentagon

5. **Capitalize names of planets, heavenly bodies, and signs of the Zodiac.**

> Andromeda   Jupiter   Corona Borealis   Canis Major   Uranus   Cancer

Do not capitalize *earth, sun,* or *moon* unless these words are used without the article ***the*** in a list of other planets.

> The solar system consists of Mercury, Venus, Earth, Mars, Jupiter, Saturn, Uranus, and Pluto revolving around the sun. Mankind has set foot only on the earth and the moon.

---

51. This biblical appellation for God (Exodus 3:14) is always in SMALL CAPS. Note that the pronoun "I" is capitalized, but the pronoun "who" is not. Conversely, the King James Version renders this name for God as "I AM THAT I AM."

6. **Capitalize brand names of commercial products but not generic words identifying products.**

    Dell computers   Ford automobiles   T-Mobile wireless communications   Popsicles

7. **Capitalize abbreviations of proper names.**

    U.A.E. (United Arab Emirates)   Tex. (Texas)   Hos. (Hosea)   NRA (National Rifle Assoc.)

8. **Capitalize names of specific academic courses but do not capitalize general school subjects unless the subjects are the names of languages. Do not capitalize words referring to school years or grade levels.**

    Geometry   graduate level   sophomore   seventh grade   theology   Portuguese

✎ **EXERCISE** Correct errors in capitalization in the following sentences. Draw double lines (_) under letters that should be capitalized. Draw a line (–) through letters that should not be capitalized.

1. Tylenol may be less harmful to the stomach than Aspirin, but tylenol is bad for the Liver.

2. Completion of the Sophomore course called algebra II is required for advanced Mathematics.

3. Jesus christ is called the alpha and omega, the beginning and the end (revelation 1:8, nkjv).

4. It is no coincidence that intel chips are manufactured by intel corporation.

5. Officials from the state department in washington, d.c., visited several areas in the balkans.

6. Our gas and electricity come from the northern indiana public service company (nipsco).

7. No one from the earth has yet set foot on mars, but several men have been on the Moon.

8. His Grandfather, the famous theologian h. bavinck, taught him the heidelberg catechism.

9. Reverend john mitchell of yorkshire, England—a Geologist and Astronomer, as well as a clergy-man—predicted the existence of Black Holes in 1784, using newtonian Physics.

10. Charles darwin's grandfather erasmus—physician, poet, philosopher, botanist, and naturalist—formulated a comparable Theory of Evolution some sixty years before charles had.

LESSON 37: TITLES AND OTHER CAPITALIZATION

1. **Capitalize titles (including abbreviations) of persons when the title comes before the person's name.**

    Mayor Rudolph Giuliani   Judge Judy   Atty. Gen. John Ashcroft   Captain Kirk

Do not capitalize titles following a name. There is only one exception, the title of President of the United States which is *always* capitalized, whether before or after a name or standing alone.

    In 1909, Ito Hirobumi, the Japanese resident general, was assassinated at Harbin railway station by Korean nationalist An Chung Gun.

2. **Capitalize the first word and all important words in the titles of books, periodicals, poems, songs and other musical compositions, stories, movies, plays, and artworks. Capitalize only words that are part of the official title.**

    Chicago Tribune   *World* magazine   *Chariots of Fire*   American Gothic

    A Sunday on La Grande   "A Mighty Fortress"   *Faith Under Fire in Sudan*

3. **Always capitalize the first word of a sentence, including sentences that are quoted within other sentences.**

    Nickolas Eicher writes, "The Republican sweep was not just another political victory. It was the first time in almost 70 years that the party of a [P]resident in his first term enjoyed gains in both houses of Congress. And the only time since 1860 that the [P]resident's party reclaimed total congressional control at the first midterm." (*WORLD* [November 23, 2002])

4. **Always capitalize the pronoun "*I*" and the interjection "*O.*"**

    Hear, O Israel: The LORD our God, the LORD is one! (Deuteronomy 6:4)

5. **Capitalize the first word of every line of a poem or song, even if it is not the beginning of a sentence.**

    Take with thee words, come to the throne of grace
    There supplicate thy God, and seek his face;
    Like to the prodigal, confess thy sin,
    Tell him where, and how vicious thou hast been.   *John Bunyan*

Note: Some modern poets have chosen to defy convention and not capitalize the first words of their lines of poetry. In fact, the poet e. e. cummings refused to use any capital letters, including those in his own name.

✎ **EXERCISE** Write one sentence to illustrate each of the five rules in this lesson. For number five, one short poem or verse will suffice.

1. _____

   _____

2. _____

   _____

3. _____

   _____

4. _____

   _____

5. _____

   _____

Note: The next few lessons include practice exercises after each point within each lesson. Study the punctuation rules below and the example sentences for each rule. After reading the example(s) given with each rule, *write a sentence of your own to illustrate the rule.*

LESSON 38: END PUNCTUATION

Sentences may be ended with one of three punctuation marks—the *period*, the *question mark*, or the *exclamation point*—depending on the kind of sentence.

THE PERIOD

1. **Use a period at the end of a declarative sentence.**

    The Bible enables the Christian to view history as something greater than a mere human process.

    _____

2. **Use a period at the end of a mild imperative sentence.**

    Don't cross the street without looking both ways.

    _____

3. **Use a period at the end of a sentence containing an indirect question.**

    Belle inquired what had happened to her father.

    _____

4. **Use a period after a standard abbreviation.**

    At 2 p.m. on St. Bartholomew's Day, the bells of Paris began to ring, signaling the massacre.

    _____

THE QUESTION MARK

1. **Use a question mark at the end of a direct question.**

    What is an enthymeme?   How many sides does a icosahedron have?

    _____

2. **If an interrogative sentence ends with an internal question, only one question mark is needed at the end.**

    "This is what Christ has done for you," declared the preacher. "What have you done for Him?"

    _____

3. **Use question marks in a series of brief questions within one sentence.**

    Your news story should answer the questions who? what? why? where? when? and how?

    _____

4. **Use a question mark in parentheses within a sentence to express doubt or uncertainty.**

    The sedan was silver with blue trim (?) and it was racing north on Halsted Street.

THE EXCLAMATION POINT

1. **Use an exclamation point at the end of an exclamatory sentence.**

    You look gorgeous in that royal blue dress!

2. **Use an exclamation point at the end of a strong imperative sentence.**

    Get off my property, now!

3. **Use an exclamation point after a strong interjection or emphatic phrase.**

    Hooray!   Well done!   What a joke!   Help!   Of course!

LESSON 39: A CAUSE TO PAUSE

THE COMMA

The *comma* (,) is only used *within* sentences, never as an ending mark. Since it is used in such a variety of ways, the comma is one of the most difficult punctuation marks to learn how to use correctly. In writing, it represents the weak, brief pauses that we make in speech. The comma is used for separating, introducing, and enclosing words, phrases, and clauses within a sentence.

1. **Use a comma to separate independent clauses joined by a coordinating conjunction: *and, but, nor, or, yet.***

    Ellie is coming to visit this weekend, but she must return on Sunday after church.

    a. **If the independent clauses are short, the comma before the conjunction may be omitted.**

        Joni thanked the clerk but he did not respond in kind.

    b. **Longer clauses may also be joined without a comma if they are closely connected in thought.**

        Josh fixed his car after school and then he drove it to youth group that night.

2. **Always use a comma before the conjunction *for* when it means *because, as,* or *since*, to avoid misreading.**

    Ricky did not invite Lucy, for something always goes wrong when she shows up.

3. **Use a comma to separate an introductory modifying clause or phrase from the rest of the sentence.**

    As the sun breaks through the rain clouds, you may see the iridescent beauty of a rainbow.

4. **Use commas to separate words, phrases, or clauses in a series.**

    He brought his tennis balls, racquets, shoes, sunglasses, and other gear to the court.

5. **Use a comma to separate contrasting expressions in a sentence.**

    The advantages, not the drawbacks, of multi-level marketing were presented to the neophytes.

6. **Use a comma to separate words or other sentence elements that might be otherwise misread.**

    The day before, I drove to Kentucky.   Of the 550, 237 were injured.

7. **Use commas to enclose non-restrictive (not essential) dependent clauses and phrases within the sentence. Do not use commas to enclose restrictive (essential) clauses and phrases.**

    Non-restrictive: The Sears Tower, which is the tallest in Chicago, is made of steel.

    Restrictive: The building that is the tallest in Chicago is the Sears Tower.

8. **Use commas to enclose parenthetical (interrupter) words, phrases, or clauses.**

    I agree, initially, that you may be right. I do not, however, want to jump to conclusions.

9. **Use commas to enclose appositives.**

    My pastor, a godly and wise man, has taught many sinners the way of salvation.

10. Use commas to enclose words used in direct address.

And now, my fellow Americans, please cast your ballot for me on Election Day.

11. Use commas to enclose second elements of places and dates.

He left on August 16, 2002, to go to college at Lookout Mountain, Georgia, for four years.

Note: Do not use a comma to enclose a number representing a year when no day of the month is mentioned.

The Church of Scotland adopted both the Larger and Shorter Catechisms in July 1648.

12. Use commas to separate two or more adjectives that equally modify the same noun.

☞ To test whether the adjectives are equal, (1) insert the word "and" between them, or (2) reverse the order of the adjectives. If the result makes sense, the adjectives are likely equal.

Note: Do not place a comma between the last adjective and the noun.

His bright, up-and-coming opponent is going to make it tough on the incumbent this election.

13. When two or more adjectives modifying the same noun are not equal, do not use commas to separate them.

Note: See hints above for testing whether adjectives are equal or unequal.

He refinished the antique rocking chair with cherry wood stain and semigloss varnish.

14. DO NOT use a comma to separate compound predicates in a simple sentence.

Tim shopped and compared options before choosing the best computer for his needs.

15. DO NOT use a comma to separate an introductory clause or phrase used as the subject of a sentence.

Who scored the winning point was a complete surprise.

16. Use commas to separate thousands, millions, etc. in numerals with four or more digits.

Earth's equatorial diameter is 7,926 miles, or 12,755 kilometers.

Note: Do not use commas in numerals representing years, telephone numbers, addresses (such as house numbers, street numbers, and postal code numbers), catalogue numbers, or part numbers.

In 2002, their phone number changed to 555-6789 when they moved to 1405 Oak Street.

17. Use a comma to separate a short quotation from the speaker to whom it is attributed.

"One must *think* in order to read and write," asserts John Robbins. "Thinking, just as everything else, is supposed to follow certain rules, if we are to think correctly."

Note: Do not use a comma when there is no specific attribution with the quotation.

In feudal times, to say someone was "in hot water" was to charge him with a capital crime.

18. Use commas to enclose initials or titles following a person's name.

Paul Lindstrom, Ph.D., labored tirelessly to reach thousands worldwide with God's Word.

THE SEMICOLON

The *semicolon* (;) has only one purpose—*to separate*. It is a stronger mark of separation than the comma; that is, it signifies a greater "break" or "pause" between elements in a sentence. It is a weaker pause or break mark than a period, however, and therefore it cannot be used as an end-of-sentence mark. Elements separated by a semicolon must be equal and coordinate.

1. Use a semicolon to separate independent clauses that are not joined by a simple coordinating conjunction (*and, but, or, nor, neither, yet*).

There was no tenderness in their relationship; there wasn't even cordiality.

2. Use a semicolon to separate independent clauses that ARE joined by a simple coordinating conjunction if the independent clauses have internal commas or if the clauses are long.

Some hotels include restaurants, shops, and other facilities; but others offer only lodging.

3. **Use a semicolon to separate independent clauses that are joined by a conjunctive adverb.**

Note: If the conjunctive adverb has two or more syllables, place a comma after it in addition to the semicolon before it.

Élyse is a sweet girl; *in fact,* she is one of the sweetest girls I have ever known.

Note: If the conjunctive adverb has only one syllable, no comma is needed.

She tried for several hours to sew a new dress; *then* she gave up and bought a new one.

4. **Use semicolons to separate items in a series when the items themselves have internal commas.**

The workbook included text, sidebars, and summaries; maps, charts, and graphs; and optional projects, exercises, and review sections.

5. **DO NOT use a semicolon to set off a dependent clause or a phrase. A semicolon represents the end of a complete thought; it might be thought of as a "weak period." Therefore, it should not be used to set off incomplete thoughts.**
    WRONG: If Saddam Hussein cannot trust anyone; how does he sleep at night?
    RIGHT: If Saddam Hussein cannot trust anyone, how does he sleep at night?

THE COLON

The *colon* (:) is used primarily as a mark of introduction. It is often used to introduce series, lists, and quotations. Occasionally, it is used as a mark of separation.

1. **Use a colon to introduce a series or list.**

Most students need the following material: paper, folders, pens, pencils, and an eraser.

2. **Use a colon to introduce a word, phrase, or clause for special emphasis.**

So that is a black hole: a place where the future only leads inward, with unpleasant results.[52]

52. Robert Kunzig, "Black Holes *Spin?*" *Discover* [July 2002], 35.

3. DO NOT use a colon to introduce such elements when there is not a clear break between the introductory words and the series, list, or emphasized material that follows.

Note: Among the indicators of this kind of break are words such as "the following" or "as follows" or "these." (See the example under #1 above.) Never use a colon after the expression "such as."

> **WRONG:**   To her guests, the kind hostess offered: tea, coffee, fruit, and pastries.
>
> **RIGHT:**   To her guests, the kind hostess offered tea, coffee, fruit, and pastries.

Write your sample sentence illustrating the sentence labeled "RIGHT" above.

4. Use a colon to introduce a clause that gives an example of, summarizes, or adds to the thought of a preceding clause.

> Exercise is good for your health: it will strengthen your heart and build your muscles.

5. Use a colon to introduce a formal or long quotation or a quotation that is placed in a separate paragraph.

> David F. Wells, in his work entitled *No Place for Truth*, states: "In theology, Protestant and Catholic modernists alike envisioned spiritual life emerging in the ideals of human civilization. And in conventional Victorian piety, daily hope was sustained by the thought that every day, in every way, things were getting better and better. Two world wars should have doused the fires of these foolish illusions, but illusions have a way of making short work of reality."

6. Use a colon following the salutation (greeting) of a formal or business letter.

> Dear Sir: Dear Mrs. Smith: Greetings: To whom it may concern:

7. Use a colon as a mark of separation in the following situations:

■ **To separate hours and minutes in time figures:**

> The lecture begins at 7:30 p.m.

■ **To separate a book title from a subtitle:**

> Norman L. Geisler coauthored *Answering Islam: The Crescent in the Light of the Cross.*

■ **To separate chapter and verse in a Bible citation:**

   Matthew 22:37–40 summarizes what the law of God requires of us.

_____

■ **To separate act and scene numbers in reference to a play:**

   Together we read the final tragic moments of *Romeo and Juliet,* V:iii.

_____

THE HYPHEN

Do not confuse the **hyphen** (-) with the **dash** (—). The *hyphen* is always placed within a word. It is therefore more a mark of spelling than of punctuation. The *dash* is placed between words and is clearly a punctuation mark.

_____

1. **Use a hyphen to separate parts of some compound words. Hyphenated combinations may consist of the following:**

■ **An adjective or noun united with a participle**

   All able-bodied citizens were called to fight the flood.   The object was cone-shaped.

_____

■ **Two adjectives**

   She was of African-American ancestry.

_____

■ **An adverb and a participle**

   She learned the afore-mentioned rules of logic.

_____

■ **Compounds with three or more words**

   My father-in-law spoke five languages fluently.

_____

■ **Words beginning with *self-*, *ex-*, *half-*, or *quarter-***

   Self-control is a gift of God.   The ex-con could not get a job.   They are half-brothers.

_____

■ **Compound numerals**

   The Good Shepherd left the ninety-nine sheep to seek the one that was lost.

_____

■ **Fractions used as adjectives**

   Passage of a constitutional amendment requires a two-thirds vote of the House, or 290 votes.

_____

■   **Words with an adverb or a preposition as the second element.**

As you write, you are involved in an on-going process of making decisions and organizing thoughts.

2. **Use a hyphen when joining a prefix to a capitalized word.**

To desecrate the flag is un-American.

3. **Use a hyphen to join a single capital letter to a noun or participle.**

Take the right fork of the Y-intersection, and turn left at the second T-street that branches off the main drive that circles the townhouse complex.

4. **Use a hyphen in improvised compounds.**

Her know-it-all attitude was unnerving.   You're invited to the come-as-you-are party.

5. **Use a dictionary to determine whether certain word combinations are hyphenated, written as a single word, or written as separate words.**

THE DASH

The *long dash*, or *em dash*, is used as a mark of introduction, separation, or enclosure. It signifies a break in thought or shift in direction of thought. In some cases, it serves the same purpose as a comma, except that the dash signifies a stronger break or shift in thought.

1. **Use a dash to introduce an emphasized word, phrase, or clause.**

He had only one goal—survival.   The insult caused him to retaliate—spouting unkind words.

The officer was quite frank in his assessment—whoever broke the law would have to pay.

2. **Use a dash to separate a final clause that summarizes a series of preceding ideas.**

Note: Do not use a *colon* for this purpose. A *colon* introduces a series. A *dash* follows a series.

Love, joy, peace, patience, goodness, kindness, self-control—these are some of the fruit of the Spirit.

3. **Use dashes in pairs to enclose parenthetical information you wish to emphasize or isolate.**

News of the President's actions—no matter what they were—could not be concealed.

4. Use dashes to indicate a major turn, shift, or break in thought.

Taking responsibility for our own actions—rather than blaming others—is a sign of maturity.

LESSON 40: SIGNS ALONG THE WAY

THE APOSTROPHE

The *apostrophe* (') is a mark of *separation* and a mark of *omission*. Like the hyphen, it is a mark of spelling, since it always is part of a word.

1. Use an apostrophe and an "s" to form the possessive of all nouns not ending in "s."

The audience's response to the performance overwhelmed the cast.

2. To form the possessive of most singular nouns ending in "s" or an "s" or "z" sound, first write the singular form and then add an apostrophe and an "s."

A box's lid was bent.   The United States's response paid off.   The bus's schedule was posted.

Note: Certain ancient names with more than one syllable and ending in "s" and certain expressions simply add an apostrophe.

Jesus' teachings	Pericles' rule	Socrates' beliefs
for conscience' sake	for righteousness' sake	Moses' leadership

3. Use an apostrophe alone to form the possessive of a plural noun ending in "s."

The doctors' office hours changed during the summer.

4. Use an apostrophe and an "s" to form the possessive of compound nouns and pronouns.

Note: Place the 's after the elements closest to the thing possessed.

She always seemed to interfere in everybody's business.

5. Use an apostrophe and an "s" after only the last word in an expression showing joint possession.

Bud Abbott and Lou Costello's performance epitomizes the "straightman"/clown act.

_____

_____

Note: The exception to this rule is as follows: If the last element in the expression of joint possession is a possessive pronoun, use an apostrophe only after the first word—not the pronoun.

Brittany's and her room is decorated with Bible verses and Christ-honoring posters.

_____

6. Use an apostrophe and an "s" after each word in an expression showing _individual_ possession.

Harry's and Jan's ideas about having a good time are completely different.

_____

7. Use an apostrophe and an "s" to form the possessive of indefinite pronouns.

Everyone's concern for homeland security bolstered voter turnout for the mid-term elections.

_____

8. Use an apostrophe in contractions to indicate omitted letters.

Our team can't lose.   Weren't they going to the meeting?   I'd like to be the first to know.

_____

9. Use an apostrophe in the contraction of "it is" to indicate the omitted letter "i."

It's his duty to defend his country.   Sue said that it's her turn to go.

_____

Note: Use only an "s" to form the possessive of _it_. EXAMPLE: A buck looses its antlers every spring.

10. Use an apostrophe to indicate other omissions as well.

The '90s wrought moral decline in America.   He's always "runnin' off at the mouth."

_____

11. Do not use an apostrophe to form the plural of letters, abbreviations used as NOUNS, letters used as WORDS, and numbers, unless it would be confusing.

Count by tens.   Mind your Ps and Qs.   Many YMCAs were remodeled in the 1990s.

_____

Note: Place the 's after confusing letters used as _nouns_, signs and symbols, and abbreviations with periods.

12. Do not use an apostrophe to form the possessive of a personal or relative pronoun.

   This invention is ours.   Hers is the best illustration.   Whose DVD is this?

_____

13. Do not use an apostrophe to form the plural of nouns.

   WRONG: The McCoy's are still fumin'.   The Hatfields swiped their car's and truck's.

   Correct the above examples:

_____

QUOTATION MARKS

Quotation marks, parentheses, and _brackets_ are marks of enclosure that are almost always used in pairs. But they each have their distinctive purposes.

There are two types of **quotation marks**: _double_ (" ... ") and _single_ (' ... '). Each type consists of a pair, one _opening_ quotation mark and one _closing_ quotation mark. The opening mark goes at the beginning of the enclosed material; the closing mark goes at the end of the material.

1. Use quotation marks to enclose direct quotations—including complete quotations, partial quotations, and each part of an interrupted quotation.

   "There are three—and only three—covenantal institutions: church, state, and family," asserts Gary North.[53]

   North argues that many evangelical Christians have been seduced by the "family first" heresy of social conservatives, when the family of God is the only family central in time and eternity.[54]

   "Anyone who calls himself an orthodox Christian theologian," North claims, "must affirm that the Christian church is more important for eternity than the non-Christian family."[55]

   Give examples of each use of quotations marks described above:

   a. _____

   _____

   b. _____

   _____

   c. _____

   _____

---

53. _Baptized Patriarchalism: The Cult of the Family_ (Tyler, TX: Institute for Christian Economics, 1994), 7.

54. Ibid., 10.

55. Ibid., 11, 12.

2. If a direct quotation extends for more than one paragraph, place opening quotation marks at the beginning of each paragraph but closing quotation marks at the end of only the last paragraph of quotation. Otherwise, always use quotation marks in pairs.

✎ **EXERCISE** Place quotation marks in the proper places in the following quotation, according to the above rule.

On pages 16 and 17 of *Shepherding a Child's Heart,* Tedd Tripp states:

Ultimately your children must internalize the message of the Gospel. Each child in a

Christian home will at some point examine the claims of the Gospel and determine whether

he will embrace the truth.

Picture the process this way: he holds the claims of the Gospel at arm's length, turning

it in the hand and determining either to embrace it or cast it away.

The parent has the marvelous opportunity to help his young adult child pursue with hon-

esty all his questions of faith. The Word of God is robust; Christian faith can withstand close,

honest scrutiny. Everyone does not have the obligation to ask every question, but everyone

has the obligation to ask every question he has.

3. Use quotation marks to enclose words with unusual, specific, or limited usages, such as illiteracies, slang, technical words, or common words used in irregular or emphasized ways.

Lisa tried to find acceptance by pleasing her friends, but she was "barking up the wrong tree."
His reputation as a "bad egg" followed him everywhere he went.
To "navigate" on the "Information Superhighway" you need a knowledge of "hypertext."

4. Use quotation marks to enclose chapter headings of books and titles of short stories, poems, songs, and similar short literary works when used in a body of prose.

Louis Haber's short story, "Pioneer in Surgery," tells of the famous surgeon, Dr. Daniel H. Williams.
Chapter two of Bahnsen's book on Van Til's apologia is entitled "The Task of Apologetics."

Note: Do not put quotation marks around a title when it is placed in the title position at the beginning of a theme paper, essay, report, or other composition.

5. **Use single quotation marks to enclose quotations, titles, etc. within a quotation.**

    "Have you read 'The Phoenix and the Turtle' by William Shakespeare?" Josh asked.

6. **Place quotation marks correctly in relation to other punctuation marks.**

■   **Commas and periods go inside the quotation marks, even when only the last word before the comma or period is enclosed.**

    "At the ninth hour," explained Cornelius, "a man stood before me in bright clothing and said, 'Cornelius, your prayer has been heard....'"   He was known as a "God-fearer."

■   **Place question marks, exclamation points, and dashes outside the quotation marks unless these punctuation marks are part of the quotation.**

    Did she say, "[T]his vast right-wing conspiracy ... has been conspiring against my husband"?

    The keeper of the prison asked Paul and Silas, "Sirs, what must I do to be saved?"

    Mom shouted, "Stop!"   You should obey when you hear the word "jump"!

    She always puts too much on her plate—"her eyes are bigger than her stomach."

■   **When listing a series of titles or words, place commas and periods inside the quotation marks. In regard to other types of punctuation, the rule above applies.**

    Only three films have swept all five "best" categories (picture, directing, actor, actress, and writing): "It Happened One Night," "One Flew Over the Cuckoo's Nest," and "The Silence of the Lambs."

    Her performance was characterized as "eccentric," "undignified," yet "entertaining."

■   **Semicolons and colons are always placed outside the quotation marks.**

    The following items are "kosher": food, vitamins, and mineral supplements blessed by a rabbi.

    His assigned topic was "My Autobiography"; but his life was drab, so he thought.

PARENTHESES AND BRACKETS

Whereas dashes are used to emphasize parenthetical material they enclose, *parentheses* (...) and *brackets* [...] are used to de-emphasize the enclosed material.

1. **Use parentheses to enclose material remotely related to a main statement.**

    Washington, Madison, Jackson, Van Buren, William Harrison, Tyler, Polk, Taylor, Pierce, Buchanan, Arthur, Cleveland, Benjamin Harrison, Theodore Roosevelt, Wilson, Coolidge, Franklin Roosevelt, Eisenhower, Ford, Reagan, George Bush (former presidents) were members of Reformed churches.

    The Organization of African Unity (OAU) was established in 1963, at Addis Ababa, Ethiopia.

2. **Use parentheses to enclose references, directions, citations, and similar material. In all these cases, place the ending period after the final parenthesis if the citation comes at the end of a sentence.**

> Garry J. Moes states, "[The Reformers] taught that man's chief aim was to bring glory to God in every endeavor" (Streams of Civilization, Vol. 2, [Arlington Heights, IL: CL Press, 1995], p. 35).

> "For the weapons of our warfare are not carnal but mighty in God for pulling down strongholds, casting down arguments and every high thing that exalts itself against the knowledge of God, bringing every thought into captivity to the obedience of Christ" (2 Corinthians 10:4, 5, NKJV).

---

3. **Use parentheses to enclose numbering figures used within written text.**

> To register your own Internet domain name, (1) you need to create a domain that suits your business; (2) search to see if your domain name is available (WHOIS Search); (3) enter your new domain with a 'registrar,' who can enter and update domain names in the master domain-name database (monthly fee is required); (4) once you have placed your order, you may have to download some sort of client software; and (5) finally, your IP service provider will activate your account and you are ready to start using your own domain.

---

4. **Use brackets to enclose parenthetical material inserted within other parenthetical material. Use parentheses to enclose parenthetical material inserted within bracketed material.**

> (The book [written by an unknown author (using the name Philo)] became a best-seller.)

---

5. **Use brackets to enclose your own comments, explanations, or corrections inserted within a quotation.**

> "Leafy, green vegetables [e.g. kale, spinach, etc.] are a good source of nutrients," she said.

---

6. **On rare occasions (usually in commercial or technical writing), use parentheses to enclose figures, chemical compounds, or formulas repeated or expanded for accuracy.**

> The experiment required the use of five milliliters (5 mil.) of saline solution.

> Most (65) of the books of the Bible mention God; only the Book of Esther does not.

> Based on the law of multiple proportions, carbon and oxygen can form two compounds—carbon monoxide (CO) and carbon dioxide (CO_2).

LESSON 41: INDENTATION AND ALTERNATIVES

It is usually quite simple to make your paragraphs mechanically correct, because there are very few rules or customs governing the appearance of paragraphs. If your sentences are correctly written and accurately punctuated, you have accomplished most of what is necessary to make a paragraph mechanically correct. Since the purpose of a paragraph is to develop a single idea through the combination of sentences, it has become the custom to indicate the beginning and end of a paragraph visually so that the reader knows instantly where there are "breaks" in thought. This helps the reader to see clearly at first glance where one specific idea ends and another begins. The device which does this is *paragraph indentation*—the offsetting of the first line of a paragraph a specified distance to the right of the left margin.

INDENTATION

The amount of space used for indentation varies, depending upon the mechanical means by which you are writing your paragraph. If you are using handwriting, it is customary to indent the first line of a paragraph about three-fourths of an inch. If you are using a standard typewriter, indent the first line of your paragraph five spaces. If you are using a computer or other electronic word processor, the word-processing software will usually have ways to pre-set paragraph indentations automatically. See your software manual for instructions on how to set indentations. Generally, the indentation will be about one-quarter of an inch. Professional printers usually indent paragraphs by a measure known as an "em"—a space approximately equal to the width of the letter "M" in whatever typeface and type size the printer is using. Here is an example of *standard paragraph indentation*:

> Robert E. Lee was a man devoted to principle in spite of personal loss in his resignation from the U.S. Army. On April 18, 1861, at the request of President Lincoln, through General Winfield Scott and Francis P. Blair, Sr., Lee could have chosen to retain his rank in the U.S. Army and later assume the position of commander of the U.S. forces in its conflict with the South; but he said that he refused to raise his sword against his family, his friends, and his native country, Virginia. Here was his golden hour of opportunity for instant glory, greatness, and fame; yet, he chose to follow the principles of duty, honor, and love of country. When war was imminent, Lee was faced with a heartrending choice; should he seek safety in cowardice and dishonor or meet possible destruction and loss in doing that which he knew was right. [*Some punctuation has been added or altered for greater clarity.*]
>
> —Charles A. Jennings, "A Character Sketch of Robert E. Lee"
> <http://www.truthinhistory.org/lee.htm>

ALTERNATIVES

While it is most commonly accepted to distinguish paragraphs by indenting the first line, modern practice and style allow for a few variations and exceptions for special purposes.

One alternative is not to indent the first line. All lines begin at the left margin. This method is often referred to as the *block style*. Paragraphs are then distinguished by leaving a *line of space* between each paragraph. The pages in the book you are now reading use the block style.

Another alternative is known as the **hanging indent**. This alignment is the opposite of the standard alignment. In a hanging indent, only the first line begins at the left margin, and all of the following lines in the paragraph are indented. Paragraphs are usually distinguished by leaving a line of space between them. Here is an example of a hanging-indent style:

Margin ➭

Lee was a man that had learned through hardship and tragedy to possess an un-relenting faith and confidence in the sovereign counsel and control of the Al-mighty God both in matters of national and personal loss. Once during the war, when the responsibilities of the survival of a whole nation rested upon his shoulders, he endured personal tragedy and loss with spiritual courage and God-given strength. Upon hearing of the death of his 23 year old daughter, Annie, in North Carolina, and unable to attend her funeral, Lee insisted that these words be carved upon her tombstone; 'Perfect and TRUE are all His ways—whom Heaven adores and earth obeys.'

Among the many virtues of this great man, he expressed foresight and serious concern for the future of our nation when he said, "I fear the liberties of our country will be buried in the tomb of a great nation." Yet he expressed faith and hope when he said, "The dominant party cannot reign forever; truth and justice will prevail at last." [*Some punctuation has been added or altered for greater clarity.*]

—Charles A. Jennings, "A Character Sketch of Robert E. Lee"
<http://www.truthinhistory.org/lee.htm>

A variation of the hanging-indent style is the **numbered paragraph**. In this alignment, a number (or letter) is placed at the beginning of the first line and at the left margin. The text of the first line and all other lines is then indented. A line of space is inserted between paragraphs. Here is an example:

The causes of this disaster, so shamefully misstated and perverted at the time, are now generally understood. No one could, at this day, repeat the misrepresentations that for the moment prevailed, without conscious, palpable guilt and ignominy. The true, controlling reasons of the Federal defeat were, briefly, these:

1. The fundamental, fatal error on that side was that spirit of hesitation, of indecision, of calculated delay, of stolid obstruction, which guided all military councils, scattering their forces and paralyzing their efforts. Had any real purpose of suppressing the rebellion been cherished by General Scott, he never would have scattered the eastern forces....

2. The flagrant disobedience and defection of General Patterson, unaccountable on any hypothesis consistent with the possession, on his part, of courage, common-sense, and loyalty.

3. The failure of General Scott to send forward with General McDowell a force adequate to provide against all contingencies. The fact that twenty thousand volunteers remained idle and useless, throughout that eventful Sunday....

4. The Confederates were kept thoroughly acquainted by their friends, left in the Union service, with all that took place or was meditated on that side, and so were able to anticipate and baffle every movement of those armies....

—Horace Greeley, *The Battle of Bull Run* (1861)

This same style may also be used for ***bulleted*** paragraphs. Instead of a number, certain devices and symbols known as "bullets" or "dingbats" are sometimes used to mark paragraphs. Here are some examples of "bullets," "dingbats," and "symbols": ❥ ✦ ❱ ➤ ♠ ➡ ➻ ¶ §. In this textbook, some of these devices are used, for instance, to indicate paragraphs containing instructions for ✎**EXERCISES**. These attention-getting devices have only limited and specialized uses, most of which you will not encounter in your school writing or in your regular writing later in life.

✎ **EXERCISE** List examples of the various types of indentation from your textbooks or other sources. Look for examples of standard indentation, hanging indentation, numbered paragraphs, bulleted paragraphs, and block style.

Title: _____

Type of Indentation: _____

Title: _____

Type of Indentation: _____

Title: _____

Type of Indentation: _____

LESSON 42: SPACING AND ALIGNMENT

SPACING

Within the paragraph, the rules are simple. If you have properly begun each sentence with a capital letter and ended each with a period, question mark, or exclamation point, the paragraph is properly constructed. It has been a custom to leave two spaces between the end of one sentence and the beginning of another when using a standard typewriter. Modern practice, especially with electronic word processors, follows the custom of professional typesetters by leaving only *one* space between sentences. This is because many electronic word processors automatically calculate word spacing within a paragraph, and putting two spaces between sentences may create an unpleasant appearance when the gap is widened further electronically. If you are handwriting your paragraph, leave sufficient space between the period at the end of one sentence and the capital letter at the beginning of the next sentence so that the reader can clearly distinguish where one sentence ends and another begins.

ALIGNMENT

Each line of your paragraph should extend from the left margin to the right margin, unless the *last line* ends before reaching to the full extent of the line. Leaving large blank spaces at the end of lines in the middle of the paragraph may mislead the reader into thinking that a new paragraph is beginning—and with it a new idea. Partially blank lines also create a jagged appearance to the page. They also force unnecessary eye movements and brain adjustments, creating extra difficulties for the reader. Also remember to keep left margins as straight as possible when handwriting your paragraph. Electronic typewriters and word processors often give you several options for aligning words along the right margin. One option, called full "justification," aligns your lines of words along a straight line on the right just as on the left margin. (To *justify* is to make right according to a fixed measure or standard.) Another option is called "flush left," in which only the left margin is aligned while lines are "jagged" at the right margin. A center alignment is not used for paragraphs but is used for titles, headlines, and sometimes subheadings.

✎ **EXERCISE** From your reading, find examples of different types of *spacing* and *alignment*. Look in instruction manuals, magazines, handbooks, advertisements, etc. Bring examples to class or write, in the spaces below, the titles of the publications or articles where you found the examples.

Instruction Manual: _____

_____

Magazine: _____

_____

Handbook: _____

_____

Advertisement: _____

_____

Novel: _____

_____

Short Story: _____

_____

Poetry: _____

_____

Other: _____

_____

LESSON 43: UNIT REVIEW

✎ **EXERCISE A** For each of the following sentences, write a **C** in the blank if the sentence is correct in its use of capitalization. Write an *X* if it contains capitalization errors. If you find an error, cross out the word or words that violate the rules and write the proper form above them.

      On Wednesday   *Chargers*   *Christian High*

1. __*X*__ ~~on wednesday~~, our team, the ~~chargers~~, defeated the team from Bethel ~~christian high~~.

2. ____ mr. kostelny, our history teacher, also coaches our Baseball team.

3. ____ This fall, the freshman class will be the largest in the history of our school.

4. ____ The World Journalism institute has a working agreement with *the asheville citizen-times*.

5. ____ frost's importance as a poet derives from "The death of the hired Man" and other poems.

6. ____ *WORLD* magazine always tries to publish articles with a Christian worldview.

7. ____ The Islamic Religion has inspired violence in some countries of the middle east.

8. ___ My great aunt wanted to learn english, but Grandpa George insisted she could not.

9. ___ The hudson bay area is known as a sanctuary for Beluga whales.

10. ___ *The reconstruction of the republic* was the last book i checked out of arlington public library.

11. ___ He graduated from Elgin High School and then attended Covenant College.

12. ___ Jordan, President of our class, has won a scholarship to attend a prestigious College in the east.

13. ___ Jakarta, the Capital of Indonesia, is situated on the Island of Java, South of the Java sea.

14. ___ Is there a Hilton Hotel on Hilton Head island?

15. ___ i cannot find any errors in this sentence. okay, i'm only joking!

✎ **EXERCISE B** Punctuate the following paragraphs by filling in the blanks. If no punctuation is needed, leave the blank empty.

Two men_ Saddam Husayn and Bakr_ increasingly dominated the [Baath] party_ Bakr_ who had been associated with Arab nationalist causes for more than a decade_ brought the party popular legitimacy_ Even more important_ he brought support from the army both among Baathist and non_Baathist officers_ with whom he had cultivated ties for years_ Saddam Husayn_ on the other hand_ was a consummate party politician whose formative experiences were in organizing clandestine opposition activity_ He was adept at outmaneuvering__and at times ruthlessly eliminating__political opponents. Although Bakr was the older and more prestigious of the two_ by 1969 Saddam Husayn clearly had become the moving force behind the party_ He personally directed Baathist attempts to settle the Kurdish question and he organized the party_s institutional structure_

In July 1973_ after an unsuccessful coup attempt by a civilian faction within the Baath led by Nazim Kazzar_ the party set out to reconsolidate its hold on power_ First_ the RCC [Revolutionary Command Council_ amended the Provisional Constitution to give the president greater power_ Second_ in early 1974 the Regional Command was officially designated as the body responsible for making policy_ By September 1977_ all Regional Command leaders had been appointed to the RCC_ Third_ the party created a more pervasive presence in Iraqi society by establishing a complex network of grass_roots and intelligence_gathering organizations_ Finally_ the party established its own militia_ which in 1978 was reported to number close to 50_000 men_

Despite Baath attempts to institutionalize its rule_ real power remained in the hands of a narrowly based elite_ united by close family and tribal ties_ By 1977 the most powerful men in the Baath thus were all somehow related to the triumvirate of Saddam Husayn_ Bakr_ and General Adnan

Khayr Allah Talfah_ Saddam Husayn_s brother_in_law who became minister of defense in 1978_ All were members of the party_ the RCC_ and the cabinet_ and all were members of the Talfah family of Tikrit_ headed by Khayr Allah Talfah_ Khayr Allah Talfah was Saddam Husayn_s uncle and guardian_ Adnan Khayr Allah_s father_ and Bakr_s cousin_ Saddam Husayn was married to Adnan Khayr Allah_s sister and Adnan Khayr Allah was married to Bakr_s daughter_ Increasingly_ the most sensitive military posts were going to the Tikritis_

Beginning in the mid_1970_s_ Bakr was beset by illness and by a series of family tragedies_ He increasingly turned over power to Saddam Husayn_ By 1977 the party bureaus_ the intelligence mechanisms_ and even ministers who_ according to the Provisional Constitution_ should have reported to Bakr_ reported to Saddam Husayn_ Saddam Husayn_ meanwhile_ was less inclined to share power_ and he viewed the cabinet and the RCC as rubber stamps_ On July 16_ 1979_ President Bakr resigned_ and Saddam Husayn officially replaced him_ as president of the republic_ secretary general of the Baath Party Regional Command_ chairman of the RCC_ and commander in chief of the armed forces_

In foreign affairs_ the Baath_s pan_Arab and socialist leanings alienated both the pro_Western Arab Gulf states and the shah of Iran_ The enmity between Iraq and Iran sharpened with the 1969 British announcement_ of a planned withdrawal from the Gulf in 1971_ In February 1969_ Iran announced that Iraq had not fulfilled its obligations under the 1937 treaty and demanded that the border in the Shatt al Arab waterway be set at the thalweg_ Iraq_s refusal to honor the Iranian demand led the shah to abrogate the 1937 treaty and to send Iranian ships through the Shatt al Arab without paying dues to Iraq_ In response_ Iraq aided anti_shah dissidents_ while the shah renewed support for Kurdish rebels_ Relations between the two countries soon deteriorated further_ In November 1971_ the shah occupied the islands of Abu Musa and the Greater and Lesser Tunbs_ which previously had been under the sovereignty of Ras al Khaymah and Sharjah_ both member states of the United Arab Emirates_

The Iraqi Baath also was involved in a confrontation_ with the conservative shaykhdoms of the Gulf over Iraq_s support for the leftist People_s Democratic Republic of Yemen _South Yemen) and the Popular Front for the Liberation of the Occupied Arabian Gulf_ The major contention between Iraq and the conservative Gulf states_ however_ concerned the Kuwaiti islands of Bubiyan and Warbah that dominate the estuary leading to the southern Iraqi port of Umm Qasr_

Beginning in the early 1970_s_ Iraq_s desire to develop a deepwater port on the Gulf led to de-

mands that the two islands be transferred or leased to Iraq_ Kuwait refused_ and in March 1973

Iraqi troops occupied As Samitah_ a border post in the northeast corner of Kuwait_ Saudi Arabia

immediately came to Kuwait_s aid and_ together with the Arab League_ obtained Iraq_s

withdrawal_

The most serious threat facing the Baath was a resurgence of Kurdish unrest in the north_ In

March 1970_ the RCC and Mustafa Barzani announced agreement to a fifteen_article peace

plan_ This plan was almost identical to the previous Bazzaz_Kurdish settlement that had never

been implemented_ The Kurds were immediately pacified by the settlement_ particularly be-

cause Barzani was permitted to retain his 15_000 Kurdish troops_ Barzani_s troops then became

an official Iraqi frontier force called the Pesh Merga_ meaning _Those Who Face Death_ _ The

plan_ however_ was not completely satisfactory because the legal status of the Kurdish territory

remained unresolved_ At the time of the signing_ of the peace plan_ Barzani_s forces controlled

territory from Zakhu in the north to Halabjah in the southeast and already had established de

facto Kurdish administration in most of the towns of the area_ Barzani_s group_ the Kurdish

Democratic Party _KDP_, was granted official recognition as the legitimate representative of the

Kurdish people_

From *Iraq: A Country Study* edited by Helen Chapin Metz
Federal Research Division_ Library of Congress_ May 1988

EXERCISE C Fill in the blanks.

1. *Indentation* is _____

_____.

2. Describe the three types of indentation, including the two variations of the third style.

a. _____

_____

b. _____

_____

c. _____

_____

1. _____

_____

_____

2. _____

_____

_____

3. Describe the two ways *spacing* is used in paragraphs.

_____

_____

4. What is the preferred method of *alignment*? Why?

_____

_____

_____

5. List various ways word processors and computers can align text.

a. _____

b. _____

c. _____

✎ **EXERCISE D** On the lines provided below, describe in a couple of paragraphs how the author used good writing mechanics in the following article. Also mention any errors you might find.

I can close my eyes and still see my father smiling and happy to be with us. In a park not so far away from this cemetery, it was a beautiful spring day many years ago. All of us children, seven in all plus my mother were sitting around him eager to learn yet another lesson. My father loved to teach us about a lot of things. My father loved to have his family around him and we loved him greatly.

This particular morning the flowers were in full bloom and it was sunny and clear. My father would look and smile at us as he prepared a surprising theme. There were butterflies and birds and lady bugs everywhere. My father cupped his hand over a flower and captured a bee. We were all surprised and frightened and got really excited. Some of my younger sisters started to scream and cry. They were afraid of bees and were concerned that my father would get stung.

But my father grabbed the bee by the wings and let the bee sting him on his arm. He pulled out the pulsating stinger from his arm and tossed it away.

Still excited and screaming, we began to see how he played with the bee. He asked me to take the bee in my hand. I was terrified. He explained that the bee could not hurt me since he had removed the venomous stinger. So, reluctantly and cautiously I began to let the bee crawl on my hand and arm and before I knew it I was laughing and giggling and showing off the bee to my brothers and sisters. I close my eyes and I see the delight in my father's eyes.

I will never forget that day. Little did we know, that the lesson we were about to learn that day, would be the greatest lesson of all. You see, almost 2,000 years ago, Jesus Christ took the sting away from death when He died on the cross. "O Death, where is thy sting? O grave, where is thy victory?" (1 Corinthians 15:55) He was almost telling us to challenge death to show its teeth. Death has none because of Jesus Christ's death on the cross for us.

Recalling that lesson would later help us to endure what was unavoidable. When my father died we all remembered that lesson that now helps us to understand that my father lives on. He lives with Jesus in eternity. Now, we all look forward to the time when we sit around my father again in heaven with Jesus. Life does not have to end in the grave. The grave can only be the beginning.

—David F. Calderon II, "O Death, Where is thy sting?"
<http://dianedew.com/bee.htm>

_____

_____

_____

_____

_____

_____

_____

_____

_____

Unit 5
Colorful Writing

In the previous unit, we considered some of the ways to make your writing mechanically correct, clear, effective, and appropriate. Still, there is more to good writing than these functional considerations. Good writing is also *creative*. To be creative means to be inventive and original, able to produce something of value that is *fresh* and *new*. In some respects, the ability to be an exceptionally creative writer is a God-given talent. That does not mean, however, that people who are not specially endowed in this area of human life cannot become better writers. This unit will outline some ideas that everyone can employ and practice to be creative and interesting in their writing.

LESSON 44: SYNONYMS AND ANTONYMS

In this lesson, we will consider words that have the same or opposite meanings. These words will help you to communicate more effectively, both in the written and spoken word. They also can breakup the dull and colorless wording that often passes as good communication. Use these words wisely.

SYNONYMS

Synonyms are words that have the same or similar meanings. Thinking of a synonym is "easy," but choosing the *right* synonym is not always as "effortless." Of course, there is no such thing as a true "synonym," since each word has its own connotation, usage, and import. As we all know, a *house* is not a *home,* all *women* are not *ladies*, and *homely* does not necessarily mean *plain*. In addition, as new words are added to the English language, they are initially used as synonyms of current words—but shortly they begin to change and take on nuances of their own. Consequently, using synonyms adds color to one's writing, but they should be chosen carefully.

ANTONYMS

Antonyms are words that have opposite meanings. Likewise, thinking of an antonym and selecting the right one are two different things. As you attempt to make your writing interesting and vivid, you should make every effort to choose the best antonym that suits your topic and fits the context. If you question the appropriateness of a particular word, be sure to consult a major dictionary to find the various definitions and connotations that the term may hold.

Sometimes antonyms are formed by the simple addition of a *prefix* which changes the meaning of a word to its opposite. Each of the prefixes below means *not.*

☞**EXAMPLES:**

un-	+	true	⇒	*un*true		im-	+	perfect	⇒	*im*perfect
dis-	+	like	⇒	*dis*like		ir-	+	reverent	⇒	*ir*reverent
mis-	+	understand	⇒	*mis*understand		il-	+	legal	⇒	*il*legal
in-	+	sincere	⇒	*in*sincere		a-	+	moral	⇒	*a*moral

Adjectives with the *suffix -ful* can often be changed to antonyms by substituting the *suffix -less*.

☞**EXAMPLES:**

joy*ful* ⇒ joy*less*   sin*ful* ⇒ sin*less*   fear*ful* ⇒ fear*less*

✎ **EXERCISE** Write *synonyms* for the first column and *antonyms* for the second column of words. If you cannot think of one from your general vocabulary knowledge, use a dictionary or thesaurus.

Synonyms		Antonyms	
1. hostile	*antagonistic*	1. arrogant	*humble*
2. apparent		2. harmful	
3. ascend		3. rough	
4. difficult		4. huge	
5. meager		5. decrease	
6. arrogant		6. adequate	
7. joyous		7. faithful	
8. rebuke		8. talkative	
9. cordial		9. refined	
10. defame		10. fruitful	

LESSON 45: HOMONYMS AND HOMOGRAPHS

In this lesson, we will consider terms that sound alike and words that are spelled alike but have different meanings. These words will also help you to communicate more effectively, both in your written and spoken pursuits. They can breakup the drab and unimaginative wording that often passes as good communication. Use these words judiciously.

HOMONYMS

Using **homonyms** correctly is also vital to good communication. Orally, they sound alike and the listener must understand the word used from context. The challenge these words present is that they sound alike but have different meanings and spellings. In writing these terms, precision in the choice of the homonym is essential to conveying the correct meaning.

HOMOGRAPHS

Homographs are two or more words that are spelled alike. However, they have different *meanings* and may have different *pronunciations.* Try to avoid using homographs together in the same sentence, unless you are doing so purposely for a certain effect, as in poetry, riddles, etc.

☞**EXAMPLES:**

AVOID: He was a terrible *bore,* but we *bore* with him as long as we could.

BETTER: He was a terrible *bore,* but we *put up* with him as long as we could.

AVOID: The *sole* reason for buying new shoes is that the *sole* of one of her shoes has a hole.

BETTER: The *only* reason for buying new shoes is that the *sole* of one of her shoes has a hole.

✎ **EXERCISE A** Write at least one *homonym* for each of the following words. Some of these words may have two homonyms. Write them both if you can.

1. peace _____
2. deer _____
3. would _____
4. herd _____
5. know _____
6. rain _____
7. who's _____
8. new _____
9. scent _____
10. flue _____

11. their _____
12. wrest _____
13. shear _____
14. sew _____
15. whether _____
16. stationary _____
17. shone _____
18. shutter _____
19. led _____
20. passed _____

✎ **EXERCISE B** Define the following *homonyms* and *near-homonyms*.

1. complement *something that completes*

   compliment *an expression of regard or praise*

2. slay _____

   sleigh _____

3. principle _____

   principal _____

4. course _____

   coarse _____

5. counsel _____

   council _____

   consul _____

6. do _____

   due _____

7. capital _____

   capitol _____

8. accept _____

   except _____

✎ **EXERCISE C** Define the following *homographs* according to their various meanings. As you look them up in a dictionary, take note of any differences in pronunciations associated with each meaning.

1. row   _____

    row   _____

    row   _____

2. air   _____

    air   _____

    air   _____

3. bow   _____

    bow   _____

    bow   _____

    bow   _____

4. lead   _____

    lead   _____

LESSON 46: TROPES

It has been said that things are not always the way they seem. This idea can be applied to writing. Words can be used in creative ways to make the meanings of our communications something brighter, grander, more clever, more subtle, or more ingenious than they might appear at first glance. The term *trope* means *the use of a word or expression in a figurative way*. In this lesson, we will consider some terms which are associated with the creative meanings of speech and written communications.

DENOTATION AND CONNOTATION

These terms apply to the *meaning* of words.

■ Denotation

Denotation is the literal, most ordinary, dictionary meaning of a word.

☞**EXAMPLE:**

> He saw a **tiger**.
> *Tiger* = a large, ferocious Asian mammal of the cat family, tawny in color with black stripes

■ Connotation

Connotation is the meaning that is implied in, suggested by, or associated with a word.

☞**EXAMPLE:**

> When he plays football, he's a real **tiger**.
> *Tiger* = a person who acts aggressively or ferociously, preys upon others, or pounces like a tiger

A good writer becomes aware of the hidden meanings of words and uses certain words in various contexts to communicate a full range of meanings. Yet, he may avoid words with certain associations so as to prevent readers from getting notions that are not intended. Train yourself to know both the **denotation** and **connotation** of the words that you use. Notice, for example, the difference in the *connotations* of the following pairs of words which have similar *denotations*:

tightfisted	—	thrifty
picky	—	discriminating
meddle	—	intervene
finicky	—	fastidious

SYNECDOCHE

A *synecdoche* (sin-EK-doh-kee) is a figure of speech in which *a part of a thing represents the whole*.

☞**EXAMPLES:**

The general summoned the **horse**.   (Meaning: The general summoned the *cavalry*.)

My brother has some new **wheels**.   (Meaning: My brother has a new *car*.)

METONYMY

Somewhat akin to synecdoche, is **metonymy** (meh-TAH-nih-mee), a term of Greek origin which means "substitute meaning." In metonymy, two different items are so closely related that they take on the characteristics of each other. The term can apply to items that may be very different in reality but may have similar appearance or qualities.

☞**EXAMPLE:**

The doctor gave up the **scalpel** in favor of medical research.   (Meaning: The doctor gave up the *practice of surgery* in favor of medical research.)

OXYMORON

An **oxymoron** is a combination or blending of two contradictory or inconsistent terms. The word itself is an example. *Oxys* is Greek for "sharp" and *moros* is Greek for "stupid or foolish." Thus an oxymoron may be said to be a cleverly foolish expression.

☞**EXAMPLE:**

They were **cautiously eager** to proceed into the dark cave.

ANTITHESIS

Antithesis is the more deliberate contrasting of two ideas or terms for the purpose of highlighting their differences.

☞**EXAMPLE:**

One man's trash is another man's treasure.

APOSTROPHE

Apostrophe is an imaginary addressing of a person or thing that is absent or dead; the addressing of an inanimate object as if it could hear and understand.

☞**EXAMPLE:**

"O Death, where is thy sting? O Grave, where is thy victory?" (1 Cor. 15:55; cf. Isaiah 25:8).

HYPERBOLE

Hyperbole is the use of gross exaggeration (not to be taken literally) for the purpose of making a point.

☞**EXAMPLE:**

> You can argue with me until doomsday, but I will never agree with you.

LITOTES

Litotes (ly-TOH-teez) is the use of understatement to convey an opposite meaning or to increase an effect.

☞**EXAMPLE:**

> The millionaire lived in a modest forty-room apartment with a meager staff of twenty servants.

SIMILE

A *simile* (SIH-mih-lee) is a comparison using *like* or *as*.

☞**EXAMPLE:**

> He runs like a deer.

METAPHOR

A *metaphor* (MEH-tah-for) is an implied comparison without the use of *like* or *as*.

☞**EXAMPLE:**

> When he plays football, he is a real tiger.

PERSONIFICATION

Personification is the giving of human characteristics to objects, ideas, or animals.

☞**EXAMPLE:**

> The waves danced along the shore.

There are two other literary devices which are not "figures of speech" in the same way that the above tropes are, but they are usually grouped with the above because they also give special distinction to speech and writing. These are *alliteration* and *onomatopoeia*.

ALLITERATION

This device involves the repetition of word sounds—particularly initial sounds.

☞**EXAMPLE:**

> "While I nodded, nearly napping, suddenly there came a tapping…" (Edgar Allen Poe)

ONOMATOPOEIA

Onomatopoeia (on-oh-mah-toh-PEE-ah) is the use of words whose pronunciation sounds like their meanings.

☞**EXAMPLES:**

> pop, sizzle, buzz, crackle, hiss, crunch

✎ **EXERCISE A** Identify the *figure of speech* or *literary device* used in each of the following sentences.

metonymy	1.	The White House issued no public statement about the incident.
_____	2.	Just then, several skiers whooshed down the hill past me.
_____	3.	Some modern thinkers are foolish sages indeed.
_____	4.	This lovely weed certainly has a fragrant stench.
_____	5.	She's not the friendliest person I know.
_____	6.	Tommy yelped like a whipped puppy after his dad punished him.
_____	7.	"Fair is foul and foul is fair" *(Shakespeare).*
_____	8.	I heard dinner calling me to the table.
_____	9.	When he saw her costume, his jaw dropped to the floor.
_____	10.	"What a tale of terror, now their turbulency tells!" *(Poe)*
_____	11.	"Give us this day our daily bread…"
_____	12.	"Rain, rain, go away, come again some other day."

✎ **EXERCISE B** Write your own examples of the following *tropes* and *literary devices* or cite examples from famous literature or other readings.

Simile

_____

_____

Hyperbole

_____

_____

Alliteration

_____

_____

Apostrophe

_____

_____

Metonymy

_____

_____

Metaphor

_____

_____

Litotes

_____

_____

Onomatopoeia

_____

_____

Oxymoron

_____

_____

Personification

_____

_____

Synecdoche

_____

_____

Antithesis

_____

_____

✎ **EXERCISE C** Write synonyms—with different connotations—for the following words. Use a thesaurus if necessary. See the examples at the top of page 143.

1. funny   _____   4. arrogant   _____

2. naive   _____   5. cunning   _____

3. wise   _____   6. deliberate _____

LESSON 47: DIALOGUE

One of the best ways to make your writing interesting is to include *dialogue*—conversations between people—and *monologue*—conversation with oneself. Obviously, not every type of writing lends itself to the use of dialogue. *Storytelling* (narrative writing) clearly does, however. If you are especially creative, you may also find ways to introduce dialogue or conversation-like sentences into other forms of writing.

MECHANICAL CONSIDERATIONS

There are some mechanical considerations which you should learn before trying to write dialogue. These have to do mostly with punctuation and paragraphing.

■ **Direct Quotation**

Enclose direct statements by your characters within *quotation marks*.

> **"What's for dinner?"** Fran asked.

■ **Attribution**

Use *attribution* (identity of the person speaking) for each quoted statement.

> "What's for dinner?" **Fran asked.**

Note: Attribution may not always be necessary. The identity of the speaker may be omitted if the source of the quotation is clear from the context.

> "What's for dinner, Mom?" Fran asked.
>
> "Guess. We're having one of your favorite dishes."

■ **Location of Attribution**

To prevent monotony, vary the location of your attribution.

> "Speak, Lord, for Your servant hears," Samuel said.
>
> Samuel said, "Speak, Lord, for Your servant hears."
>
> "Speak, Lord," Samuel said, "for Your servant hears."

However, do not put attribution in the middle of a quotation if the result would be awkward or would disrupt the natural flow of the quotation.

AWKWARD:	"We shall not," the protesters chanted, "be moved."
BETTER:	"We shall not be moved," the protesters chanted.

■ **Punctuation**

Place commas and ending punctuation marks *inside* the closing quotation marks. (See previous examples.)

■ **Paragraphing**

Use a new paragraph each time the speaker changes.

■ **Quotation Marks**

If a quotation is longer than one sentence, place quotation marks only at the beginning of the first sentence and the end of the last sentence. Do not enclose each sentence individually.

■ **Long Quotations**

If a speaker changes subjects during a long quotation, start a new paragraph with quotation marks at the beginning. Place closing quotation marks only at the end of the entire quotation.

> "And that," the chairman said, "is a summary of our plans for this project.
>
> "Before I close, however," he added, "let me discuss one more subject...."

■ **A Quotation within a Quotation**

Use single quotation marks (' ... ') to enclose a quotation within a quotation.

> Eli said to Samuel, "Go, lie down; and it shall be, if He calls you, that you must say, 'Speak, Lord, for Your servant hears.'" (I Samuel 3:9, NKJV)

■ **Capitalization**

Use a small letter to begin the second part of a sentence in a quotation that is interrupted by its attribution. Use a capital letter if the second part of the quotation is a new sentence.

> "I have been thinking for awhile," she said, "but I can't remember the name of that book."
>
> "I have been thinking for awhile," she said. "Regrettably, I can't remember the name of that book."

RHETORICAL CONSIDERATIONS

■ Choosing Appropriate Verbs

The word *said* is a good, all-purpose word for use with attribution and may be used repeatedly in dialogue. However, for variety, you may wish to consider other *appropriate* verbs as substitutes to more accurately relate the style of the expression. Here are some possibilities, which obviously depend on the context of the dialogue:

added	cried	howled	muttered	snapped	stated
agreed	declared	indicated	remarked	sobbed	stuttered
announced	giggled	laughed	shouted	sputtered	whispered

On the other hand, do not be so eager to avoid "said" that you inappropriately use stilted words such as *declaimed, articulated, phonated, marked*, etc.

■ Gestures and Facial Expressions

Written dialogues are records of conversations. You probably are aware that conversations usually consist of more than words. Since most people use gestures and facial expressions as part of their conversations, your dialogues will be more realistic if you intersperse such elements among your quotations.

Randy's brow furled for several moments. Then, raising his arm and pointing a finger upward, he said, "Pardon me, ma'am?"

"Yes, sir?"

"Could you recommend a suitable perfume for an older woman?"

"How old?"

"A great-grandmother."

With a nod and blink of understanding, the clerk reached under the glass counter. "This has been a favorite for many years," she said, holding a "Gardenias & Lace" sampler to Randy's nose.

✎ **EXERCISE** On a separate sheet of paper, write brief dialogues that might take place in the following settings: (1) on the basketball floor, (2) at Starbucks, and (3) on the debate team.

LESSON 48: PARAPHRASING

Paraphrasing is the process of putting into your own words the thoughts and expressions of other writers—the rewording of a piece of writing. When paraphrasing, you should seek to retain all the ideas of the original text, but to put those ideas into another form. Good paraphrasing is more than mere substituting of synonyms for each word of the original author. Instead, it recasts the original idea as a fresh, new expression.

ADVANTAGES

Paraphrasing has several advantages as a practice exercise in creative writing. Beyond the practice advantages, paraphrasing also is useful in your actual writing.

➢ It forces you to stretch your vocabulary by learning the meaning of words used by the original author and by searching for other words which express the ideas in a new light.

➢ It stretches your thinking by making you fully appreciate the meaning of other people's writings.

➢ It provides an opportunity to make difficult or obscure passages easier to read.

➢ It provides an opportunity to shorten lengthy or wordy passages or to expand overly concise ones with fuller meaning.

GUIDELINES

Here are some guidelines for paraphrasing:

Paraphrasing Guidelines
1. Give proper credit to the original author when using his ideas.
2. Carefully read the original writing. Reread it until you completely understand what the author is trying to say. Find all of his ideas. Look up definitions for words you do not understand.
3. Unless no substitute words can be found, avoid reusing the language of the original. Choose your own words. Rework the sentences, clauses, and phrases in a way that naturally expresses the ideas as you would think them.
4. Keep all of the original ideas. Do not leave out significant facts or meanings, even those that are implied rather than expressed. Do not add ideas which are not in the original or insert your own opinions. If you paraphrase a direct quotation, do not keep the quotation marks.
5. Try to preserve the original author's "tone"—humor, formalness, informality, sarcasm, etc.
6. Check your paraphrase after you have written it to make sure it meets the above requirements. Rewrite it if necessary.

PARADIGMS

Original:

Therefore you are inexcusable, O man, whoever you are who judge, for in whatever you judge another you condemn yourself; for you who judge practice the same things. But we know that the judgment of God is according to truth against those who practice such things. And do you think this, O man, you who judge those practicing such things, and doing the same, that you will escape the judgment of God?

—Paul, the Apostle, (Romans 2:1-3, NKJV)

Paraphrase:

No matter who you are, if you judge anyone, you have no excuse. When you judge another person, you condemn yourself, since you, the judge, do the same things. We know that God's judgment is right when He condemns people for doing these things. When you judge people for doing these things but then do them yourself, do you think you will escape God's judgment?

—Romans 2:1-3, "God's Word," God's Word to the Nations Bible Society

Note: Great care must be given when paraphrasing the Bible. Many who have tried to do this have **NOT** preserved the original meaning, but have inserted their own opinions about what God has said. *No paraphrase of the Bible should ever be considered God's inspired Word.* That claim can only be made for the original text and those translations which have been faithfully carried out under God's special care in preserving His truth through the ages.

✎ **EXERCISE** Reread the guidelines for paraphrasing in this lesson and then paraphrase the following on-line news articles. Use separate sheets of paper to do this exercise.

1. As unions have made good on their initial objectives—shorter work days, safe working conditions, and so on—many have moved on to funding liberal causes such as abortion-on-demand and school-based sexual-health clinics, opposing conservative causes such as school choice and welfare reform, and strongly supporting liberal candidates. Federal Election Commission records show that union political action committees over the past decade gave more than $362 million to Democrats and only $25 million to Republicans. Union leaders say they're representing their members, but about one third of union members voted Republican in the [November 2002] elections. (<http://www.worldmag.com/world/issue/11-30-02/cover_1.asp>)

2. The Constitution is quite clear on the matter. It says copyrights are to be granted for "limited times." I don't know any definition of "limited" that would mean 75 years plus a 20-year extension plus the chance of getting another extension later. The whole issue was argued three centuries ago, and it was established as a principle of democracy that, when the author is dead, his work becomes the property of all. This was modified slightly to allow the first generation after his death to continue to collect royalties, presumably to protect widows and children. But that's all that was intended. There was no argument ever made for a third- or fourth-generation royalty, much less a perpetual assignment of royalties to a corporation that never dies. (<http://www.nationalreview.com/comment/comment-bloom112202.asp>)

LESSON 49: AMPLIFYING MEANING

Throughout much of your writing in life you will find it necessary to explain the meaning of some of the words and ideas about which you are writing. In fact, the writing of *extended definitions* or "amplified meanings" can be seen as a whole category of creative writing. Inexperienced writers often resort to dictionary definitions. For example, if writing about "liberty," they might say something like: "According to Webster, liberty is...." That is not very creative, although there are times when literal, denotative meanings are useful.

WAYS TO EXTEND DEFINITIONS

Here are some ways to write more significant *meaning* into your literary efforts:

Ways of Amplifying Meaning
1. Work *synonyms* into your writing to show the meaning of a word or topic. A thesaurus (printed or electronic) is a good source of synonyms. Many dictionaries also list synonyms.
2. Use *antonyms* to show what the word or idea does not mean.
3. Provide the reader with the *word's history*, its origins in other languages, or how the meaning has changed through the passage of time. An unabridged dictionary has information about each word's history.
4. Use *illustrations*, *stories*, and *examples* to show what the word means in the lives of real people.
5. *Quote from other writers* who have given particular context or meaning to the word or idea about which you are writing. You might also expand upon the quotation or paraphrase it to further bring out the meaning you intend.
6. Use a combination of the above methods to reinforce the meaning.

Read the following example in which the nineteenth-century English preacher Charles Haddon Spurgeon explores the meaning of the word "trust" as it is used in Psalm 62:8—"Trust in Him at all times."

☞**EXAMPLE:**

> Faith is as much the rule of temporal as of spiritual life; we ought to have faith in God for our earthly affairs as well as for our heavenly business. It is only as we learn to trust in God for the supply of all our daily need that we shall live above the world. We are not to be idle, that would show we did not trust in God, who works hereto, but in the devil, who is the father of idleness. We are not to be imprudent or rash; that were to trust chance, and not the living God, who is a God of economy and order. Acting in all prudence and uprightness, we are to rely simply and entirely upon the Lord at all times.
>
> Let me commend to you a life of trust in God in temporal things. Trusting in God, you will not be compelled to mourn because you have used sinful means to grow rich. Serve God with integrity, and if you achieve no success, at least no sin will lie upon your conscience. Trusting God, you will not be guilty of self-contradiction. He who trusts in craft, sails this way today, and that way the next, like a vessel tossed about by the fickle wind; but he that trusts in the Lord is like a vessel propelled by steam; she cuts through the waves, defies the wind, and makes one bright silvery straightforward track to her destined haven. Be you a man with living principles within; never bow to the varying customs of worldly wisdom. Walk in your path of integrity with steadfast steps, and show that you are invincibly strong in the strength which confidence in God alone can confer. Thus you will be delivered from anxious care, you will not be troubled with evil tidings, your heart will be fixed, trusting in the Lord. How pleasant to float along the stream of providence! There is no more blessed way of living than a life of dependence upon a covenant-keeping God. We have no care, for He cares for us; we have no troubles, because we cast our burdens upon the Lord.

Notice the different ways that the author explains the meaning of trust. Among other things, he uses the *synonyms* "faith" and "confidence" along with related words and phrases such as "rely," "fixed," "steadfast," and "cast our burdens." He uses a number of phrases and clauses which contain fairly straightforward *denotative meanings* of trust ("… to rely simply and entirely upon the Lord …"). He also shows *what trust is not*: it does not mean idleness or acting rashly according to our own wits. He uses the *illustration* of two kinds of ships to show how trust works and does not work. He shows the *consequences* of both trust and unbelief, thereby showing more about what these mean. He uses an imperative sentence at one point ("Walk in your path of integrity….") to instruct the reader how to trust.

✎ **EXERCISE** Write a paragraph or paragraphs exploring the meaning of "God's grace." Try to incorporate some or all of the ways of amplifying meaning listed on page 150 to your writing. Use separate sheets of paper to do this exercise.

LESSON 50: DESCRIPTIVE WRITING

Good writing often includes *description*. Description is writing that gives the reader a mental image of a scene, person, situation, etc. Some writing is "pure description"; that is, its sole purpose is to paint a mental picture of the chosen subject. But description can also be used to enhance other forms of writing, such as the narrative, expository writing, or even argumentation.

To write descriptions well, you must go beyond simply telling readers what you see, hear, or feel. You must get the reader to sense and experience what you experience. Description, by definition, involves the senses. Good description will involve as many of the senses as are appropriate and possible: sight, sound, smell, taste, and touch.

WRITING DESCRIPTIVELY

Here are some suggestions for good descriptive writing:

■ **Determining Your Point of View**

There are two classifications of "point of view": physical and mental. "Physical point of view" refers to the position from which you (and your readers) are observing your subject. It may be from a hillside, a seashore, or through a window. If you are describing a mountain scene, is your vantage point from the top of the mountain looking down, from a valley looking up, from an airplane, or from a mountain trail? Is the view distant or nearby? "Mental point of view" refers to your attitude, intellectual ideas, or emotional feelings about your subject: like or dislike, boredom or enthusiasm, happiness or gloom, etc.

■ **Selecting Appropriate Details**

Especially select details that appeal to the senses. You should include only details that can be observed from your point of view. If you can't "see" it, you can't adequately describe it. Be selective of details. You may "see" many details, but you do not need to include everything. Choose only those details that add something significant to the mental point of view. Which details will best contribute to the impression you want to leave with your reader? Of course, always be honest; do not deliberately deceive your reader by hiding details which *are necessary to an honest, focused impression.*

■ **Arranging Details Carefully**

A random listing of anything and everything in sight will not focus your reader on the precise impression you wish to leave. Guide the reader by writing details in an order that is easy for him to mentally follow: right to left, left to right, top to bottom, bottom to top, near to far, far to near, order of prominence in the scene, general to particular, etc. If you change the order or point of view during the course of the description, be sure to alert the reader to that fact.

■ **Emphasizing Nouns and Verbs**

Using concrete nouns and verbs is usually better than using many adjectives and adverbs. Amateur writers tend to rely too heavily on modifiers. *Choose nouns and verbs with descriptive meanings built in.* For example, instead of an ordinary adjective-noun combination such as "red, crested bird," use a concrete noun that includes that description, "cardinal." Instead of "fell straight down," say "plunged."

■ **Using Comparisons and Contrasts**

Often things can be described by comparing them with or contrasting them to other objects or scenes. Metaphors and similes can be useful in this regard.

Read the following historic description of the capital city of the Mediterranean island of Sardinia.

☞**EXAMPLE:**

Cagliari is its capital city. It is situated on the northeast shore of a large bay on the south coast of the island, has a spacious and safe harbor defended by several forts, and is the emporium of all the trade of the island. Cagliari is very picturesque when viewed from the sea, as it covers the slope and summit of a promontory, the highest part of which is crowned by a noble castle.

The streets of the city are narrow, steep, and poorly paved. In the early morning they are swept by galley slaves, the dull clink of whose heavy fetters jars on the nerves. There is a loveliness in the fresh, gentle breeze of the early morning, which is peculiar to warm climates. But, as in other lands, the richer people do not value these fresh, calm hours, and it is only the poorer ones who are astir. The church bells are ringing for early mass, and the worshipers, chiefly of the peasant class, look very gay in their endless variety of dresses—for each class, and each trade, has its distinctive costume.

The little streets are a universal workshop, for everyone plies his trade in the open air: the carpenter, the cobbler, the tinman, and the tailor—all hard at work. Everybody seems to be acquainted with everybody else, and what a chattering there is! Pretty girls are picking grain to be ground in the family mill, and old women are busily spinning, while little children are eating figs and bread in the sunshine, and rolling round in the dirt, as childhood delights in doing the world over.

Down in the market place the noise increases and the scene defies description. Numerous dogs, lank, starved-looking creatures, roam about in all directions. Every morning, when the city gates are opened, crowds of them are waiting to enter. They go to the market and all round the town, devouring the refuse which they find.

As noon approaches, doors are shut and locked, shutters are closed, and quiet reigns everywhere. "Cagliari dines, and after dinner Cagliari sleeps." The Sardinian is fond of the good things of the table, and he is also a firm believer in the siesta. Later in the day, the city wakes up; and the people take a turn in the public walk that winds around the castle-crested hill on which the city stands. Lovely views are obtained of the surrounding country. There lies the great salt lake, where in the winter season may be seen large flocks of brilliant flamingoes. At sunset, the drums beat as a signal for the soldiers to retire to their quarters. There is no twilight here, for the sun goes down quickly.

—Dunton Larkin, *Australia and the Islands of the Sea*

Notice that the author begins by stating his **initial point of view** ("... when viewed from the sea..."). He then switches to a closer view: the streets. He also uses activity to describe the scene. Notice that he adds to his *physical point of view* a **time-related point of view**, following the scenes of the city from morning to nightfall. There are many examples of *sense-related* words and phrases: bells ringing, people chattering, dull clink of slave chains, fresh and gentle breezes, drums beating. At one point, he cleverly describes the chaotic marketplace by saying that it "defies description," but then goes on to give some details of the chaos by focusing selectively on the many roaming dogs. In the last paragraph, after "the city wakes up," he illustrates how it does: the people take walks. Near the end, after making a general statement about "lovely views," he adds the details of the "great salt lake" and "brilliant flamingoes."

Examine also how the author sometimes supplies **deeper meanings**, as we discussed in the last lesson. For example, after saying that the harbor is "safe," he explains that word by adding that the harbor is "defended by several forts." In another example, he uses descriptive details to explain what he means when he calls the streets a "universal workshop."

✎ **EXERCISE A** List some concrete, *descriptive nouns* and *verbs* used in the example above.

1. Nouns_____

2. Verbs_____

✎ **EXERCISE B** On a separate sheet of paper, write a couple of *descriptive paragraphs* of your own. Select a "live" scene or situation, or find a painting or photographic image (still or video) to describe. (A travelogue video from your local library or video store may be used.) You might even describe an interesting place you have visited, if your memory is strong and vivid enough to supply details.

LESSON 51: SKETCHES

Whereas *descriptions* usually deal with scenes and situations, *sketches* are descriptions of people. There are two types of sketches: *character sketches* and *type sketches*. Character sketches are word portraits of *specific people*. They present information that sets off the person being described from others. They describe individual personality traits and physical or historical features of that particular person. A type sketch does the opposite. It describes a general class of people, rather than an individual. This description has also been called a *stereotype*.

CHARACTER SKETCHES

Here are some guidelines for writing *character sketches*:

■ **Choosing a Suitable Character**

You might consider someone you know well—a friend, family member, relative, or notable public figure. Or you might choose someone who is especially interesting because of his unique personality, appearance, or qualities. You will have to do some research, if the person is obscure.

■ **Disclosing a General Impression**

Consider the general impression you wish to give the reader about this person. Put this general impression in a sentence at or near the beginning of your sketch. Then provide the reader with details to support this general impression.

■ **Selecting Details Carefully**

Use some of the same techniques you learned in the previous lesson on descriptions. Choose details which bring out the general impression but which set the person apart from others of the same sex, age, profession, etc. Include necessary details; exclude unnecessary details.

■ **Enlarging the Character**

Develop the character by using a variety of methods, including *description of appearance, examples of activities, quotations, how others view the person,* and *how the individual reacts* to situations or other people. Verbally place the individual in his typical environment or surroundings. Be sure that, as you develop your character, you avoid descriptions that could apply to anyone. Your goal is to describe this unique individual.

Writing character sketches is similar to writing biography, which is generally a longer character sketch. Someone has made the following observations and warning about this type of writing:

> Biography is a quicksilver art. Setting the task to know men from the past, it forces its practitioners to find their subjects from a cold trail, to revive ideas from documents, to bring life from shadows. Whether this proves easy or hard depends on the subject. Great men, men who bestride their times and shape them by their presence, appear easy to portray—but appearances are often deceiving. Great men usually create copious records, leave many trails, and generate a personal mythology. And in that very bulk of evidence lies a pitfall of plenty to trap the biographer.
>
> —Frank Vandiver

TYPE SKETCHES

Here are some guidelines to keep in mind when writing a stereotype or *type sketch:*

■ **Choosing a General Class of People**

Select a **general class** of people, not a specific person: typical sports fans, gossips, practical jokers, used car salesmen, bookworms, health-food fanatics, etc. You might choose a class of people whom you admire or dislike—those who amuse you or annoy you. Last but not least, select a class of people who will be understood or recognized by your readers.

■ **Disclosing a General Impression**

Begin with a **broad description** or **impression**. It is not necessary to make long introductions.

■ **Developing the Subject's Character**

Describe typical appearances. Use comparisons, vivid words (especially nouns and verbs), and words that appeal to the senses. Note actions typical of these kinds of people. Use anecdotes, incidents, and examples. You might use quotations or sayings that are typical of these people. Humor and sarcasm are often effective tools in type sketches (*Note, however, "Being Honest and Fair" below*).

■ **Selecting Details Carefully**

Remember, *you are trying to leave an impression* on your reader concerning your subject. **Select details** that contribute to that impression and avoid those that distract from the impression or prove your stereotype to be false. This is particularly true *if you are trying to highlight some specific trait* of your subject. Details related to specific physical characteristics probably will not be needed, because you are not describing a specific individual. Physical descriptions should be limited to those which are typical of the class about which you are writing.

■ **Being Honest and Fair**

It is not right to take overly broad brushstrokes in your portrait of a stereotype. All geniuses are not sloppy dressers, of course. If you suggest that geniuses typically are slovenly in their personal appearance, make sure you remind your reader in some way that others may not be. It is easy to hurt people by stereotyping specific individuals. Avoid being unkind in your use of humor or sarcasm.

Here is an example of a character sketch that also includes material that qualifies as a type sketch. This example shows how the two kinds of sketches can be used together to increase their individual effectiveness.

☞**EXAMPLE:**

No golden eagle, warm from the stamping press of the mint, is more sharply impressed with its image and superscription than was the formative period of our government by the genius and personality of Thomas Jefferson.

Standing on the threshold of the nineteenth century, no one who attempted to peer down the shadowy vista, saw more clearly than he the possibilities, the perils, the pitfalls and the achievements that were within the grasp of the Nation. None was inspired by purer patriotism. None was more sagacious, wise and prudent, and none understood his countrymen better.

By birth an aristocrat, by nature he was a democrat. The most learned man that ever sat in the [P]resident's chair, his tastes were the simple ones of a farmer. Surrounded by the pomp and ceremony of Washington and Adams' courts, his dress was homely. He despised titles and preferred severe plainness of speech and the sober garb of the Quakers.

"What is the date of your birth, Mr. President?" asked an admirer.

"Of what possible concern is that to you?" queried the President in turn.

"We wish to give it fitting celebration."

"For that reason, I decline to enlighten you; nothing could be more distasteful to me than what you propose, and, when you address me, I shall be obliged if you will omit the 'Mr.'"

If we can imagine … , a sheet of paper resting on the crowns of Washington and Jefferson would have lain horizontal and been six feet two inches from the earth, but the one was magnificent in physique, of massive frame and prodigious strength, … the other was thin, wiry, bony, active, but with muscles of steel, while both were as straight as the proverbial Indian arrow.

Jefferson's hair was of sandy color, his cheeks ruddy, his eyes of a light hazel, his features angular, but glowing with intelligence and neither could lay any claim to the gift of oratory.

Washington lacked literary ability, while in the hand of Jefferson, the pen was as masterful as the sword in the clutch of Saladin or Godfrey of Bouillon. Washington had only a common school education, while Jefferson was a classical scholar and could express his thoughts in excellent Italian, Spanish, and French, and both were masters of their temper.

Jefferson was an excellent violinist, a skilled mathematician and a profound scholar. Add to all these his spotless integrity and honor, his statesmanship, and his well curbed but aggressive patriotism, and he embodied within himself all the attributes of an ideal [P]resident of the United States....

—Edward S. Ellis, *Great Americans of History: Thomas Jefferson, A Character Sketch*
<http://www.pinkmonkey.com/dl/library1/digi267.pdf>

✎ **EXERCISE A** On a separate sheet of paper, write a *character sketch* of at least 125 words about a friend, relative, famous person, historical figure, or literary character.

✎ **EXERCISE B** On a separate sheet of paper, write a *type sketch* of at least 125 words. Choose a stereotype of interest to you or select one of the following: truck drivers, grandfathers, librarians, today's young professionals, TV addicts, computer whizzes, garden-club ladies, cynics, the Pharisees, golfers, bowlers, high school football players, typical cheerleaders, homeschoolers, "super-moms," the "virtuous wives" of Proverbs 31:10-31, or the Christian husbands of Ephesians 5:25-33.

LESSON 52: UNIT REVIEW

✎ **EXERCISE A** Underline the correct word in parentheses to fit the meaning of the sentence.

1. It is extremely important not to (altar, alter) the meaning of Scripture by paraphrasing.

2. The thane of Cawdor was greedy and wanted the (throne, thrown) of England for himself.

3. We will begin reading the play (hear, here), at the beginning of the second act.

4. A proverb is a statement of (principle, principal) more than a rule of law.

5. The heels of her feet were (course, coarse) due to the dry, winter weather.

6. My youth leader (cent, scent, sent) me a reminder about the Saturday mission project.

7. The company name was printed at the top of his business (stationery, stationary).

8. Our freedom has allowed us to forget that (their, there, they're) is a price to follow Christ.

9. To start a business of your own, you need an adequate amount of (capital, capitol).

10. In A.D. 155, Polycarp, the faithful elder of the church at Smyrna, was burned at the (steak, stake).

✎ **EXERCISE B** In the blank at the end of each sentence, write a synonym for the word in **dark print**.

1. The birth of a baby is always a miraculous **event** in a family's life. _____

2. The **sense** of the cryptic message was hard to discern. _____

3. The **job** of building a coalition of nations to stop terrorism was immense. _____

4. You must follow the **rules** of the game if you wish to play. _____

5. The business **stores** inventory in various locations all over the county. _____

6. The **main** event will be held in the Grand Ballroom of the Palmer House. _____

7. He felt quite **fatigued** after his transplant surgery. _____

8. A beluga whale **consumes** about 40 to 80 pounds of food a day. _____

9. The young man **pursued** his dreams to the neglect of his family. _____

10. The programers **developed** a database designed for their unique needs. _____

✎ **EXERCISE C** Test your vocabulary and spelling ability by underlining the correct word in parentheses in each of the following sentences. Check a dictionary if necessary.

1. A (dairy, diary) is a book used to record (personal, personnel) thoughts.

2. There is a (statue, statute, stature) of Stonewall Jackson on the grounds of the West Virginia State (Capitol, Capital) building.

3. Christians have formed many interpretations of the (prophecy, prophesy) of Daniel.

4. The Seventh Commandment requires (marital, martial) faithfulness.

5. San Diego's (climatic, climactic) conditions are often described as ideal.

6. The film director employed a variety of amazing special (affects, effects).

7. The movie was (all together, altogether) hilarious.

8. The Israelites wandered for forty years in the (deserts, desserts) of the Sinai Peninsula.

9. The fugitive was able to (allude, elude) the police for four days.

10. Chocolate syrup is the perfect (complement, compliment) for vanilla ice cream.

11. The children were (anxious, eager) to see their loving grandparents.

12. The climbers' (descent, decent) from the mountain was slow and treacherous.

✎ **EXERCISE D** Fill in the blanks for the following:

1. The term *trope* means _____.

2. *Denotation* is _____.

3. *Connotation* is _____.

4. Give definitions or descriptions of the following figures of speech or literary devices:
    Synecdoche

    _____

    Metonymy

    _____

    Oxymoron

    _____

Antithesis

_____

Apostrophe

_____

Hyperbole

_____

Litotes

_____

Simile

_____

Metaphor

_____

Personification

_____

Alliteration

_____

Onomatopoeia

_____

5. _Attribution_ in dialogue is _____
    _____ .

6. If a quotation is longer than one sentence, place quotation marks _____
    _____ .

7. Paraphrasing is _____
    _____ .

8. List three ways to add _meaning_ to your writing.

    a. _____

    b. _____

    c. _____

9. In writing description, it is wise to use words that appeal to the five _____.

10. The two kinds of sketches are _____ sketches and _____ sketches. What is the
    difference between these two?

    _____

    _____

    _____

    _____

✎ **EXERCISE E** In the following article, identify the various elements that make it a *character sketch*.

Joshua Redivivus ["Joshua brought back to life"]: That is to say, Moses' spy and pioneer, Moses' successor and the captain of the Lord's covenanted host come back again. A second Joshua sent to Scotland to go before God's people in that land and in that day; a spy who would both by his experience and by his testimony cheer and encourage the suffering people of God. *For all this Samuel Rutherford truly was* [italics added]. As he said of himself in one of his letters to Hugh Mackail, he was indeed a spy sent out to make experiment upon the life of silence and separation, banishment and martyrdom, and to bring back a report of that life for the vindication of Christ and for the support and encouragement of His people. It was a happy thought of Rutherford's first editor, Robert M'Ward, his old Westminster Assembly secretary, to put at the top of his title-page, Joshua risen again from the dead, or, Mr. Rutherford's Letters written from his place of banishment in Aberdeen.

In selecting his twelve spies, Moses went on the principle of choosing the best and the ablest men he could lay hold of in all Israel. And in selecting Samuel Rutherford to be the first sufferer for His covenanted people in Scotland, our Lord took a man who was already famous for his character and his services. For no man of his age in broad Scotland stood higher as a scholar, a theologian, a controversialist, a preacher and a very saint than Samuel Rutherford. He had been settled at Anwoth on the Solway in 1627, and for the next nine years he had lived such a noble life among his people as to make Anwoth famous as long as Jesus Christ has a Church in Scotland. As we say Bunyan and Bedford, Baxter and Kidderminster, Newton and Olney, Edwards and Northampton, Boston and Ettrick, M'Cheyne and St. Peter's, so we say Rutherford and Anwoth.

His talents, his industry, his scholarship, his preaching power, his pastoral solicitude and his saintly character all combined to make Rutherford a marked man both to the friends and to the enemies of the truth. His talents and his industry while he was yet a student in Edinburgh had carried him to the top of his classes, and all his days he could write in Latin better than either in Scotch or English. His habits of work at Anwoth soon became a very proverb. His people boasted that their minister was always at his books, always among his parishioners, always at their sick-beds and their death-beds, always catechising their children and always alone with his God. And then the matchless preaching of the parish church of Anwoth. We can gather what made the Sabbaths of Anwoth so memorable both to Rutherford and to his people from the books we still have from those great Sabbaths: *The Trial and the Triumph of Faith*; *Christ Dying and Drawing Sinners to Himself*; and such like. Rutherford was the 'most moving and the most affectionate of preachers,' a preacher determined to know nothing but Jesus Christ and Him crucified, but not so much crucified, as crucified and risen again—crucified indeed, but now glorified. Rutherford's life for his people at Anwoth has something altogether superhuman and unearthly about it. His correspondents in his own day and his critics in our day stumble at his too intense devotion to his charge; he lived for his congregation, they tell us, almost to the neglect of his wife and children. But by the time of his banishment his home was desolate, his wife and children were in the grave. And all the time and thought and love they had got from him while they were alive had, now that they were dead, returned with new and intensified devotion to his people and his parish....

—Alexander Whyte, "Joshua Redivivus"
<http://www.puritansermons.com/ruth/rwhyte01.htm>

Unit 6
Nouns and Pronouns

The English language has more than 600,000 words. New words are being created as time goes by, and the need arises to name and describe new things and activities. Yet all of these words can be classified into eight groups, known as the **parts of speech**. The eight parts of speech are *noun, pronoun, verb, adjective, adverb, preposition, conjunction,* and *interjection*.

Within most of these categories there are some **subgroups**. For example, there are at least two types of nouns, several types of pronouns, three types of verbs, and several categories of conjunctions. Even among the subgroups, words can take a variety of different forms. In addition, some of the eight main parts of speech can be used as if they were another part of speech. In this unit, we will study the eight parts of speech.

Most of the eight parts of speech have numerous uses, and in some cases each use requires a change in the form of the part of speech. In addition, some of the words which are normally identified as one part of speech can also be used as another part of speech. In this unit, we will study the variety of ways **nouns** and **pronouns** can be used.

LESSON 53: NOUNS

A **noun** is a word that names a person, place, thing, quality, or idea.

Person	Place	Thing	Quality	Idea
teacher	camp	book	justice	capitalism
Michael	country	bolt	love	Christianity
secretary	neighborhood	desk	friendliness	wisdom
Queen Anne	Lake Erie	star	devotion	duty
plumber	Columbia	telephone	peace	socialism
gymnast	yard	shelf	joy	philosophy

There are two main categories of nouns: **common** and **proper**. Common nouns name persons, places, things, qualities, or ideas *in general*. Proper nouns name *specific* persons, places, things, qualities, or ideas. Proper nouns always begin with a capital letter. Common nouns always begin with a small letter unless they come at the beginning of a sentence or quotation.

Common Nouns	man	city	make (car)	book	pen	denomination
Proper Nouns	John Knox	Tokyo	Cadillac	Bible	Parker	Reformed Church

Nouns can also be classified as *single* or *compound*. A single noun consists of one word. Compound nouns are composed of more than one word, or of two or more words joined into one word. Some compound nouns are hyphenated and some are not.

Single Nouns	man	language	spaghetti	robin	pen	Maria
Compound Nouns	Ian Smith	storybook	green beans	meadowlark	PaperMate	sister-in-law

Most nouns have different forms depending on their *number*. "Number" is a grammatical term indicating whether a word refers to one or more than one. If a noun refers to one person, place, thing, quality, or idea, it is singular. If it refers to more than one, it is plural. Some nouns use the same form for both singular and plural.

Singular Nouns	prisoner	candy	wolf	Bible	toy	switch
Plural Nouns	prisoners	candies	wolves	Bibles	toys	switches

A few nouns name a group even when they are singular in form. These nouns are called *collective* nouns. Collective nouns can also be plural when they name more than one collective group.

Singular Nouns	crowd	team	jury	committee	assembly	congregation
Plural Nouns	crowds	teams	juries	committees	assemblies	congregations

✎ **EXERCISE A** Underline all the *nouns* in the ensuing paragraph about the first American Huguenots.

Spanish <u>forces</u> under <u>Pedro Menéndez de Avilés</u> captured the French Huguenot settlement of Fort Caroline, near present-day Jacksonville, Florida. The French, commanded by René Goulaine de Laudonniere, lost 135 men in the first instance of colonial warfare between European powers in America. Most of those killed were massacred on the order of Avilés, who allegedly had the slain hung on trees beside the inscription: "Not as Frenchmen, but as heretics." Laudonniere and some [forty] other Huguenots escaped. In 1564, the French Huguenots (Protestants) had settled on the Banks of May, a strategic point on the Florida coast. King Philip II of Spain was disturbed by this challenge to Spanish authority in the New World and sent Menéndez de Avilés to Florida to expel the French heretics and establish a Spanish colony there. In early September 1565, Avilés founded San Augustin on the Florida coast, which would later grow into Saint Augustine—the oldest city in North America. Two weeks later, on 20 September, he attacked and destroyed the French settlement of Fort Caroline. The decisive French defeat [compelled] France to refocus its colonial efforts in America far to the north, in what is now Quebec and Nova Scotia in Canada.

—Events, Deaths, Births on 20 Sep, *HISTORY "4" "2" DAY* (Web site)
<http://www.jcanu.hpg.ig.com.br/history/h4sep/h4sep20.html>

✎ **EXERCISE B** In the spaces below, write all the *proper nouns* from the paragraph above.

1. *Avilés (appears 4 times)*   9. _____   17. _____

2. *Fort Caroline (appears twice)*   10. _____   18. _____

3. *Jacksonville*   11. _____   19. _____

4. _____   12. _____   20. _____

5. _____   13. _____   21. _____

6. _____   14. _____   22. _____

7. _____   15. _____

8. _____   16. _____

✎ **EXERCISE C** In the spaces below, write all the *compound nouns* from the paragraph above.

1. *Pedro Menéndez de Avilés*   5. _____   9. _____

2. *Fort Caroline*   6. _____   10. _____

3. _____   7. _____   11. _____

4. _____   8. _____   12. _____

✎ **EXERCISE D** In the spaces below, write at least three *collective nouns* from the paragraph above.

1. *forces*   3. _____   5. _____

2. _____   4. _____   6. _____

LESSON 54: PLACING NOUNS

The term ***substantive*** (sŭb´ stan• tĭv) may be used to refer to any word, phrase, or clause that *has the qualities and uses of a noun.* Substantives, in their capacity as nouns to name persons, places, things, qualities, or ideas, can be used in seven different ways in sentences. These seven ways are: *subject, direct object, indirect object, object of a preposition, objective complement, predicate nominative* (subjective complement), and *appositive.*

☞**EXAMPLES:**

Subject:	**Bees** have wings.
Direct object:	Bees have **wings.**
Indirect object:	God gave **bees** wings.
Object of a preposition:	God gave wings to **bees.**
Objective complement:	God made this bee a **carpenter bee.**
Predicate nominative:	This bee is a **carpenter bee.**
Appositive:	This bee, a **carpenter bee**, has wings.

NOUNS USED AS SUBSTANTIVES

1. A *subject* is a substantive about which a sentence makes a statement.

☞**EXAMPLES:**

>   The **bank** is closed on Saturday.   The **Bible** is the Word of God.

2. A *direct object* is a substantive that "receives" the action of a verb or verbal expression or shows the result of the action. It answers the questions *whom?* or *what?* after the verb.

☞**EXAMPLES:**

>   She opened the **letter**. (*opened what?*)   I love **babies**. (*love whom?*)

3. An *indirect object* is a substantive that tells "to *or* for whom" or "to *or* for what" the action of the verb is done. The words "to" and "for" are implied before an indirect object. If the word *to* or *for* is *stated*, the noun becomes *an object of a preposition* (see below).

☞**EXAMPLES:**

>   Mrs. Anderson gave **Jim** a scolding. (*gave [to] Jim*)   Do your **mother** a favor. (*do [for] mother*)

4. An *object of a preposition* is a substantive that follows a preposition and is related by the preposition to some other word in the sentence.

☞**EXAMPLES:**

>   Mrs. Anderson gave a scolding *to* **Jim**.   Do a favor *for* your **mother**.

5. An *objective complement* is a substantive used *after a direct object* to complete its meaning.

Note: *Adjectives* can also be used sometimes as *objective complements*, as stated in Lesson 65 (*page 206*).

☞**EXAMPLES:**

>   They elected *him* **president** of the class.   His captors made *John Newton* a **slave**.

6. A *predicate nominative* is a substantive that follows a linking verb and renames or identifies the subject of the verb. A predicate nominative is one of two kinds of *subjective complements* because it completes the meaning of the subject.

Note: *Predicate adjectives* are the other kind of *subjective complement*, as stated in Lesson 65 (*page 206*).

☞**EXAMPLES:**

>   He *is* **president** of the class.   I *am* a **student**.

7. An *appositive* is a substantive following another substantive to further identify or explain the first substantive. The appositive signifies the same thing as the substantive to which it is added. The appositive is usually set off with commas, but no punctuation is needed if its relationship to the first substantive is "close," especially when the appositive is a one- or two-word name.

☞**EXAMPLES:**

>   Jerry, the **president** of our class, is fourteen years old.
>
>   Her husband **Dave** is an insurance salesman.

NOUNS USED AS ADJECTIVES

In addition to their uses as substantives, words that are normally nouns can be used as *adjectives*, modifying other nouns.

☞**EXAMPLES:**

She mopped the **kitchen** floor.   Where is the **telephone** book?

Nouns in their *possessive form* are considered to be *adjectives*.

☞**EXAMPLES:**

Bob's bicycle has a flat tire.   The calf was allergic to its **mother's** milk.

✎ **EXERCISE** Identify the use of the words in **dark print** by writing above the noun *S* if it is a subject, *DO* if it is a direct object, *IO* if it is an indirect object, *OP* if it is an object of a preposition, *OC* if it is an objective complement, *PN* if it is a predicate nominative, *A* if it is an appositive, or *Adj.* if it is used as an adjective.

       S   OP   DO

1. The **natives** of **Australia** are called **aborigines**.

2. The natives are **aborigines**.

3. Aborigines, **natives** of Australia, use a **weapon** known as a boomerang.

4. **Mr. Edwards** told his **grandsons** a **story** about his **experiences** in the **war**.

5. The **change** of **caterpillars** into **butterflies** is a fascinating **phenomenon**.

6. **Gerald** was chosen **employee** of the **year**.

7. The **company president** named **Gerald employee** of the year.

8. Those who are wise experience **wisdom's benefits**.

9. **Years** passed after the **tragedy**, but the bitter **memories** remained.

10. The **music club** offered its **members** more free **selections** than ever before.

LESSON 55: PLURALS OF NOUNS

Nouns have **number**. *Number* is a grammatical term indicating whether a part of speech refers to one (**singular**) or *more than one* (**plural**). It is important to know the *number* of a noun because many nouns change their form or spelling depending on whether they are singular or plural. In addition, it is important to know the *number* of a noun because number may affect the form of a verb or pronoun that is used with the noun.

PLURALS OF NOUNS

The following rules govern how the **plurals of nouns** are formed. Most nouns are pluralized by simply adding *-s* or *-es*, or changing the final "y" to "i" and then adding *-es*. Others are pluralized by changing the final "f" or "fe" to "v" and adding *-es*. A few nouns may become plural by either adding *-s* or *-es*. Some nouns, however, change form completely to become plural in number. Finally, some foreign words retain their original plural endings, such as *media* (the plural of *medium*). Study the following **rules** and **exceptions** to forming the plurals of nouns.

	Rule or Exception to the Rule	Example(s)
Rule 1	The plural of most nouns is formed by adding *-s*.	bag ⇨ bags
Rule 2	The plural of nouns ending with a silent "e" is formed by adding *-s*.	college ⇨ colleges
Rule 3	The plural of nouns ending with *-s, -z, -x, -ch,* or *-sh* is formed by adding *-es.*	bush ⇨ bushes
Rule 4	The plural of nouns ending with a *-y* preceded by a consonant is formed by changing the "y" to "i" and adding *-es.*	army ⇨ armies
Exception to Rule 4	The plural of *proper names* ending with a *-y* preceded by a consonant is formed by adding *-s.*	Mary ⇨ Marys
Rule 5	The plural of nouns ending with *-quy* is formed by changing the "y" to "i" and adding *-es.*	colloquy ⇨ colloquies
Note:	The plural of nouns ending with *-y* or *-o* preceded by a vowel is formed by adding *-s. (See Rule 1 above.)*	quay ⇨ quays chimney ⇨ chimneys ploy ⇨ ploys
		video ⇨ videos studio ⇨ studios kangaroo ⇨ kangaroos
Rule 6	The plural of nouns ending with an *-o* preceded by a consonant usually is formed by adding *-s.*	ego ⇨ egos piano ⇨ pianos silo ⇨ silos
		burro ⇨ burros hippo ⇨ hippos poncho ⇨ ponchos
Exception to Rule 6	Some nouns ending with *-o* preceded by a consonant form their plurals by adding *-es*. Check your dictionary to be certain of spelling.	hero ⇨ heroes echo ⇨ echoes potato ⇨ potatoes embargo ⇨ embargoes tomato ⇨ tomatoes

	Rule or Exception to the Rule	Example(s)
Another Exception to Rule 6	Still other such nouns can form their plurals either by adding -s or -es. Check your dictionary to be certain of spelling.	banjo ⇨ banjos, banjoes buffalo ⇨ buffalos, buffaloes cargo ⇨ cargos, cargoes tornado ⇨ tornados, tornadoes
Rule 7	Most nouns ending with -i form their plurals by adding -s.	macaroni ⇨ macaronis
Exception to Rule 7	Some nouns ending with -i, however, form their plurals by adding either -s or -es. Check your dictionary to be certain of spelling.	taxi ⇨ taxis, taxies alkali ⇨ alkalis, alkalies
Rule 8	Nouns ending with -f or -fe usually form their plurals by changing the "f" to "v" and adding -es.	loaf ⇨ loaves knife ⇨ knives

IRREGULAR PLURALS OF NOUNS

■ Some nouns form their plurals by changing their form or spelling.

☞**EXAMPLES:**

mouse ⇨ mice	goose ⇨ geese	child ⇨ children
brother ⇨ brethren	ox ⇨ oxen	louse ⇨ lice
man ⇨ men	woman ⇨ women	tooth ⇨ teeth

■ A few nouns do NOT change their form from singular to plural.

☞**EXAMPLES:**

kin ⇨ kin	sheep ⇨ sheep	deer ⇨ deer

PLURALS OF TWO-PART COMPOUND NOUNS

Some *two-part compound nouns* add a plural ending to the first word in the compound; others add the plural ending to the second word. In others, the plural ending can be added to either part of the compound. In still others plural endings are added to both parts.

☞**EXAMPLES:**

heir apparent	⇨	**heirs** apparent
brigadier general	⇨	brigadier **generals**
attorney general	⇨	**attorneys** general, attorney **generals**
court-martial	⇨	**courts**-martial, court-**martials**
thing-in-itself	⇨	**things**-in-**themselves**

PLURALS OF THREE-PART COMPOUND NOUNS

Three-part compound nouns usually make a plural of the first word in the compound.

☞**EXAMPLES:**

attorney-at-law ⇨ **attorneys**-at-law   man-of-war ⇨ **men**-of-war

sister-in-law ⇨ **sisters**-in-law   coat of mail ⇨ **coats** of mail

PLURALS OF FOREIGN WORDS

Many nouns of foreign origin or with origins in ancient languages still retain their foreign or ancient plural forms. However, in modern usage, it is now acceptable for a few of these words to use standard modern English plural forms (shown in parentheses).

☞**EXAMPLES:**

Latin:	alumnus ⇨ alumni	cactus ⇨ cacti
	formula ⇨ formulae (formulas)	medium ⇨ media
Greek:	analysis ⇨ analyses	nemesis ⇨ nemeses
	parenthesis ⇨ parentheses	crisis ⇨ crises
	thesis ⇨ theses	phenomenon ⇨ phenomena
	criterion ⇨ criteria	genesis ⇨ geneses
	basis ⇨ bases	
French:	beau ⇨ beaux	plateau ⇨ plateaux (plateaus)
	bureau ⇨ bureaux (bureaus)	
Hebrew:	cherub ⇨ cherubim	seraph ⇨ seraphim
Spanish:	señor ⇨ señores	
Italian:	tempo ⇨ tempi (tempos)	solo ⇨ soli (solos)
	concerto ⇨ concerti (concertos)	

	Rule or Exception to the Rule	**Example(s)**
Rule 9	The plural of letters, abbreviations used as NOUNS, letters used as WORDS, and numbers is usually formed by adding only an "s," unless it would be confusing to the reader.	the three Rs IBMs, ABCs, IOUs ifs, ands, or buts the late 1850s count by twos
Exception to Rule 9	When "s" alone is confusing, use an *apostrophe* and an "s"—for certain lower case letters used as NOUNS, certain capital letters, signs and symbols, and abbreviations with periods.	a's, i's, u's A's, I's, U's p's and q's $'s and ='s Ph.D.'s and I.Q.'s

✎ **EXERCISE** Write the plural form of the following. Check a dictionary, if necessary.

☞**EXAMPLE:**

	solo		_soli_ or _solos_

1.	crutch	_____	11.	plaque	_____
2.	loaf	_____	12.	codex	_____
3.	bulrush	_____	13.	capacity	_____
4.	Jones	_____	14.	B.S.	_____
5.	alto	_____	15.	notary public	_____
6.	providence	_____	16.	key	_____
7.	area	_____	17.	bureau	_____
8.	cockatoo	_____	18.	Kathy	_____
9.	&, #, +	_____	19.	grandchild	_____
10.	plague	_____	20.	aide-de-camp	_____

LESSON 56: MORE ABOUT NOUNS

GENDER

Nouns have **gender**. Gender is a grammatical term indicating the sex of the person, place, thing, quality, or idea. While there are only two sexes for people, animals, or other living organisms, English nouns belong to one of four possible genders. These are _masculine_, _feminine_, _neuter_, and _common_.

■ Masculine Gender

The **masculine gender** refers to individuals of the male sex.

☞**EXAMPLES:**

man	Harold	nephew	stallion	Mr. Pitt	boy

■ Feminine Gender

The **feminine gender** refers to individuals of the female sex.

☞**EXAMPLES:**

woman	Sally	niece	mare	Mrs. Pitt	girl

■ Neuter Gender

The **neuter gender** refers to things, places, ideas, or qualities that are neither male nor female.

☞**EXAMPLES:**

book	love	floor	sky	computer	fist

■ Common Gender

The **common gender** refers to individuals of unknown sex or to words naming individuals who may be either male or female.

☞**EXAMPLES:**

individual	mankind	chairman	leader	person	people

The gender of English nouns is grammatically irrelevant *except* when the noun serves as an antecedent for a personal pronoun. Personal pronouns take different forms in some cases, depending on gender (*he, him, she, her, it*). In order to choose the correct gender form of pronouns, *it is necessary to know the gender of the noun antecedent.*

Masculine pronouns refer to masculine nouns. *Feminine pronouns* refer to feminine nouns. *Neuter pronouns* refer to neuter nouns. *Common pronouns* are usually the same in form as masculine pronouns, although in some cases common-gender nouns can serve as antecedents for pronouns that are the same in form as neuter pronouns.

EXAMPLES:

> Mr. Pitt said **he** would be home at 6 p.m. (*masculine*)
>
> Mrs. Pitt told **her** neighbor about the new product. (*feminine*)
>
> The tree has lost all of **its** leaves. (*neuter*)
>
> Mankind[56] seems to have lost **its** moral bearings. (*common*)
>
> The student must apply **himself** to **his** studies. (*common*)

CASE

Nouns have *case*. *Case* is a grammatical term referring to the form substantives take to indicate their relation to other words in a sentence. English nouns have three cases. They are *nominative* (also called *subjective*), *objective* (also called *accusative*), and *possessive* (also called *genitive*).

■ *Nominative Case*

Nouns used as *subjects* and *predicate nominatives* are in the **nominative case**.

EXAMPLES:

> The **manager** approved the purchase. (*subject*)
>
> Lee Brown is the **manager** of the store. (*predicate nominative*)

■ *Objective Case*

Nouns used as *direct objects, indirect objects, objects of prepositions,* or *objective complements* are in the *objective case*.

EXAMPLES:

> He took his **medicine**. (*direct object*)
>
> The doctor gave **Fred** his medicine. (*indirect object*)
>
> The top of the **table** is marble. (*object of a preposition*)
>
> They appointed him **secretary-general**. (*objective complement*)

■ *Nouns That Rename*

Nouns used as *appositives* are in the same case as the nouns which they rename.

EXAMPLES:

> Washington, our first **President**, was quite tall. (*nominative*)
>
> He took his medicine, a foul-tasting **substance**. (*objective*)

---

56. When this word is pronounced with the accent on the second syllable (man • kind'), it means all of humankind, including males and females, and is common in gender. When it is pronounced with the accent on the first syllable (man' • kind), it refers only to men (males) and is masculine in gender.

■ *Possessive Case*

Nouns in the nominative and objective cases have the same form. Nouns, however, in the ***possessive case*** have a slightly altered form.

☞**EXAMPLES:**

> The **family** had a backyard barbecue. (*nominative*)
>
> Backyard barbecues gave the **family** hours of fun. (*objective*)
>
> The **family's** favorite pastime is backyard barbecues. (*possessive*)

The following are rules for writing the ***possessive case form*** of nouns:

	Rule or Exception to the Rule	Example(s)
Rule 10	Use an *apostrophe and "s"* to form the possessive of any noun (singular or plural) NOT ending in "s."	a **man's** home the **men's** department
Rule 11	Use an *apostrophe alone* to form the possessive of a PLURAL noun ending in "s."	the **students'** projects two **weeks'** notice
Rule 12	To form the possessive of a noun naming a *nonhuman object*, it is preferred that a prepositional phrase beginning with *of* be used.	the cover **of the atlas** [*not the atlas's cover*] the color **of the carpet** [*not the carpet's color*]

A number of other common expressions relating to time or measure, which use the possessive form but do not show real ownership, are exceptions to this rule.

☞**EXAMPLES:**

a day's work	a moment's notice	two years' experience
a dollar's worth	a stone's throw	at his wit's end
today's fashion	tomorrow's weather	

Certain non-personal nouns ending with an "s" or "s-sound" form their possessives by adding an ***apostrophe alone***.

☞**EXAMPLES:**

> for **righteousness'** sake   for **conscience'** sake

Rule 13	To form the possessive of a *one-syllable proper name* ending with an "s" sound, add an *apostrophe and "s."*	Robert **Burns's** poetry **Charles's** bowling ball Karl **Marx's** philosophy
Rule 14	To form the possessive of *proper names with more than one syllable* and ending with an "s," add an *apostrophe alone*.	**Jesus'** parables The **Cummings'** family car **Pericles'** role in ancient Athens
Rule 15	To form the possessive case of *compound words* or of *words showing joint possession*, make only the last element possessive.	his **mother-in-law's** carrot cake **Harper and Row's** latest publication

	Rule or Exception to the Rule	Example(s)
Exception to Rule 15	If the second element is a *possessive pronoun*, the first substantive must be in the possessive case form.	**Jane's and her** bedroom [not *Jane and her bedroom*] **Tom's and my** house [not *Tom and my house or Tom and I's house*]
Rule 16	To show *individual possession*, make each word in a group possessive.	**Darwin's and Freud's** ideas **Mr. Brown's and Mr. Green's** classrooms

PERSON

Nouns have **person**. Person is a grammatical term indicating whether a word refers to the one speaking (**first person**), the one spoken to (**second person**), or the one spoken about (**third person**). The *person* of a substantive used as a subject is significant in the selection of the correct verb form, because verbs change their form according to person.

The *person* of nouns is easy to determine: nouns are almost always in the third person. The exception is when a noun is an *appositive* to a pronoun that is in the first or second person. In any event, the form of the noun is **always the same**, regardless of its person.

☞**EXAMPLES:**

The **girls** *are* having a party. (*usual third person*)

We **girls** *are* having a party. (*first person, appositive*)

The **boys** *are* not leaving until they are finished. (*third person*)

You **boys** *are* not leaving until you finish. (*second person, appositive*)

John Mason *is* telling the truth. (*third person*)

I, **John Mason**, *am* telling the truth. (*first person, appositive*)

✎ **EXERCISE A** Indicate the gender of the following nouns by writing *M* for masculine, *F* for feminine, *N* for neuter, or *C* for common in the blanks.

_N_	1. endorsement	____	6. upgrade	____	11. writer
____	2. computer	____	7. doe (deer)	____	12. garçon
____	3. empress	____	8. thesaurus	____	13. actress
____	4. man	____	9. musician	____	14. jeans
____	5. referee	____	10. master	____	15. shoe

✎ **EXERCISE B** In the blank, write *N* for nominative, *O* for objective, or *P* for possessive to indicate the case of the nouns in **dark print** in each of the following sentences.

_N_ 1. The job **opening** is no longer available.

____ 2. They can tolerate another **night's** stay.

____ 3. The lines on the **parking lot** need repainting.

____ 4. **Earth** is covered mostly with water.

____ 5. Give her another **opportunity**.

_____ 6. Give **Renee** another opportunity.

_____ 7. Do you have your **parents'** approval?

_____ 8. He always tries to put in his two **cent's** worth.

_____ 9. The top of the **building** has an antenna.

_____ 10. The **top** of the building has an antenna.

_____ 11. The top of the building has an **antenna**.

_____ 12. That man is a **relative** of my father.

_____ 13. The **women's** Bible study meets every Tuesday afternoon.

_____ 14. My **GameBoy®** needs a new battery.

_____ 15. My GameBoy® needs a new **battery**.

_____ 16. She gave the **bellboy** a large tip.

✎ **EXERCISE C** Write the *possessive case* form of each of the following singular or plural nouns.

_____*branch's*_____ 1. branch
_____ 2. peninsula
_____ 3. father
_____ 4. lawyers
_____ 5. Mrs. Lukes
_____ 6. doctor
_____ 7. Bea and Doris[a]
_____ 8. Australia
_____ 9. branches
_____ 10. sister-in-law

_____ 11. firemen
_____ 12. Moses
_____ 13. moth
_____ 14. Sam Cass
_____ 15. children
_____ 16. confidant
_____ 17. Aldolphe Sax
_____ 18. sectarian
_____ 19. Edwards
_____ 20. apostles

a. joint ownership

LESSON 57: PRONOUNS

A *pronoun* is a word that is used in the place of a noun—that is, a noun substitute. Without pronouns, we would have to repeat nouns again and again with every reference to a person, place, thing, quality, or idea. Notice the difference between the following sentences:

☞**EXAMPLES:**

1. When Bob and Carol visited the museum, Bob and Carol saw the museum's Egyptian treasures and grew to appreciate the museum's Egyptian treasures and the Egyptian treasures' significance.

2. When Bob and Carol visited the museum, **they** saw **its** Egyptian treasures and grew to appreciate **them** and **their** significance.

In the second example, the words in **dark print** (*they, its, them, their*) are pronouns used as substitutes for the nouns *Bob* and *Carol, museum,* and *treasures.*

Pronouns do not have a clear meaning unless we know what they stand for. When using pronouns, you must make clear to which noun or nouns the pronouns refer. The noun to which a pronoun refers is called its **antecedent**. In the second example above, *Bob* and *Carol, museum,* and *treasures* are antecedents to the pronouns *they, its, them,* and *their.*

KINDS OF PRONOUNS

There are seven different kinds of pronouns: *personal, personal-possessive, compound, interrogative, demonstrative, indefinite,* and *relative.*

TYPES	PRONOUNS
Personal	I, me, you, he, him, she, her, it, we, us, they, them
Personal-possessive	my, mine, your, yours, his, her, hers, its, our, ours, their, theirs
Compound	myself, yourself, himself, herself, itself, ourselves, yourselves, themselves
Interrogative	who, whom, whose, whoever, whomever, what, whatever, which
Demonstrative	this, that, these, those, such
Indefinite	each, either, neither, one, everyone, everybody, no one, nobody, anyone, anybody, someone, somebody, both, few, several, many, some, any, none, all, most
Relative	who, whom, whose, which, that

■ **Personal Pronouns**

Personal pronouns are the most common direct noun substitutes and may refer to the person speaking (**first person**), the person spoken to (**second person**), or the person spoken about (**third person**).

PERSONAL PRONOUNS	
First Person	I, me, we, us
Second Person	you
Third Person	he, him, she, her, it, they, them

■ **Personal-possessive Pronouns**

Personal-possessive pronouns are personal pronouns that show ownership.

☞**EXAMPLES:**

　　　my ideas, **your** talents, **his** horse, **her** song, **its** color, **their** house

■ **Compound Pronouns**

Compound pronouns combine a personal pronoun with the suffix *-self* (singular) or *-selves* (plural). There are two types of compound pronouns: **reflexive** and **intensive**. The form is the same for both, but the usage is different. Reflexive pronouns "reflect" the action of a verb back to an antecedent which is the subject of the verb. Intensive pronouns follow their antecedents and give them special emphasis or "intensity."

☞**EXAMPLES:**

　　Reflexive:　　Jesus offered **Himself** as our Redeemer.

　　Intensive:　　Jesus **Himself** offered to be our Redeemer.

Do not use the improper forms: *hisself* or *theirselves*. These incorrectly combine a personal-possessive pronoun with a *-self* or *-selves* suffix. Also, do not use compound pronouns alone as personal pronouns; they must have a reflexive or intensive idea.

☞**EXAMPLES:**

> **Wrong:**   John and **myself** hereby volunteer for the job.
>
> **Right:**   John and **I** hereby volunteer for the job.

■ **Interrogative Pronouns**

Interrogative pronouns ask or introduce a question.

☞**EXAMPLES:**

> **What** is this?   **Who** will go?

■ **Demonstrative Pronouns**

Demonstrative pronouns point out a person, place, thing, etc. to which they refer.

☞**EXAMPLES:**

> **This** is good food.   Don't say **that** again.
>
> **Those** who wish to leave may now do so.

■ **Indefinite Pronouns**

Indefinite pronouns do not refer to any particular named antecedents but refer only to generally understood persons or things.

☞**EXAMPLES:**

> **Nobody** knows the trouble I've seen.
>
> **Many** are called but **few** are chosen.

■ **Relative Pronouns**

Relative pronouns are used only to introduce dependent clauses that modify nouns (*adjective clauses*).

☞**EXAMPLES:**

> He is the man **who** bought my car.
>
> The dog **that** bit my sister did not have rabies.

✎ **EXERCISE A** Underline all the pronouns in the following sentences.

1. One never knows what will happen next.

2. Everyone who wants it should simply ask for it.

3. What is the name of the man who spoke to our class?

4. The islands are known for their white beaches, which I hope to visit next year.

5. She cut herself on a sharp blade of grass.

6. He told me what he wanted for his birthday, but I have forgotten what it was.

7. Who is on the Lord's side?

8. To whom was that gift given?

✎ **EXERCISE B** Write a sentence using at least one of each of the following types of pronouns.

Personal

_____

Personal-possessive

_____

Compound (reflexive)

_____

Compound (intensive)

_____

Interrogative

_____

Demonstrative (Do NOT use demonstrative pronouns as adjectives: *this* car, *those* boys.)

_____

Indefinite

_____

Relative

_____

LESSON 58: PLACING PRONOUNS

You will recall from previous lessons that **pronouns** are also *substantives*, words with noun-like qualities which can be used in the place of nouns. The grammatical rules governing pronouns are much the same as those governing nouns. The rules are more difficult to apply to pronouns, in some cases, because pronouns have more changes in form than nouns do; therefore, it is sometimes more difficult to make pronouns agree in form with other words in a sentence.

CASE

Like nouns, some pronouns have *case*—nominative, objective, and possessive. Unlike nouns, *some pronouns have different forms for nominative and objective cases*. These changes occur only in personal, interrogative, and relative pronouns. Indefinite, demonstrative, and compound pronouns, however, have the same form in nominative and objective cases.

Personal, interrogative, relative, and indefinite pronouns all have separate forms for possessive case. Compound and demonstrative pronouns do not have a possessive-case form. The following chart will help to illustrate these rules:

PRONOUNS	Nominative	Objective	Possessive
Personal	I, you, he, she, it, we, they	me, you, him, her, it, us, them	my, mine, yours, his, her, its, our, ours, their, theirs
Interrogative	who, whoever, what, whatever, which, whichever	whom, whomever, what, whatever, which, whichever	whose, whosoever
Relative	who, which, that	whom, which, that	whose
Indefinite	each, either, neither, one, everyone, everybody, no one, nobody, anybody, anyone, someone, somebody, both, few, several, many, some, any, none, all, most	each, either, neither, one, everyone, everybody, no one, nobody, anybody, anyone, someone, somebody, both, few, several, many, some, any, none, all, most	either's, neither's, one's, everyone's, everybody's, no one's, nobody's, anybody's, anyone's, someone's, somebody's[a]
Compound	myself, yourself, himself, herself, itself, ourselves, yourselves, themselves	myself, yourself, himself, herself, itself, ourselves, yourselves, themselves	
Demonstrative	this, that, these, those, such	this, that, these, those, such	

a. Use an "of" phrase when appropriate to show possession in other indefinite pronouns. For example, *servant of all* is correct, rather than *all's servant*.

Just as with nouns, pronouns in the **nominative** case may be used as *subjects* or *predicate nominatives* (subjective complements).

Pronouns in the **objective** case may be used as *direct objects, indirect objects, objects of prepositions*, or *objective complements*.

Pronouns in the **possessive** case are used as *adjectives*.

☞**EXAMPLES:**

■ Nominative Case:

> **He** is a good swimmer. (*subject*)
>
> **Who** are the winners? **We** are **they**. (*subject/predicate nominative*)
>
> **This** is a good steak. (*subject*)

■ Objective Case:

> Tell **him** to come here. (*indirect object*)
>
> Eve ate **it**. (*direct object*)
>
> To **whom** was the Law of the Lord given? (*object of a preposition*)

■ Possessive Case:

> **Everyone's** excuse was illness. (*used as adjective*)
>
> **Its** name is Gibraltar. (*used as adjective*)
>
> **Whose** reputation has been damaged the most? (*used as adjective*)

PERSON

Pronouns have **person**—first, second, and third. Whereas *person* is usually not a significant grammatical factor in nouns, it is very important in some pronouns. Some **personal pronouns** use distinctive forms for first, second, and third persons, as the following chart shows. Notice that a pronoun-subject in the third person requires a change in the form of the verb (an "s" added) when the verb is in the present tense (also in the present perfect tense).

Case ➠	NOMINATIVE		OBJECTIVE	
Number ➠	**Singular**	**Plural**	**Singular**	**Plural**
First Person	*I* like	*We* Like	helped *me*	helped *us*
Second Person	*You* like	*You* like	helped *you*	helped *you*
Third Person	*He* likes *She* likes *It* likes	*They* like	helped *him* helped *her* helped *it*	helped *them*

Person is not a significant grammatical consideration for other types of pronouns, just in the case of personal pronouns.

GENDER

Personal pronouns, including personal-possessive and compound personal, have **gender** (*masculine, feminine, neuter,* or *common*) and must agree with their antecedents in gender. Other types of pronouns do not have gender.

Study the following chart:

Masculine	Feminine	Neuter	Common
Use with reference to males	Use with reference to females	Use with reference to things with no sex	Use with reference to entities of unknown sex or which include both sexes
he, him, his himself	she, her, hers herself	it, its itself	I, me, my, myself, mine, you, your, yours, yourself, yourselves, he,[a] him,[a] his,[a] himself,[a] it, its, itself, we, us, our, ours, ourselves, they, them, themselves, their, theirs

    a. In certain contexts, these pronouns include both males and females in nouns having common gender.

NUMBER

Personal, personal-possessive, compound, and indefinite pronouns have **number** (*singular* or *plural*). Likewise, demonstrative pronouns (*this, that, these, those*) have number. The following chart illustrates the *number* of personal, personal-possessive, and compound pronouns.

PRONOUNS	Singular	Plural
Personal	I, me, you, he, him, she, her, it	we, us, you, they, them
Personal-possessive	my, mine, your, yours, his, her, hers, its	our, ours, your, yours, their, theirs
Compound	myself, yourself, himself, herself, itself	ourselves, yourselves, themselves

Most of the problem people have with *number* when using pronouns is related to the fact that pronouns must agree with their antecedents and verbs in *number*. This is particularly a problem when the pronoun is an **indefinite pronoun**, because one cannot tell from the spelling of some of them whether they are singular or plural. Memorize the following chart.

INDEFINITE PRONOUNS		
Always Singular	**Always Plural**	**Either Singular or Plural**
each, either, neither, one, everyone, everybody, no one, nobody, anyone, anybody, someone, somebody	both, few, several, many	some, any, none, all, most

The indefinite pronouns in the column at the right in the above chart can be either singular or plural, depending on the context of the sentence. If they refer to singular antecedents, they are singular and require singular verbs. If they refer to plural antecedents, they are plural and require plural verbs.

☞**EXAMPLES:**

> **Some** of the *men* are Christians. (*plural*)
>
> **Some** of the *milk* is spilled. (*singular*)
>
> **Most** of the *rabbits* are white. (*plural*)
>
> **Most** of the *grass* is brown. (*singular*)
>
> **All** of the *women* are attending. (*plural*)
>
> **All** of the *wheat* has been harvested. (*singular*)

✎ **EXERCISE A** For each sentence, underline the correct pronoun in parentheses. In the blank write *N* if the pronoun needed is in the nominative case, *O* if it is in the objective case, or *P* if it is in the possessive case.

___O___ 1. It was probably (we, <u>us</u>).

_____ 2. Jay and (he, him) are both going out for basketball.

_____ 3. Jessica has been ill, but (he, him, she, her) feels better today.

_____ 4. Mr. Lindstrom told Grant and (I, me) to give our report on euthanasia.

_____ 5. (We, Us) girls are planning a slumber party.

_____ 6. "Hello! Is Brian home?" ... "Yes, this is (he, him)."

_____ 7. The ROTC commander is (he, him).

_____ 8. Everyone should pay (his, her, their) own way.

_____ 9. (They, Them) and (we, us) are facing off in the tournament.

_____ 10. The sparring partners were Manuel and (she, her).

_____ 11. Both men were cognizant of (his, their) roles in the offense.

_____ 12. May Joni and (I, me) order a pizza tonight?

_____ 13. Do you and (him, he) expect to graduate?

_____ 14. Give (she, her) a portion of the business.

_____ 15. God (Himself, Hisself) will be with you forever.

✎ **EXERCISE B** Fill in the blank spaces in the following chart with all of the correct personal pronouns.

CASE ➠	Nominative		Objective	
NUMBER ➠	Singular	Plural	Singular	Plural
First Person				
Second Person				
Third Person				

LESSON 59: UNIT REVIEW

✎ **EXERCISE A** Fill in the blanks.

1. _____ nouns are always capitalized.

2. A _____ is a word that is used as a noun substitute.

3. Name the seven types of *pronouns*:

   a. _____   e. _____

   b. _____   f. _____

   c. _____   g. _____

   d. _____

4. In the space below, write a paragraph of about 75 words using **nouns** and **pronouns**, *at least one of each kind* (i.e., **nouns**: *common, proper, compound, collective;* **pronouns**: *personal, personal-possessive, compound* (reflexive and intensive), *interrogative, demonstrative, indefinite, relative*).

   _____

   _____

   _____

   _____

   _____

   _____

   _____

   _____

   _____

   _____

   _____

   _____

   _____

5. From the paragraph you have written above, write an example of each of the following items.

Common Noun: _____   Personal Pronoun: _____

Proper Noun: _____   Personal-possessive Pronoun: _____

Compound Noun: _____   Compound (reflexive) Pronoun: _____

Collective Noun: _____   Compound (intensive) Pronoun: _____

Indefinite Pronoun: _____   Interrogative Pronoun: _____

Relative Pronoun: _____   Demonstrative Pronoun: _____

✎ **EXERCISE B** Answer the following questions by filling in the blanks:

1. What is a substantive?

    _____

    _____

    _____

2. A _____ is a substantive about which a sentence makes a statement.

3. An _____ is a substantive (or adjective) used after a direct object to complete its meaning.

4. _____ is the grammatical term indicating whether a part of speech refers to one or more than one.

5. The plural of nouns ending with a -y preceded by a consonant is formed by

    _____ .

6. How many genders are possible for English nouns? _____ They are:

    _____

7. The three cases of English nouns are: _____, _____, and _____.

8. Nouns used as *subjects* and *predicate nominatives* are in the _____ case.

    Nouns used as *objects* are in the _____ case.

    Nouns that show *ownership* are in the _____ case.

9. The indefinite pronouns that are always plural are _____, _____, _____, and _____.

Unit 7
Verbs, Verbals,
and Participles

This unit is a review of the part of speech called the **verb**. *Types of verbs* (action, linking, helping, and state-of-being verbs), *qualities of verbs* (tense, tone, voice, and mood), *verbals* (participles used as nouns, adjectives, and adverbs), and *principal parts of verbs* (present, present participle, past, and past participle) will be covered. In addition, the various subgroups under each of the four qualities of verbs will be discussed (e.g., *tone*—simple, progressive, and emphatic).

LESSON 60: VERBS

A *verb* is a word that shows action or existence, that links another word to a subject, or that helps another verb complete its meaning. There are four types of verbs: *action, linking, helping,* and *state-of-being* (existence) verbs.

☞**EXAMPLES:**

Action:	President Bush **pursues** the same common-sense approach and bipartisan spirit that he used in Texas.
Linking:	The argument **seemed** implausible.
Helping:	Kurt Busch **had** been on a raging hot streak in racing.
State-of-being:	The vehicles **are** in the garage.

Sometimes a verb may consist of a single word. At other times, two or more words may serve the purposes of a verb. In this latter case, the construction is called a ***verb phrase***. A verb phrase consists of a main verb plus one or more helping verbs.

☞**EXAMPLES:**

Single verb:	She **abhors** his hypocritical attitude.
	The narrator **read** the Bible story while the actors **performed** their parts.
Verb phrase:	The message **was e-mailed** to all the employees.
	As of September 1, Ellen **will have served** as a deaconess for seven years.

ACTION VERBS

The "action" of a verb may be either physical or mental. Sometimes the "action" might involve both physical or mental effort.

☞**EXAMPLES:**

Physical:	eat, kick, run, give, stand, construct, rake, carry
Mental:	think, ponder, realize, consider, wonder, hope, imagine
Both:	read, buy, criticize, speak, call

Verbs can be described as **transitive** or **intransitive**. *Transitive* is a term applied to a verb that passes its action to a *receiver* which is necessary to complete the verb's meaning. *Intransitive* verbs have no receiver for their action but have a meaning that is complete in themselves. State-of-being verbs (forms of *to be* when they mean *to exist*) are considered intransitive. Some action verbs can be transitive or intransitive, depending on how they are used. Other action verbs are always transitive.

☞**EXAMPLES:**

In each sentence below, the capitalized WORD is the noun which *receives* the verb's action.

> **Transitive:** Washington **fought** the WAR for American Independence.
>
> His wife **desired** God's PEACE in her heart.
>
> The BOOK, *Grace and Glory*, **was written** by Geerhardus Vos.

In the following sentences, there is *no receiver* of the verb's action.

> **Intransitive:** The wind **blew** through the willows.
>
> The results of the November election **were** still **being resolved**.
>
> In June, my family **ferried** from Manitowoc, Wisconsin, to Ludington, Michigan.
>
> God **exists**.

LINKING VERBS

Linking verbs (sometimes called "coupling" verbs) link their subject(s) to another word in the sentence, usually one which follows the verb. The word thus linked either renames/identifies the subject or describes/modifies the subject. If it renames or identifies the subject, it will be a noun, pronoun, or noun-like expression called a **predicate nominative**. If it describes or modifies the subject, it will be an adjective or adjective-like expression called a **predicate adjective**.

☞**EXAMPLES:**

> **Linking:** The car **is** a Honda. (*links a predicate nominative to the subject*)
>
> Her hair **is** auburn. (*links a predicate adjective to the subject*)

The verb **to be**—along with its various forms: *am, is, are, was, were, be, being, been*—is the most common linking verb. Words that are used in much the same way that the verb "to be" is used are also common linking verbs. These include *seem, become, appear, taste, feel, smell, sound, look, grow, remain,* and *stay*. Some of these words can also be action verbs, depending on how they are used. If a form of **to be** can be substituted logically for any of these verbs, they are likely linking verbs; if not, they are likely action verbs.

☞**EXAMPLES:**

> **Linking:** This lemon **tastes** (*is*) sour.
>
> The article **appeared** (*was*) satisfactory.
>
> Baking bread **smells** (*is*) scrumptious.
>
> His outreach plan **sounded** (*was*) tenable.
>
> **Action:** Jay **tasted** the lemon to see if it were sour.
>
> His essay **appeared** in the Op-Ed section of the *Chicago Tribune*.
>
> Joelle **smelled** the baking bread.
>
> He **sounded** the rallying cry to declare the Gospel message.

HELPING VERBS

Helping verbs—also called *auxiliary verbs*—assist other verbs to complete their meaning. The verbs in the following examples are commonly used as helping verbs. *Shall, will, should, would, may, might, must, can,* and *could* are verbs that are **always** used as helping verbs. *Be, being, been, am, is, are, was, were, have, has, had, do, does,* and *did* can be used as helping verbs but also may stand alone as linking, state-of-being, or action verbs.

☞**EXAMPLES:**

Helping:	She **was** *painting* a still-life scene.
	He **was being** *persecuted* for his faith.
	Barb **has been** *memorizing* her part for the school play.
	You **did** not *finish* your assignment on time.
Linking:	The Pilgrims **were** brave and adventurous.
Action:	Samuel **did** his studies before supper.
	I **had** a difficult time after the surgery.

STATE-OF-BEING VERB

Forms of the verb **to be** are *linking verbs* when they "link" a predicate nominative or predicate adjective to a subject. The same verb forms are **state-of-being verbs** when they mean "to exist." When these forms of "to be" are state-of-being verbs, they are not followed by a predicate nominative or predicate adjective.

☞**EXAMPLES:**

Linking:	Elyse **was** unkind to her sister.
Being:	There **is** no God but Jehovah.
	They **were** near the place of the crime.
	How **was** she after the loss of her mother?

✎ **EXERCISE A** Underline all the verbs in the following sentences. Above each verb, write *A* if the verb is an action verb, *L* if it is a linking verb, *S* if it is a state-of-being verb, or *H* if it is a helping verb.

      H   *A*   *H* *L*
1. He <u>has</u> never <u>asked</u> for anything that <u>would</u> <u>be</u> a burden on his family.

2. It has been said that he who does not plan for the future will be woebegone—beset by woes.

3. Today you broke my heart in a place that was not broken.

4. Actions speak louder than words.

5. "For by one Spirit we were all baptized into one body" (1 Corinthians 12:13a).

6. The theory of evolution is one of the greatest evidences of man's rebellion against God.

7. Someone once wrote that the two greatest "abilities" are availability and dependability.

8. The team commemorated its outstanding season by honoring its coach.

9. Each year they have given us a bonus at the end of the year.

10. It could be said that things are not always as we would have them.

✎ **EXERCISE B** Underline all the *verbs* or *verb phrases* in the following sentences. Above each one write *T* if the verb is transitive or *I* if the verb is intransitive. Consider verb phrases as if they were a single verb. If the verb is transitive, double-underline the receiver of the action. (HINT: The receiver of the action of a transitive verb may be either the subject or the direct object of the verb.)

1. The solo was sung by the young girl.

2. Sue assembled all the parts for her science project.

3. A DVD will generate a clearer picture than a video will.

4. Either he runs to win or he does not run at all.

5. "The wicked borrows and does not repay, but the righteous shows mercy and gives" (Psalms 37:21).

6. God shines the light of His Gospel over the whole earth.

7. Steve only flew over well-charted routes.

8. My father works for a not-for-profit ministry.

9. The student delivered his speech in front of the entire school body.

10. "For the earth shall be full of the knowledge of the LORD as the waters cover the sea" (Isaiah 11:9).

LESSON 61: PLACING VERBS

Verbs have qualities known as **tense**, **tone**, **voice**, and **mood**. To express these qualities, verbs often change their forms.

TENSE

Tense is a grammatical term signifying the **time frame** in which the action or condition expressed by a verb takes place—*past time, present time*, or *future time*. The English language is also capable of expressing action or a state of being which has been or will be completed at a given time in the past, present, or future. The six tenses of English verbs are **past**, **present**, **future**, **past perfect**, **present perfect**, and **future perfect**.

■ **Past Tense**

The *past tense* expresses action or being which took place during a definite time before now.

☞**EXAMPLES:**

> World War IV began on September 11, 2001.
> She **downloaded** the game from <gamehouse.com>.

■ **Present Tense**

The *present tense* expresses action or being taking place now.

☞**EXAMPLES:**

> Samuel **runs** for Big Rapids High's track team.
> The mountains **are** rugged.

■ **Future Tense**

The *future tense* expresses action or being during a time after now.

☞**EXAMPLES:**

> The cold front **will shift** northeast in about a day or two.
>
> I **shall design** a set for the community theater.

Note: When using the helping words *shall* and *will* in future-tense constructions, it is preferred to use *shall* with the first person and *will* with the second and third persons. You may use *shall* with second and third persons to express strong determination. In modern usage, however, the distinction between *shall* and *will* is not strictly observed.

■ **Past Perfect Tense**

The *past perfect*[57] *tense* expresses action or being which began sometime in the past and was completed at some later point in the past.

☞**EXAMPLES:**

> Tom **had visited** his grandmother twice a year until her death in May 2002.
>
> The socialist focus group **had misled** the masses by its disinformation campaign.

■ **Present Perfect Tense**

The *present perfect tense* expresses action or being which began in the past and is still taking place now.

☞**EXAMPLES:**

> Nick **has been traveling** for two weeks.
>
> We **have seen** His star in the East and **have come** to worship Him.

■ **Future Perfect Tense**

The *future perfect tense* expresses action which began in the past, present, or near future and will be completed sometime later in the future.

☞**EXAMPLES:**

> Julie **will have completed** the report by week's end.
>
> By noon, she **will have been baking** for two hours.

Number ➠	Singular	Plural
Tense ➠	Present	
First Person	I *see*	we *see*
Second Person	you *see*	you *see*
Third Person	he (she, it) *sees*	they *see*
Tense ➠	Past	
First Person	I *saw*	we *saw*
Second Person	you *saw*	you *saw*
Third Person	he (she, it) *saw*	they *saw*

---

57. In this context, the word "perfect" means "complete."

Number ➠	Singular	Plural
Tense ➠	**Future**	
First Person	I *shall see*	we *shall see*
Second Person	you *will see*	you *will see*
Third Person	he (she, it) *will see*	they *will see*
Number ➠	**Singular**	**Plural**
Tense ➠	**Present Perfect**	
First Person	I *have seen*	we *have seen*
Second Person	you *have seen*	you *have seen*
Third Person	he (she, it) *has seen*	they *have seen*
Tense ➠	**Past Perfect**	
First Person	I *had seen*	we *had seen*
Second Person	you *had seen*	you *had seen*
Third Person	he (she, it) *had seen*	they *had seen*
Tense ➠	**Future Perfect**	
First Person	I *shall have seen*	we *shall have seen*
Second Person	you *will have seen*	you *will have seen*
Third Person	he (she, it) *will have seen*	they *will have seen*

TONE

Tone is a characteristic of some verb tenses indicating simple or progressive time or emphasis. Thus the three tones of English verbs are **simple**, **progressive**, and **emphatic**.

■ **Simple Tone**

Simple tone is the normal, straightforward way of expressing the six tenses—like snapshots of action or being in fixed time frames.

Note: *Voice* will be covered in the next section. However, it is included in the following "example charts" to show the various forms that the verb "to see" takes according to *active* and *passive voice*.

☞**EXAMPLES:**

Tense	Active Voice	Passive Voice
Present	He sees.	He is seen.
Past	He saw.	He was seen.
Future	He will see.	He will be seen.
Present Perfect	He has seen.	He has been seen.
Past Perfect	He had seen.	He had been seen.
Future Perfect	He will have seen.	He will have been seen.

■ **Progressive Tone**

Progressive tone indicates action or state of being in progress or *ongoing* in each of the six tenses. It requires an appropriate form of the helping verb *to be* and the present participle (-**ing** form of the verb (for *active voice*).

☞**EXAMPLES:**

Tense	Active Voice	Passive Voice
Present	He **is seeing.**	He **is being seen.**
Past	He **was seeing.**	He **was being seen.**
Future	He **will be seeing.**	
Present Perfect	He **has been seeing.**	
Past Perfect	He **had been seeing.**	
Future Perfect	He **will have been seeing.**	

■ **Emphatic Tone**

Emphatic tone is used to express emphasis or to ask a question. It is used only in the present and past tenses. It requires an appropriate form of the helping verb *to do.*

☞**EXAMPLES:**

Tense	Emphasis	Question
Present	I (you, we) **do see.**	**Do** I (you, we) **see?**
	He (she, it, they) **does see.**	**Does** he (she, it) **see?**
Past	I (you, we) **did see.**	**Did** I (you, we) **see?**
	He (she, it, they) **did see.**	**Did** he (she, it, they) **see?**

VOICE

Voice is a grammatical term indicating whether the subject of a sentence is doing the action of the verb (*active voice*) or receiving the action (*passive voice*)—in other words, whether the subject is acting or being acted upon.

In *active voice*, the subject is the doer and the direct object is the receiver. In **passive voice**, the subject is the receiver. The doer follows the verb and is an expressed or implied noun which is preceded by the preposition *by*, either expressed or implied.

Passive voice is formed by using an appropriate tense form of the helping verb *to be* plus the past participle of the main verb. Only *transitive verbs* have passive voice. As you learned in Lesson 60, transitive verbs pass their action from a *doer* to a *receiver.*

☞**EXAMPLES:**

Active: Jesus saves **sinners.**

Jordan plays **baseball.**

Passive: **Sinners** are saved by **Jesus.**

Baseball is played by **Jordan.**

Most **constituents** were misled. (*by a source not named in the sentence*)

MOOD

Mood is a grammatical term indicating the *state of mind* or *manner* in which a statement is being made. *Mood*, also called **mode**, is expressed through verbs. English has three moods—*indicative*, *imperative*, and *subjunctive*.

■ Indicative Mood

Indicative mood is the usual way a statement of fact, opinion, or idea is made or a question is asked.

☞EXAMPLES:

Southern yellow pine **is** harder than eastern white pine.

The children's Christmas program **was** wonderful.

Will Amy **be** exhausted after her wilderness trek?

■ Imperative mood

Imperative mood is used to express a command, a request, or an order. It uses verbs in only one (tense) form in both singular and plural: *the present* (infinitive form without the introductory *to*).

☞EXAMPLES:

Stop whining at once!

Please **ask** me if you have any questions.

Remember the Alamo!

■ Subjunctive mood

Subjunctive mood is used to express a condition contrary to fact, a supposition, a doubt or uncertainty, a desire, an improbability, a necessity.

☞EXAMPLES:

If I **were** you, I would change my ways.

Should I **produce** the evidence, they will need to retract their false allegations.

The most significant change in form required by subjunctive mood involves the verb **to be**. We would normally say "I was," not "I were." Because of the construction of "supposition" using the phrase "*if I …*" the form changes from *was* to *were*. Distinctive forms for expressing verbs in subjunctive mood have largely gone out of fashion in modern English usage. Current usage prefers to express subjunctive ideas through such helping verbs as *should, would, can, could, may, might, must, ought, let, dare, need,* and *used.*

☞EXAMPLES:

Former:	If the fugitive **come**, he will be apprehended.
	If she **debate** me, I shall be happy to prove it.
Current:	If the fugitive **should come**, he will be apprehended.
	If she **dare debate** me, I shall be happy to prove it.

Modern English usage, however, retains a number of common expressions which still reflect the former tendency to use distinct subjunctive forms.

☞EXAMPLES:

Heaven **forbid!**	**Suffice** it to say…
Thy Kingdom **come**…	**Come** what may…
…if need **be**…	

The following chart illustrates the differences between indicative and subjunctive moods for the verb *to be:*

MOOD ➠	INDICATIVE		SUBJUNCTIVE	
Number ➠	**Singular**	**Plural**	**Singular**	**Plural**
Tense ➠	*Present*			
First Person	I *am*	we *are*	(if) I *be*	(if) we *be*
Second Person	you *are*	you *are*	(if) you *be*	(if) you *be*
Third Person	he (she, it) *is*	they *are*	(if) he (she, it) *be*	(if) they *be*
Tense ➠	*Past*			
First Person	I *was*	we *were*	(if) I *were*	(if) we *were*
Second Person	you *were*	you *were*	(if) you *were*	(if) you *were*
Third Person	he *was*	they *were*	(if) he *were*	(if) they *were*
Tense ➠	*Future*			
First Person	I *shall be*	we *shall be*	*(same as indicative)*	
Second Person	you *will be*	you *will be*		
Third Person	he *will be*	they *will be*		

✎ **EXERCISE A** Underline all the verbs and verb phrases in the following sentences. Identify the tense, voice, tone, and mood of each by writing the correct numbers in the boxes, using the following key.

TENSE	VOICE	TONE	MOOD
1. Present	1. Active	1. Simple	1. Indicative
2. Past	2. Passive	2. Progressive	2. Imperative
3. Future		3. Emphatic	3. Subjunctive
4. Present Perfect			
5. Past Perfect			
6. Future Perfect			

1.   They <u>have seen</u> many historical sites during their vacation.

Tense: 4	Voice: 1	Tone: 1	Mood: 1

2.   Please, do not hesitate to call.

Tense:	Voice:	Tone:	Mood:

3.   The eucalyptus leaves were eaten by a koala bear.

Tense:	Voice:	Tone:	Mood:

4.   Please do not shout at each other.

Tense:	Voice:	Tone:	Mood:

5. Dave has been laying tile in our home.

| Tense: | Voice: | Tone: | Mood: |

6. She will have been waiting for an hour.

| Tense: | Voice: | Tone: | Mood: |

7. The play had been seen by several hundred students.

| Tense: | Voice: | Tone: | Mood: |

8. We shall not be affected by mere emotion.

| Tense: | Voice: | Tone: | Mood: |

9. They were being deceived by the liberal media.

| Tense: | Voice: | Tone: | Mood: |

10. Thy will be done, Lord.

| Tense: | Voice: | Tone: | Mood: |

✎ **EXERCISE B** Rewrite the following sentences, changing the verbs from active to passive voice or from passive to active voice. Keep the tense and tone as they are.

1. Jesus was seen by more than 500 people after His resurrection.

   More than 500 people saw Jesus after His resurrection.

2. Jerry faithfully taught the youth God's Word.

3. She is being awarded by her peers.

4. Bob produced the Web page in a few hours.

5. The congregants are being shepherded by the elders at all times.

6. E. Margaret Clarkson wrote the hymn "O Father, You Are Sovereign."

7. A memorable performance was achieved by the drama club during the fall semester.

8. Some of her expenses as a missionary will be provided by the congregation.

LESSON 62: VERBALS

Verbs are normally used to show action or a state of being or to link a subject to a subject complement. When used in this way they are called **predicate verbs**. Predicate verbs and verb phrases serve as the main verb of a sentence or clause, as in the following example:

☞**EXAMPLE:**

Before Jim **became** a Christian,	he often **kept** bad company.
[main verb of a dependent clause]	[main verb of the sentence (*independent clause*)]

Verbs may also be used as other parts of speech. When they do so, they are called **verbals**. There are three types of verbals: *participles* (present and past), *infinitives*, and *gerunds*.

VERBALS USED AS NOUNS

Two types of verbals may be used as **nouns**: *infinitives* and *gerunds*.

■ Infinitives

Infinitives are formed by using the present form of the verb preceded (usually) by the word **to**: *to see, to eat, to run, to pray, to worship, to fret, to sing, to whisper, to sit*, etc.

☞**EXAMPLES:**

To love God above all is the first commandment. (*subject*)

The Bible teaches us **to love** one another. (*direct object*)

■ Gerunds

Gerunds are formed by using the infinitive form of the verb and adding the suffix **-ing**: *seeing, eating, running, praying, worshipping, fretting, singing, whispering, sitting*, etc.

☞**EXAMPLES:**

Fretting is not healthy. (*subject*)

This lesson is about **using** verbals. (*object of a preposition*)

He gave **practicing** the piano his highest priority. (*indirect object*)

She loves **reading**. (*direct object*)

VERBALS USED AS ADJECTIVES

Three types of verbals may be used as **adjectives**: *present participles, past participles*, and *infinitives*.

■ Present Participles

Present participles are formed by using the infinitive form of the verb and adding the suffix **-ing**. Present participles look exactly like gerunds. Remember, however, that gerunds are used as *nouns*. Present participles are used as *adjectives*.

☞**EXAMPLES:**

Adopt a **forgiving** attitude.

The marine mammal presentation included **dancing** dolphins and whales.

How many **speeding** tickets did you receive?

■ Past Participles

Past participles of many verbs end with the suffixes **-d**, **-ed**, or **-t**. The past participle form of many other verbs, however, follows no set pattern. You must simply memorize these irregular forms or find them in a dictionary. The past participle is the form which is used with the helping verbs *have, has,* or *had* when the verb is a predicate verb: (*have*) *eaten,* (*has*) *pounded,* (*had*) *wondered.* This same form may be used as an adjective.

☞**EXAMPLES:**

I do not like **burned** toast.   The candy bar is **melted**.

■ Infinitives

Infinitives, in addition to their uses as nouns, may also be used as adjectives, modifying nouns or pronouns.

☞**EXAMPLES:**

The time **to pray** is anytime.   She gave them some grapes **to eat**.

A VERBAL USED AS AN ADVERB

One type of verbal may be used as an **adverb**, modifying verbs, adjectives, or other adverbs: the **infinitive**.

☞**EXAMPLES:**

Be quick **to praise** and slow **to criticize**.   She ran **to meet** the bus.
The words ran across the screen too fast **to read**.

SUMMARY

1. **Infinitives** are verb forms (verbals) used as *nouns, adjectives,* or *adverbs*.

2. **Gerunds** are verb forms (verbals) used as *nouns*.

3. **Participles** (present and past) are verb forms (verbals) used as *adjectives*.

✎ **EXERCISE A** Write the correct verbal form for the following verbs.

	INFINITIVE	GERUND	PRESENT PARTICIPLE	PAST PARTICPLE
1. build	*to build*	*building*	*building*	*built*
2. display				
3. spoil				
4. anger				
5. dispute				
6. fancy				
7. continue				
8. guess				
9. bewilder				
10. scurry				

✎ **EXERCISE B** Identify the verbals in **dark print** by writing in the blanks *I* for infinitive, *G* for gerund, *PS* for present participle, or *PP* for past participle. If the verbal is an infinitive, write *ADJ.*, *ADV.*, or *N* above it to indicate if it is used as an *adjective*, *adverb*, or *noun*. HINT: To decide whether an **-ing** word is a present participle or a gerund, you will have to decide whether it is used as a noun (gerund) or adjective (present participle).

   N
   I   1. He claimed not **to know**.

_____ 2. **Glorifying** God is man's chief end.

_____ 3. My family ate **barbecued** burgers around the picnic table.

_____ 4. The chicken casserole was served in a **baking** dish.

_____ 5. **Buying** time was his only hope of escape.

_____ 6. She needed **to collect** her thoughts.

_____ 7. The geologists searched for fossils **to collect**.

_____ 8. Jessica was ready **to execute** her plan.

_____ 9. He received his information from a **posted** news bulletin.

_____ 10. The Gregorian order is renowned for its **chanting** monks.

✎ **EXERCISE C** Select three of the verbs listed in Exercise A. Write four sentences for each, using the verbal forms specified below.

Sentence 1:	*Infinitive*
Sentence 2:	*Gerund*
Sentence 3:	*Present Participle*
Sentence 4:	*Past Participle*

Verb: *build*

1. *To build a towering edifice someday is my dream.*
2. *Building a typical skyscraper, however, is not my greatest desire.*
3. *I often construct models with building material of various shapes and sizes.*
4. *I presented a built prototype with my proposal.*

Verb:_____

1. _____
2. _____
3. _____
4. _____

Verb:_____

1. _____
2. _____
3. _____
4. _____

Verb:_____

1. _____

2. _____

3. _____

4. _____

LESSON 63: PRINCIPAL PARTS OF VERBS

As you have already seen, verbs take a wide variety of forms, depending upon their tense, voice, tone, mood, or use as verbals. All of the forms are constructed by using one of the four *principal parts* each English verb has. By choosing the correct principal part of each main verb and each helping verb used with a main verb, you will be able to apply or construct exactly the right form of the verb needed to communicate what you want to say or write.

FOUR PRINCIPAL PARTS

The *four principal parts* of a verb are the *present, present participle, past,* and *past participle.*

☞**EXAMPLES:**

1st Principal Part: Present	2nd Principal Part: Present Participle	3rd Principal Part: Past	4th Principal Part: Past Participle
trot	trotting	trotted	(have) trotted
use	using	used	(have) used
stand	standing	stood	(have) stood
wait	waiting	waited	(have) waited
go	going	went	(have) gone

You may notice some patterns in the forms of the examples above. Notice, for instance, that the **present form** is the form used in infinitives, without the introductory word "**to**." It is the form used for the *first person, present tense, indicative mood, active voice* of predicate verbs.

Secondly, notice that all **present participles** end with the suffix **-ing**. You may have to slightly change the spelling of some root words before adding the "-ing" ending, such as doubling a final consonant or dropping a silent final "e"; but the present participle of all verbs is always formed by adding **-ing** to the present form of the verb.

Thirdly, notice also that many verbs form their **past** and **past participle** forms by adding the suffix **-ed**. Some other verbs, however, change their form or spelling completely when forming their third and fourth principal parts. Verbs that form their third and fourth principal parts by adding *-ed, -d,* or *-t* are called **regular verbs**. Verbs that form their third and fourth principal parts by radically changing their spelling or form are called **irregular verbs**. In some cases, the third and fourth principal parts of irregular verbs are alike (although different from the first and second parts); in other cases, the third and fourth principal parts are different from each other; in still other cases, the first, third, and fourth principal parts are all identical. There is no way to "figure out" how to form the third and fourth principal parts of irregular verbs. You must simply memorize the correct part of each individual verb after consulting a dictionary, grammar textbook, or other source. (*See Appendix for a list of many common irregular verbs.*)

■ *How Participles Are Used*

Present participles and *past participles* have two uses:

1. They may be part of a verb phrase used as a *predicate verb.*

Notice in the following examples that the *present* and *past participles* are in **dark print** while the *verb phrase* is in brackets.

☞**EXAMPLES:**

Present Participles:	The motor [is **running**].
	The butcher [was **cutting**] the meat.
	I [am **writing**] a letter to my sister.
Past Participles:	The candles [have been **lit**].
	I [have **eaten**] my lunch.
	She [had **taken**] the book back to the library.

2. As you learned in Lesson 62, participles may also be used as *adjectives.*

☞**EXAMPLES:**

Present participles:	**Running** water is usually safer than stagnant water.
	She suffered from an **eating** disorder.
	His views were on the **cutting** edge of philosophy.
Past participles:	He was not much of a **skilled** hunter.
	The door had a **broken** hinge.
	They were among the **chosen** few.

FORMING TENSES, TONES, AND VOICES

Different *principal parts* of verbs are used in forming various predicate verb *tenses, tones,* and *voices*:

Voice ⏩	Active		Passive
Tone ⏩	**Simple**	**Progressive**	**Simple**
Present Infinitive	to go	to be going	to be gone
Perfect Infinitive	to have gone	to have been going	to have been gone
Present Participle	going	—	being gone
Past Participle	gone	—	—
Perfect Participle	having gone	having been going	having been gone
Present Gerund	going	—	being gone
Past Gerund[a]	gone	—	—
Perfect Gerund	having gone	having been going	having been gone

a. Even though Past gerunds are not common, they are used of persons or things which have been acted upon. The gerund "seen" may be used as follows: They were numbered among the seen. By definition, these verbals are always used as nouns. Past gerunds normally end with the suffix -ed, unless they take an irregular ending.

■ *Active Voice*

Simple Tone

The *present tense* is formed by using the first principal part of the verb. All forms in singular and plural are alike, except the third person singular, which adds -*s* or -*es*.

☞**EXAMPLES:**

I go.	I do.	I write.	I call.	I run.
He goes.	He does.	He writes.	He calls.	He runs.

The *past tense* is formed by using the third principal part of the verb. Except for *was* and *were* (I was, we were), singular and plural forms are alike.

☞**EXAMPLES:**

I went.	I did.	I wrote.	I called.	I ran.
He went.	He did.	He wrote.	He called.	He ran.

The *future tense* is formed by the helping verb "shall" or "will," followed by the first principal part of the main verb.

☞**EXAMPLES:**

I shall go.	I shall do.	I shall write.	I shall call.	I shall run.
He will go.	He will do.	He will write.	He will call.	He will run.

The *present perfect tense* is formed by the helping verb "have" or "has," followed by the fourth principal part of the main verb.

☞**EXAMPLES:**

I have gone.	I have done.	I have written.	I have called.	I have run.
He has gone.	He has done.	He has written.	He has called.	He has run.

The *past perfect tense* is formed by the helping verb "had," followed by the fourth principal part of the main verb.

☞**EXAMPLES:**

I had gone.	I had done.	I had written.	I had called.	I had run.
He had gone.	He had done.	He had written.	He had called.	He had run.

The *future perfect tense* is formed by the helping verb "shall" or "will," followed by the helping verb "have," followed by the fourth principal part of the main verb.

☞**EXAMPLES:**

I shall have gone.	I shall have done.	I shall have written.
He will have gone.	He will have called.	He will have run.

Progressive Tone

The *present tense* is formed by using an appropriate present form of the helping verb "be," followed by the second principal part of the main verb.

☞**EXAMPLES:**

I am going.	You are calling.	He is writing.

The *past tense* is formed by using an appropriate past form of the helping verb "be," followed by the second principal part of the main verb.

☞**EXAMPLES:**

      I was going.   You were calling.   He was writing.

The *future tense* is formed by using the helping verb "shall" or "will," followed by the first principal part of the helping verb "be," followed by the second principal part of the main verb.

☞**EXAMPLES:**

      I shall be going.   You will be calling.   He will be writing.

The *present perfect tense* is formed by using the helping verb "have" or "has," followed by the fourth principal part of the helping verb "be," followed by the second principal part of the main verb.

☞**EXAMPLES:**

      I have been going.   You have been calling.   He has been writing.

The *past perfect tense* is formed by using the helping verb "had," followed by the fourth principal part of the helping verb "be," followed by the second principal part of the main verb.

☞**EXAMPLES:**

      I had been going.   You had been calling.   He had been writing.

The *future perfect tense* is formed by using the helping verb "shall" or "will," followed by the helping verb "have," followed by the fourth principal part of the helping verb "be," followed by the second principal part of the main verb.

☞**EXAMPLES:**

      I shall have been going.   You will have been calling.

      He will have been writing.   They will have been running.

Emphatic Tone

The *present tense* is formed by using the first principal part of the helping verb "do," followed by the first principal part of the main verb.

☞**EXAMPLES:**

      I do go.   You do call.   He does write.

The *past tense* is formed by using the third principal part of the helping verb "do," followed by the first principal part of the main verb.

☞**EXAMPLES:**

      I did go.   You did call.   He did write.

Note: There are no other tenses in emphatic tone.

■ *Passive Voice*

Simple Tone

The passive voice tenses are formed by using an appropriate tense form of the helping verb "to be" followed by the fourth principal part of the main verb—i.e., the *simple tone*, passive voice.

☞**EXAMPLES:**

I am called.	You are called.	He is called.
I was called.	You were called.	He was called.
I shall be called.	You will be called.	He will be called.
I have been called.	You have been called.	He has been called.
I had been called.	You had been called.	He had been called.
I shall have been called.	You will have been called.	He will have been called.

Progressive Tone

The passive voice tenses are formed by using an appropriate tense form of the helping verb "be," followed by the second principal part of the helping verb "be," followed by the fourth principal part of the main verb. There are no perfect tenses in *progressive tone*, passive voice.

☞**EXAMPLES:**

I am being called.	You are being called.	He is being called.
I was being called.	You were being called.	He was being called.

Emphatic Tone

There are no emphatic tone forms for verbs in passive voice.

✎ **EXERCISE A** Memorize the principal parts of the *irregular verbs* in the table in the *Appendix*.

✎ **EXERCISE B** Write the other three principal parts of the following verbs, spelling all parts correctly. Some are regular verbs and some are irregular. Use a dictionary if necessary.

	First	Second	Third	Fourth
1.	twist	*twisting*	*twisted*	*twisted*
2.	spin			
3.	see			
4.	give			
5.	worry			
6.	spy			
7.	mean			
8.	burn			
9.	taint			
10.	shake			
11.	lie (recline)			
12.	cover			
13.	fumble			
14.	worship			

✎ **EXERCISE C** Write sentences using the form of the verb specified below. Use indicative mood unless instructed otherwise.

☞**EXAMPLE:**

play: *future perfect tense, active voice, progressive tone*

After taking a year's worth of private flute lessons, she will have been playing much better.

1. **show**: *past tense, passive voice, simple tone*

_____

_____

2. **speak**: *present perfect tense, active voice, progressive tone*

_____

_____

3. **choose**: *past perfect tense, passive voice, simple tone*

_____

_____

4. **eat**: *past tense, active voice, emphatic tone*

_____

_____

5. **bite**: *present perfect tense, passive voice, simple tone*

_____

_____

6. **steal**: *present tense, active voice, emphatic tone, imperative mood*

_____

_____

LESSON 64: UNIT REVIEW

✎ **EXERCISE A** Fill in the blanks.

1. The four main *types of verbs* are:

   a. _____   c. _____

   b. _____   d. _____

2. _____ is a grammatical term signifying the time frame in which the action or condition expressed by a verb takes place.

3. Write the *six tenses* of the verb "to be," using the first person singular form:

   _____   _____

   _____   _____

   _____   _____

4. The *three tones* of English verbs are _____, _____, and
   _____.

5. When the subject is the doer of the action, the verb is in _____ voice. When the subject is the receiver of the action, the verb is in _____ voice.

6. *Mood* is the grammatical term indicating the _____ or

   _____ in which a statement is being made by a verb. The *three moods* of English

   verbs are _____, _____, and _____.

7. Verbs used as another part of speech are called _____. The three types are

   _____,_____,_____.

8. *Infinitives* may be used as _____.

9. *Gerunds* are used as _____.

10. *Participles* are used as _____.

11. The *four principal parts* of verbs are _____, _____,

    _____, and _____.

12. In the space below, write a paragraph of about 75 words using verbs, verbals, and participial phrases—*at least **three** times* each.

    _____

    _____

    _____

    _____

    _____

    _____

    _____

    _____

    _____

    _____

    _____

    _____

13. From the paragraph you have written above, write examples of *verbs*, *verbals*, and *participles*.

Verb: _____   Verbal: _____

Verb: _____   Participle: _____

Verb: _____   Participle: _____

Verbal: _____   Participle: _____

✎ **EXERCISE B** Underline all the *verbs* or *verb phrases* in the following sentences. Above each one write *T* if the verb is transitive or *I* if the verb is intransitive. Consider verb phrases as if they were a single verb. If the verb is transitive, double-underline the receiver of the action.

1.   The thief stole from the convenience store but, in haste, left incriminating evidence behind.

2.   The church choir will perform the cantata before the congregation.

3.   His poem was read by his literature teacher.

4.   So you care deeply for the lost, or you do not care at all.

5.   The satellite beamed information gathered by the astronauts in the space station.

6.   She walked to Starbucks for a cup of coffee, where she ran into a friend from work.

7.   The missionary challenged the young people to "put feet to their faith."

✎ **EXERCISE C** In the chart below, conjugate the irregular verb "to begin" in the active voice only. NOTE: This exercise continues on the next page.

Number ⟹	Singular	Plural
Tense ⟹	Present	
First Person		
Second Person		
Third Person		
Tense ⟹	Past	
First Person		
Second Person		
Third Person		
Tense ⟹	Future	
First Person		
Second Person		
Third Person		
Tense ⟹	Present Perfect	
First Person		
Second Person		
Third Person		

Number ⟹	Singular	Plural
Tense ⟹	**Past Perfect**	
First Person		
Second Person		
Third Person		
Tense ⟹	**Future Perfect**	
First Person		
Second Person		
Third Person		

✎ **EXERCISE D** In the chart below, conjugate the verb "to be."

MOOD ⟹	INDICATIVE		SUBJUNCTIVE	
Number ⟹	Singular	Plural	Singular	Plural
Tense ⟹	**Present**			
First Person				
Second Person				
Third Person				
Tense ⟹	**Past**			
First Person				
Second Person				
Third Person				
Tense ⟹	**Future**			
First Person				
Second Person				
Third Person				

✎ **EXERCISE E** Write the other three principal parts of the following verbs, spelling all parts correctly. Some are regular verbs and some are irregular. Use a dictionary if necessary.

	First	Second	Third	Fourth
1.	wake			
2.	read			
3.	blink			
4.	take			
5.	envy			
6.	bid (command)			
7.	drink			

Unit 8
Five Other Parts of Speech

Unit 8 covers the final *five parts of speech*—*adjectives, adverbs, prepositions, conjunctions,* and *interjections.* The various subgroups of these parts of speech will be included in our discussion, as well as their placement in a sentence.

LESSON 65: ADJECTIVES

An *adjective* is a word used to modify or describe a noun or pronoun. To **modify** means to *limit.* When we say an adjective modifies a noun or pronoun, we mean that it limits or narrows a general noun to a more particular one. For example, the noun "clothes" refers to all items of apparel. But if we use the adjective "dirty" with the noun "clothes" ("dirty clothes"), we have limited our reference to only those garments which are soiled. The adjective "dirty" *modifies* the noun "clothes." That is to say, adjectives make nouns or pronouns more *definite.*

Further, we must ask *how an adjective modifies* a noun or pronoun. You can identify how an adjective is used if it answers the question *which one? what kind? how many? how much?* or *whose?* about a noun or pronoun.

☞**EXAMPLES:**

Which one?	the **clever** student, the **cowardly** boy, the **aforementioned** idea
What kind?	a **rough** road, **purple** grapes, a **sour** lemon
How many?	
or **how much?**	a **half** dollar, **some** tools, **less** space, **several** candidates
Whose?	**our** honor, **Gloria's** afghan, **my** CD Walkman

ARTICLES

The most commonly used adjectives are *a, an,* and *the.* These adjectives are called *articles.* They are considered adjectives because they "limit" the nouns which they precede.

☞**EXAMPLES:**

Which one?	**the** car, **a** tree, **an** apple

Note: When you are asked to identify or work with *adjectives* in the exercises in this workbook, you may ignore *articles* since they are so common.

PROPER ADJECTIVES

A *proper adjective* is an adjective formed from a proper noun or a proper noun used as an adjective. Proper adjectives begin with a capital letter.

☞**EXAMPLES:**

Japanese ingenuity   **Reformation** weekend   **Turkish** delight   **Polish** sausage

PLACEMENT OF ADJECTIVES

Adjectives can be placed in different locations in a sentence, depending on how they are used. Most **simple adjectives** come *immediately before the words they modify.*

☞**EXAMPLES:**

The Lord loves a **cheerful** giver.   His **favorite** snack is **salty, crisp** chips.

Some adjectives come *after the words they modify.* There are three situations when this is common: (1) when the adjective is a **predicate adjective** following a linking verb, (2) when the adjective is in an **appositive** position, and (3) when the adjective is an **objective complement**.

■ Placing Predicate Adjectives

A **predicate adjective** is an adjective which follows a linking verb and modifies the subject of the linking verb. Because it "completes" the meaning of the subject, it is sometimes called a *subjective complement.*

☞**EXAMPLES:**

The student never seemed **discouraged**.   Father was **anxious** about my health.

■ Placing Appositive Adjectives

An **appositive adjective** is an adjective which follows immediately after a noun and adds a description of the noun.

☞**EXAMPLES:**

Steak Kabob, **lean** and **tender**, takes on a truly delicious flavor when braised for many hours.

■ Placing Objective Complements

An adjective used as an **objective complement** is an adjective which follows a grammatical object and completes the meaning of that object.

☞**EXAMPLES:**

They built the structure **solid**.   His son's choice made him **proud**.

✎ **EXERCISE A** Underline all the words used as *adjectives* in the following sentences. (*Skip articles.*)

1. The supersonic jet is sleek and swift.

2. The football team scored several goals during the second half of the game.

3. The ambitious woman seemed fond of using remarks to portray rivals' ideas as nocuous.

4. A simple adjective is usually placed immediately before the word it modifies.

5. Eric was convinced that the theological argument would persuade the most incredulous skeptic.

6. Wars, foreign and domestic, have taken the lives of many young American men.

✎ **EXERCISE B** In the first column, write each of the *adjectives* you underlined in Exercise A. In the second column, write the *noun* or *pronoun* that is modified by the adjective. In the third column, write *SA* if the adjective is a simple adjective, *PA* if it is a predicate adjective, *AA* if it is an appositive adjective, *OC* if it is an objective complement, or *Pro. Adj.* if it is proper adjective.

	ADJECTIVE UNDERLINED	WORD MODIFIED	TYPE OF ADJECTIVE
1.	supersonic	jet	SA
	sleek	jet	PA
	swift	jet	PA
2.			
3.			
4.			
5.			
6.			

LESSON 66: ADVERBS

An *adverb* is a word that modifies a verb, adjective, or another adverb.

☞**EXAMPLES:**

Modifies verb:	He went **promptly** to the interview.
Modifies adjective:	Ellen is an **altogether** capable parent.
Modifies adverb:	She spoke **fairly** deliberately.

An *adverb* tells something about the word that it modifies, making the verb, adjective, or adverb modified more specific. It usually answers one of the following questions about that word: *how? where? when? how often?* or *to what extent?*

☞**EXAMPLES:**

How?	Megan selected the produce **carefully**.
Where?	She could not meet him **there**.
When?	Tom wrote me **yesterday**.
How often?	Pastor **frequently** plays the piano in the worship service.
To what extent?	We are **seldom** taken in by telemarketing.

Many adverbs end with the suffix *-ly*. However, some words that do end with *-ly* are **adjectives**, rather than adverbs. When trying to identify an adverb, the *-ly* ending may be a clue, but do not conclude from the ending that the word is always an adverb. To be an adverb, the word must modify a *verb, adjective,* or *another adverb*. If it modifies a noun or pronoun, it is an adjective.

☞**EXAMPLES:**

-ly adverbs:	partially, anxiously, carefully, loudly, proudly
-ly adjectives:	friendly, costly, manly, brotherly, neighborly
Other adverbs:	now, seldom, there, up, not, never, always, why

LOCATION OF ADVERBS

Adverbs can be placed in many different locations in a sentence as listed below.

1. **If they modify verbs**, they may be *immediately before* or *after* the verb; they may be *in the middle* of a verb phrase; or they may be at the *beginning* or *end* of the sentence—nowhere near the verb.

2. **If they modify adjectives**, they are placed *immediately before* those adjectives.

3. **If they modify adverbs**, they are placed *immediately before* those adverbs.

☞**EXAMPLES:**

■ Modifying a verb—"responded":

She **quickly** and **accurately** has responded to the question.
She has responded **quickly** and **accurately** to the question.
She has **quickly** and **accurately** responded to the question.
Quickly and **accurately**, she has responded to the question.
She has responded to the question **quickly** and **accurately**.

■ Modifying an adjective—"fine":

This is an **especially** fine specimen.

■ Modifying an adverb—"rapidly":

The epidemic is spreading **very** rapidly.

✎ **EXERCISE** Circle each adverb in the following sentences and draw an arrow to the word that it modifies. If the adverb modifies a verb phrase, draw arrows to all the words in the verb phrase.

1. That was the most precious gift she had ever received.

2. The moon appeared suddenly in the sky as they spryly hiked through the mountains.

3. The prospectus almost always outlines the company's projected earnings.

4. Jesus was always sympathetic toward the needy.

5. Anxiously the wives of the trapped miners awaited news of their rescue.

6. The boys eagerly looked forward to learning the manly art of self-defense.

7. The negotiators said they were cautiously optimistic about the outcome of their talks.

LESSON 67: PREPOSITIONS

A *preposition* is a word that shows how a noun or pronoun is related to another word in the sentence. In the following examples, the prepositions in **dark print** tell how the underlined words are related to each other:

☞**EXAMPLES:**

the <u>clouds</u> **in** the <u>sky</u>   the <u>phone</u> **by** the <u>computer</u>   <u>fell</u> **down** the <u>stairs</u>

In each of the examples above and in all other cases, the noun or pronoun that follows the preposition is called the ***object of the preposition***. The preposition tells what relationship its object has to another word in the sentence. A preposition may have more than one object.

A group of words beginning with a preposition and ending with the object of the preposition is called a prepositional phrase.

Here is a list of some of the most common prepositions:

COMMON PREPOSITIONS			
aboard	beneath	into	till
about	beside	like	to
above	besides	near	toward
across	between	notwithstanding	under
after	beyond	of	underneath
against	but (meaning *except*)	off	until
along	by	on	unto
alongside	concerning	outside	up
amid	despite	over	upon
amidst	down	per	with
among	during	past	within
around	except	regarding	without
at	excepting	save	
before	for	since	NOTE: Some of these words can also be used as adverbs or conjunctions.
behind	from	through	
below	in	throughout	

A preposition that consists of more than one word is called a ***compound preposition***. Here are some examples:

COMPOUND PREPOSITIONS			
according to	due to	in company with	owing to
as for	exclusive of	in favor of	pertaining to
as to	except for	in front of	regardless of
aside from	for fear of	in regard to	with a view to
because of	for the sake of	in spite of	with reference to
by means of	in accordance with	instead of	with regard to
by reason of	in addition to	in view of	with respect to
by way of	in behalf of	on account of	with the exception of
contrary to	in case of	out of	

✎ **EXERCISE** Underline each preposition in the sentences below one time and every object of each preposition two times.

1. He makes me to lie down in green pastures.

2. He leads me beside the still waters.

3. He leads me in the paths of righteousness for His name's sake.

4. Yea, though I walk through the valley of the shadow of death, I will fear no evil;

    for You are with me.

5. You prepare a table before me in the presence of my enemies.

6. You anoint my head with oil.

7. Surely goodness and mercy shall follow me all the days of my life.

8. I shall dwell in the house of the Lord forever.

9. The preceding sentences were all taken from Psalm 23.

LESSON 68: CONJUNCTIONS

A *conjunction* is a word that joins other words or groups of words such as phrases, clauses, and occasionally sentences. There are two main classifications of conjunctions: *coordinating* and *subordinating*. *Coordinating conjunctions* join words or groups of words that are of equal grammatical rank. *Subordinating conjunctions* join groups of words that are of unequal grammatical rank; that is, they join dependent clauses to independent clauses.

COORDINATING CONJUNCTIONS

There are two main classifications of coordinating conjunctions: *simple* and *correlative*.

■ **Simple Conjunctions**

Simple coordinating conjunctions perform the usual simple task of joining words, phrases, or clauses of equal grammatical rank. They are *and, but, or, nor,* and *yet.* (Some grammarians also include *for* and *so.*)

☞**EXAMPLES:**

Mike **and** Joe rebuilt the engine.   I am not angry, **nor** will I seek revenge.

She was old, **but** she was spry.   She was hurt, **yet** she did not say anything.

You can eat now **or** later.

■ **Correlative Conjunctions**

Correlative coordinating conjunctions are always used in pairs. They are used to join (correlate) only two ideas, not more than two. They are *both ... and, either ... or, neither ... nor, not only ... but also,* and *whether ... or.*

☞**EXAMPLES:**

Both my father **and** my mother are Dutch.   **Neither** rain **nor** snow are forecast for today.

You can **either** buy **or** rent this house.   She is **not only** talented **but also** kind.

■ **Conjunctive Adverbs**

There is a third classification of words that are used to join sentence elements of equal grammatical rank. This group of words consists of adverbs that serve as coordinating conjunctions. For this reason they are called *conjunctive adverbs*. Conjunctive adverbs are used to connect (or coordinate) two independent clauses (*see glossary: independent clause*).

☞**EXAMPLES:**

I forgot; **therefore**, I am not ready.	God is with you; **so** do not worry.
You are too old; **however**, we let you in.	He is very liberal; **in fact**, he is a socialist.

Here is a list of conjunctive adverbs:

CONJUNCTIVE ADVERBS			
also	furthermore	likewise	otherwise
anyhow	hence	meanwhile	so
as a result	henceforth	moreover	still
besides	however	namely	then
consequently	in fact	nevertheless	therefore
for example	indeed	notwithstanding	thus

■ **Punctuating Conjunctive Adverbs**

When writing sentences with conjunctive adverbs, place a **semicolon** before the *conjunctive adverb* and a **comma** after it if the *conjunctive adverb* has two or more syllables or is made up of more than one word. If the *conjunctive adverb* has only one syllable, place a **semicolon** before it and no punctuation after it. (*See examples above.*)

SUBORDINATING CONJUNCTIONS

Subordinating conjunctions have only one purpose: to join an adverb clause (a dependent clause that is used as an adverb) to an independent clause. (*See glossary for definitions of independent clause, dependent clause, adverb clause.*) They are called *subordinating conjunctions* because they join a clause that is of lesser (*dependent, subordinate*) grammatical rank to a clause of superior (*independent*) rank.

☞**EXAMPLES:**

Independent clauses	*Dependent clauses*
She was sleeping	**when** I called.
I tried to tell her	**why** I disagreed with her.
God will hear us	**whenever** we pray in faith.

Here is a list of subordinating conjunctions:

SUBORDINATING CONJUNCTIONS			
after	because	than	where
although	before	that	wherever
as	·if	though	whether
as if	in order that	unless	while
as much as	lest	until	
as long as	since	when	
as soon as	so that	whenever	

✎ **EXERCISE** Underline all the conjunctions and conjunctive adverbs in the following sentences. Above each conjunction, write *SC* if the conjunction is a simple conjunction, *CC* if the conjunctions are correlative (write *CC* over both parts of the pair), *CA* if the word is a conjunctive adverb, or *Sub.* if the word is a subordinating conjunction. In the blank, write *W* if the conjunction joins words, *P* if it joins phrases, or *C* if it joins clauses.

                                               CC   *CC*

  P   1. You are a citizen <u>not only</u> of America <u>but also</u> of the Kingdom of God.

_____   2. Your term paper is excellent; furthermore, you could submit it for publication.

_____   3. Some people act as if they own the world.

_____   4. As long as you are donating the car, why don't you donate it to me?

_____   5. Although he was young, Timothy was an effective witness for the Gospel.

_____   6. Either you are with me or you are against me.

_____   7. Both Rita and Mary Anne flew to Montreal for the conference.

_____   8. George W. Bush and Richard B. Cheney were running mates in 2000.

_____   9. June was a "civil" person, but her actions betrayed her true personality.

_____ 10. You cannot go until you finish your homework assignment.

LESSON 69: INTERJECTIONS, ETC.

The eighth part of speech is the *interjection*—an exclamatory word or words that are not grammatically related to any other word in a sentence. It is an independent sentence element that has *no grammatical function* in a sentence, although, of course, it has purpose and meaning. Sometimes, an interjection can stand alone as a single-word "sentence."

☞**EXAMPLES:**

    Behold!   Ouch!   Wow!   Certainly!   Oh, my!   Listen!

An interjection is usually followed by an *exclamation point*. A mild interjection, however, may be followed by a *comma* or *period*. If the interjection is followed by an exclamation point or period, the next word should be capitalized.

☞**EXAMPLES:**

    Ouch! That hurts!   **Okay.** Will the next contestant come forward?

    Oh, I hope I didn't offend you.   **Ah,** there you are.

    Excellent! I think you have it!

Here is a list of some common interjections, including some words (*marked* *) which are usually another part of speech but which may be used as interjections:

INTERJECTIONS				
ah	botheration	hey	my*	so*
aha	bravo	hi	never*	tut
ahoy	certainly*	ho	no*	what*
alas	encore	huh	nonsense*	why*
amen	excellent*	humbug	O	whoa
ay	goodness*	hurrah	oh	whoopee
bah	gracious*	hush	okay, OK	whoops
baloney	ha	indeed	ouch	woe
behold*	hello	listen*	phooey	wow
boo	hem	lo	pshaw	yes*

DIRECT ADDRESS

A *noun of direct address* names the person or persons to whom a statement is directed. Although it is not a separate part of speech, this type of noun is, like the interjection, an independent sentence element having no grammatical function in a sentence. Sometimes, a noun of direct address is used with an interjection.

☞**EXAMPLES:**

Mom, what do you want for Mother's Day?   Hey, **Jim**, wait for me!

He has shown thee, **O man**, what is good and what the Lord requires of thee (*Micah 6:8*).

Note: A noun of direct address is set off with a *comma* or *commas*.

✎ **EXERCISE** Write four sentences using *interjections* and four sentences using *nouns of direct address*.

1. _____

_____

2. _____

_____

3. _____

_____

4. _____

_____

5. _____

_____

6. _____

_____

7. _____

_____

8. _____

_____

LESSON 70: UNIT REVIEW

✎ **EXERCISE A** Fill in the blanks.

1. _____ modify nouns or pronouns; _____ modify verbs, adjectives, or

    other _____.

2. A group of words beginning with a preposition and ending with a noun or pronoun is called

    a _____ _____.

3. What are the two main classifications of *conjunctions*?

    a. _____   b. _____

4. What three types of words can be used to connect sentence elements that are of equal gram-
    matical rank?

    a. _____   c. _____
    b. _____

5. Give four examples of *interjections*.

    a. _____   c. _____
    b. _____   d. _____

6. In the space below, write a paragraph of 75 words or less using each of the eight parts of speech
    *at least **three** times*. Use a separate piece of paper if necessary.

    _____

    _____

    _____

    _____

    _____

    _____

    _____

    _____

    _____

    _____

    _____

    _____

7. From the paragraph you have written above, write three examples of each of the *eight parts of speech*.

Noun: _____   Adverb: _____

Noun: _____   Adverb: _____

Noun: _____   Adverb: _____

Pronoun: _____   Preposition: _____

Pronoun: _____   Preposition: _____

Pronoun: _____   Preposition: _____

Verb: _____   Conjunction: _____

Verb: _____   Conjunction: _____

Verb: _____   Conjunction: _____

Adjective: _____   Interjection: _____

Adjective: _____   Interjection: _____

Adjective: _____   Interjection: _____

✎ **EXERCISE B** Identify which part of speech each word in **dark print** is by writing above each word *N* for noun, *P* for pronoun, *V* for verb, *Adj.* for adjective, *Adv.* for adverb, *Prep.* for preposition, *C* for conjunction or conjunctive adverb, or *Int.* for interjection.

           N   *Adj.*   *Prep.*

1. Mr. **George W. Bush** is a **high-principled** man who is esteemed **by** his constituents.

2. **His** report needs to be **submitted** by the **end** of the week.

3. **Your** account will be activated **automatically** by pressing **the** return key.

4. **She** does **not** want to come **for** the holiday.

5. Obeying the **Bible** may be difficult, **but** it **will lead** you in the way of salvation **in** the end.

6. **Wow!** What **kind** of attitude the **children** have displayed **before us**!

7. **I** am **only** trying to be **practical**.

8. They were **entirely mistaken concerning** what he did; **however**, they were **likely** misinformed.

9. The **agile**, brown **antelope** jumped away **from** the **crouching** lion's hideout.

10. **Those** species of creatures **usually** exhibit an incredible **means** of survival.

11. **It** is **easy** to see where she **got** her good **looks**.

12. **My** cousin **works** for a **large** media company **in** the Loop.

13. The **train** will be stopping **automatically** at each station **during** rush hour.

14. She was a **thoughtful** person **who** was well-liked **by** her colleagues.

15. "Sweatin' to the **Oldies**" may be amusing, **but** it makes **exercising** fun.

16. **Tell** me! Why did your **Op-Ed** piece **not** appear in the paper **today**?

17. Ted **ordered** his staff to roll the **press**, but **they** were not **ready** to start.

18. He was **totally** embarrassed **about** what **they** said; **yet**, they kept **badgering** him **unmercifully**.

19. The **tall**, heavy **man** waddled **over** to the **chair** to **rest** his legs.

20. **What** set of books **does** the **child** want **for** his **birthday**?

Unit 9
Phrases and Clauses

The parts of speech may be combined to form groups of words. Some word groups express ideas or thoughts that are complete in themselves; some are expressions that are incomplete and must depend upon other words or groups of words to make their thoughts complete. English writing has three major word groupings: **phrases**, **clauses**, and **sentences**. In this unit, you will work with the first two groups of words.

LESSON 71: PHRASES

A **PHRASE** is a group of related words, containing neither a subject nor a predicate. A phrase does not express a complete thought in itself. *Phrases* are classified in two ways—according to their **function** and according to their **structure**. As to function, phrases may be used as single parts of speech—*nouns, verbs, adjectives,* and *adverbs*. When classified according to structure, phrases fall into five main categories: *prepositional, verb, participial, gerundial,* and *infinitive*.

PREPOSITIONAL PHRASES

As you learned in Lesson 67, a **prepositional phrase** is a group of words beginning with a *preposition* and ending with a substantive called the *object of the preposition*. The phrase may also include words that modify the object. Furthermore, the object of a preposition may be compound.

☞**EXAMPLES:**

> The bush **by the house** needs to be replaced.
>
> The student was rewarded **for her achievements**.

■ Adjectival Prepositional Phrase

A prepositional phrase may be used as an **adjective**, modifying a substantive.

☞**EXAMPLES:**

> Anyone **with the right credentials** can apply. (*modifies "Anyone," a pronoun*)
>
> The book **on the table** was mine. (*modifies "book," a noun*)

■ Adverbial Prepositional Phrase

A prepositional phrase may be used as an **adverb**, modifying a verb, adjective, or adverb.

☞**EXAMPLES:**

> **In 1517,** Luther nailed his *95 Theses* to the door of the Castle Church. (*modifies the verb "nailed"*)
>
> Saving money is impossible **with his income**. (*modifies the adjective "impossible"*)
>
> We arrived early **in the morning**. (*modifies the adverb "early"*)

■ *Nounal Prepositional Phrase*

A prepositional phrase may occasionally be used as a *noun*.

☞**EXAMPLES:**

> **By the fountain** is a coffee shop. (*subject*)
>
> The best time to exercise would be **before you eat**. (*predicate nominative*)
>
> The hiding place, **under the doormat**, was not the best location to stash the key. (*appositive*)

VERB PHRASES

A *verb phrase* consists of a main verb and all of its helping verbs. Verb phrases are used as *predicate verbs* in the same way that single verbs are used.

☞**EXAMPLES:**

> I **shall** not **be preaching** this weekend.
>
> The little boy **had been rescued** by the police.

At times, a verb phrase may be *interrupted* by an adverb(s) which modifies the verb phrase.

☞**EXAMPLES:**

> The athletes **do** not always **compete** with one another.
>
> We **have been** cautiously **analyzing** your argument.

PARTICIPIAL PHRASES

A *participial phrase* consists of a *participle* and any related *complements* and *modifiers*. Like single participles, participial phrases are used as **adjectives**.

Remember that a participle is a *verb form* used as an *adjective*. Participles and participial phrases therefore have the characteristics of both verbs and adjectives.

■ As VERBS, they can have *complements* such as direct and indirect objects.

■ As VERBS, they can be *modified* by single adverbs or phrases used as adverbs.

■ As ADJECTIVES, they can *modify* nouns or pronouns.

☞**EXAMPLES:**

> *(part.)(ind. obj.)(dir. obj.)*
> **Giving troops an order**, the sergeant expected obedience. (*phrase modifies "sergeant"*)
>
> *(part.)   (adverb)*
> **Answering correctly**, the student passed the oral exam. (*phrase modifies "student"*)
>
> *(part.)(adv. phrase)*
> **Confiding in me**, she divulged what actually happened. (*phrase modifies "she"*)

GERUNDIAL PHRASES

A *gerundial phrase* consists of a *gerund* and any related *complements* and *modifiers*. Like single gerunds, gerundial phrases are used as **nouns**.

Remember that a gerund is a *verb form* used as a *noun*. Gerunds and gerundial phrases therefore have the characteristics of both verbs and nouns.

- As VERBS, they can have *complements* such as direct and indirect objects.

- As VERBS, they can be *modified* by adverbs or adverb phrases.

- As NOUNS, they can by used as *subjects, objects, predicate nominatives* or *appositives.*

☞**EXAMPLES:**

(gerund) (dir. obj.)(adv. phrase)
Reading your Bible before bedtime is a good habit. (*phrase used as subject*)

(gerund)(dir. obj.)
He enjoys **building birdhouses**. (*phrase used as direct object*)

(gerund)(dir. obj.)
Her hobby is **sewing quilts**. (*phrase used as predicate nominative*)

(gerund)(dir. obj.)
He demonstrated his piety by **obeying God's Word**. (*phrase used as object of a preposition*)

(adverb) (gerund)   (dir. obj.)
His task, **carefully checking the text**, was vital for publication. (*phrase used as appositive*)

INFINITIVE PHRASES

An **infinitive phrase** consists of an *infinitive* and any related *complements* and *modifiers*. Like single infinitives, infinitive phrases can be used as **nouns, adjectives**, and **adverbs**.

Remember that infinitives are *verb forms* used as *nouns, adjectives*, and *adverbs*. Infinitives and infinitive phrases therefore have characteristics of all of these parts of speech.

- As VERBS, they can have *complements* such as direct and indirect objects.

- As VERBS, they can be *modified* by adverbs or adverb phrases.

- As NOUNS, they can be used as *subjects, objects, predicate nominatives*, or *appositives.*

- As ADJECTIVES, they can *modify* nouns or pronouns, directly or as predicate adjectives.

- As ADVERBS, they can *modify* verbs, adjectives, or adverbs.

☞**EXAMPLES:**

(infinitive)(ind. obj.)(dir. obj.)
To give God your best is a worthy goal. (*phrase used as subject*)

(infinitive) (dir. obj.)
I hate **to say good-bye**. (*phrase used as direct object*)

(inf.)(dir. obj.)(adv. prep. phrase)
God's purpose is **to save us from sin**. (*phrase used as predicate nominative*)

(infinitive)(dir. obj.)(adv. prep. phrase)
He was the only one **to finish the race without help**. (*phrase used as adjective*)

(infinitive) (dir. obj.)
We go to church **to worship God**. (*phrase used as adverb*)

✎ **EXERCISE A** Identify the type of phrase in **dark print** by writing *Prep.* (for prepositional), *Part.* (for participial), *Ger.* (for gerundial), *Inf.* (for infinitive) or *V* (for verb) in the blank at the end of each sentence.

1. We donated ten copies of the Bible **to the mission**. *Prep.*

2. **Practicing daily** is the smart way to increase your music skills. _____

3. Henry tried **to convince him immediately**. _____

4. The girl **combing her hair** is my sister. _____

5. **Putting feet to your faith** is the best way to fulfill the Great Commission. _____

6. **Do** you always **tell** the truth?_____

7. We ordered ten copies **of the book** from the publisher. _____

8. *Hamlet* **has been seen** by countless people. _____

9. The time **to bow the knee** to God is now. _____

10. **From the airport** we will go home. _____

11. Washington crossed the river **to attack the British.** _____

12. One difficulty of **becoming a missionary** is learning a new language. _____

13. One difficulty of becoming a missionary is **learning a new language.** _____

14. One difficulty **of becoming a missionary** is learning a new language. _____

_____ 15. The man **learning a new language** is a missionary. _____

✎ **EXERCISE B** Identify the function of the phrases in **dark print** by writing *N* (noun), *Adj.* (adjective), *Adv.* (adverb), or *V* (verb) in the blank. If the phrase is a *noun phrase*, tell how it is used by writing *S* (subject), *DO* (direct object), *PN* (predicate nominative), *OP* (object of a preposition), or *A* (appositive) above the phrase. If it is an *adjective* or *adverb phrase*, draw an arrow to the word it modifies.

1. ___*Adj.*___   The race car **rounding the curve** is likely to win.

            DO
2. ___*N*___   Scott Metzger enjoys **reading fantasy fiction**.

3. _____   His dream, **to become a surgeon**, will require many years of schooling.

4. _____   He **will be coming** on the weekend.

5. _____   **To be a successful entrepreneur** takes more perspiration than inspiration.

6. _____   **To be a successful entrepreneur**, he knew he needed to work hard.

7. _____   **Being a successful entrepreneur**, he devoted himself to his business.

8. _____   **Being a successful entrepreneur** gave him the ability to support many missionaries.

9. _____   By **winning second place**, the Olympian received a silver medal.

10. _____   His philosophy is difficult **to explain simply**.

11. _____   He does not make enough **to save for retirement**.

12. _____   Benjamin learned the art of **folding paper**, known as origami.

13. _____   I must stop **eating late at night**.

14. _____   Are you smart enough **to pass this exam**?

15. _____   **Going to church** does not make you a Christian any more than being baptized does.

LESSON 72: CLAUSES

A *clause* is a group of words containing both a subject and a verb and used as a part of a sentence. There are two types of clauses: *independent* and *dependent*.

INDEPENDENT CLAUSES

An *independent clause* expresses a complete thought; that is, it could stand alone as a complete sentence.

☞**EXAMPLES:**

[**She wanted to thank the man**] who saved her life.

[**He is not here**]; [**He is risen**].

DEPENDENT CLAUSES

A *dependent clause* does *not* express a complete thought and can*not* stand alone as a complete sentence.

☞**EXAMPLES:**

She wanted to thank the man [**who saved her life**].

I have been wondering [**whether I should attend the meeting**].

Dependent clauses are classified according to their function within a sentence. The three classifications are: *noun, adjective,* and *adverb*.

■ *Noun Clauses*

A noun clause is a dependent clause that serves the function of a noun within a sentence: *subject, direct object, predicate nominative, object of a preposition,* or *appositive*.

Noun clauses are usually introduced by *signal words* that often serve a grammatical function within the clause. Common signal words include: *that, whether, if, who, whom, whose, which, what, when, where, why, how, whoever, whomever, whichever,* and *whatever*.

Note: The signal words *that, whether,* and *if* often do not have a grammatical function within their clause but serve only as introductory words.

☞**EXAMPLES:**

[**Why he suddenly departed**] was a mystery. (*clause used as subject*)
  • The signal word "Why" is used as an adverb within the clause.

I do not know [**whose book this is**]. (*clause used as direct object*)
  • The signal word "whose" is used as an adjective within the clause.

My question is [**whether this is right**]. (*clause used as predicate nominative*)
  • The signal word "whether" has no grammatical function in this clause.

By [**what you have said**], I can tell you are honest. (*clause used as object of a preposition*)
  • The signal word "what" is used as a direct object within the clause.

Sometimes the signal word "*that*" is only implied rather than expressed.

☞EXAMPLE:

> I mistakenly believed {**that**} **you were my friend.**

■ *Adjective Clauses*

An ***adjective clause*** is a dependent clause that modifies a *noun* or *pronoun*.

Adjective clauses are introduced by words known as **relatives**. *Who, whom, which,* and *that* are ***relative pronouns***. *Whose* and (sometimes) *which* are ***relative adjectives***. *When* and *where* are ***relative adverbs***.

These introductory words are called "*relatives*" because they "relate" the adjective clause to the noun or pronoun they modify. In addition to "relating" the clause they introduce to the word they modify, relatives have two other characteristics:

■ **They have a grammatical function within their own clause.**

■ **They refer to an antecedent (i.e., a *noun* or *pronoun*) in another clause.**

☞EXAMPLES:

> The man [**who answered the phone**] had a raspy voice. (*clause modifies "man"*)
>
> > • The relative pronoun "who" is the subject of the dependent clause. Its antecedent within the independent clause of the sentence is "man."
>
> This is the place [**where we agreed to meet**]. (*clause modifies "place"*)
>
> > • The relative adverb "where" modifies the infinitive "to meet" within the dependent clause. Its antecedent within the independent clause of the sentence is "place."
>
> The number [**that you called**] was the wrong one. (*clause modifies "number"*)
>
> > • The relative pronoun "that" is a direct object of "called" within the dependent clause. Its antecedent within the independent clause of the sentence is "number."
>
> The boy [**whose hat you took**] is looking for you. (*clause modifies "boy"*)
>
> > • The relative adjective "whose" modifies "hat" within the dependent clause. Its antecedent within the independent clause of the sentence is "boy."

Sometimes the relative is *implied* rather than expressed.

☞EXAMPLE:

> The book {**that**} **I needed** was not in the library.

■ *Adverb Clauses*

An ***adverb clause*** is a dependent clause that modifies a *verb, adjective,* or *adverb* in another clause of the sentence. Like single adverbs and adverb phrases, adverb clauses usually answer the questions *where? when? how? why? to what extent?* or *under what condition?*

Adverb clauses are introduced by words known as ***subordinating conjunctions*** (see Lesson 68). Their only function is to connect an adverb clause to the rest of the sentence. Here is a list of the most common subordinating conjunctions:

SUBORDINATING CONJUNCTIONS			
after	because	only	until
although	before	since	when
as	else	so ... as	whence
as ... as	except that	so that	whenever
as if	for	than	where
as much as	if	that	wherever
as long as	in order that	though	whereupon
as soon as	inasmuch as	till	whether
as though	lest	unless	while

☞**EXAMPLES:**

We will start the dinner [**when all the guests arrive**]. (*clause modifies the verb "will start"*)

[**Because God is our refuge and strength**], we will not be afraid. (*modifies "will be afraid"*)

[**After all is said and done**], I still think you made the right decision. (*modifies "think"*)

You must study hard, [**else you will fail the test**]. (*clause modifies "must study"*)

It is clear [**that you do not know the facts**]. (*clause modifies the adjective "clear"*)

She learns more quickly [**than I do**]. (*clause modifies the adverb "quickly"*)

An adverb clause placed at the beginning of a sentence is set off with a comma (*see examples 2 and 3 above*). Adverb clauses elsewhere in a sentence usually are not set off with commas unless they are "nonessential" (*see examples 1* [essential] *and 4* [nonessential] *above*).

Sometimes certain words in an adverb clause may be omitted and *implied* rather than *expressed* if the omitted words can be easily understood from similar words expressed in the sentence's independent clause. Such an adverb clause is called an *elliptical clause.*

☞**EXAMPLE:**

Bobbi usually works faster [**than I**]. = Bobbi usually works faster [**than I {work}**].

IDENTIFYING DEPENDENT CLAUSES

You may have noticed that some words can be used to introduce different types of dependent clauses. For example, *"that"* can be a *relative pronoun* (introducing an adjective clause), a *signal word* (introducing a noun clause), or a *subordinating conjunction* (introducing an adverb clause). The lesson to be learned from this is that it is not always possible to determine which kind of clause a dependent clause is simply from the introductory word. To decide which kind of clause a given clause is, you must determine **how the clause is used in the sentence**.

☞**EXAMPLES:**

The idea [**that faith and reason are mutually exclusive**] was hotly debated. (*noun clause used as an appositive to the subject "idea"*)

The idea [**that you gave me**] was a good one. (*adjective clause modifying the noun "idea"*)

He ran so fast [**that no one could catch him**]. (*adverb clause modifying the adverb "fast"*)

✎ **EXERCISE A** Underline the dependent clauses in the following sentences. In the blanks, write **N** if the clause is a noun clause, **Adj.** if the clause is an adjective clause, or **Adv.** if the clause is an adverb clause. REMEMBER: Some clauses may have *implied* introductory words.

N   1.   <u>What you wear</u> is a reflection of your personal walk with God.

_____   2.   Ask me which commandment is the first with a promise.

_____   3.   Aaron is the one who is wearing a white shirt and tie.

_____   4.   That she is dedicated to our cause is quite clear from her actions.

_____   5.   I am dismayed that you thought it necessary to remind me of my duty.

_____   6.   While I was waiting, I did my homework.

_____   7.   She would not reveal which person was responsible for the debacle.

_____   8.   As bright as he was, Professor Nash had few social skills.

_____   9.   When he awoke, he could not remember much.

_____   10.   When he awoke could not be ascertained.

✎ **EXERCISE B** The following sentences all contain noun clauses. Underline the clauses. In the blank, write how the clause is used in the sentence. Use the following symbols: **S** for subject, **DO** for direct object, **OP** for object of a preposition, **PN** for predicate nominative, **A** for appositive.

S   1.   <u>How I lead</u> is important to them.

_____   2.   Please tell me what you think.

_____   3.   I often cannot tell what you think.

_____   4.   She told me about what you think.

_____   5.   So this is what you think!

_____   6.   An important fact—what you think—has been ignored by all of them.

_____   7.   How you care has been ignored by all of them.

✎ **EXERCISE C** The following sentences all contain noun clauses. Underline the signal word. In the blank, write how the introductory word is used *within* the dependent clause. Use the same symbols as you used for Exercise B, plus **Adj.** for adjective and **Adv.** for adverb. If the signal word has no grammatical function in the clause, write **X**.

DO   1.   <u>Whom</u> the commander chose was the best man for the job.

_____   2.   Serving is what the soldier enjoyed the most.

_____   3.   This brave man, whose vehicle was strafed, was not wounded in the crossfire.

_____   4.   He dared not tell us how he arranged to elude the enemy.

_____   5.   He convinced us that all would be fine.

_____   6.   He did whatever was necessary to escape.

_____   7.   That is why he was chosen to lead our outfit.

✎ **EXERCISE D** The following sentences all contain dependent clauses. Put parentheses (...) around each dependent clause. Underline the subject of the clause. Double-underline the clause's verb (including all words in verb phrases).

1. A Christian is a person (who obeys Christ as his Lord and Savior).

2. A Christian is a person whose sins have been forgiven by God through Christ.

3. A Christian is a person for whom Christ died.

4. Whether you have faith in Christ is essential to your salvation.

5. Unless you are eighteen years old, you cannot vote in the upcoming election.

6. We visited the battlefield where Custer and his men died.

7. "If you love Me, keep My commandments."

8. Jesus is the Savior whose blood covers all the sins I have ever committed.

LESSON 73: UNIT REVIEW

✎ **EXERCISE A** Fill in the blanks:

1. A phrase is _____ .

2. Phrases may be classified according to _____ or according to _____ .

3. As to function, phrases may be used as _____, _____, _____, or _____ .

4. The five main categories of phrases, as to structure, are _____, _____,

   _____, _____, and _____ .

5. A prepositional phrase consists of _____

   _____ .

6. A verb phrase consists of _____

   _____ .

7. A participial phrase consists of _____

   _____ .

8. A gerundial phrase consists of _____

   _____ .

9. An infinitive phrase consists of _____

   _____ .

10. A clause is _____

   _____ .

11. The three types of dependent clauses are _____, _____, and _____.

12. Adverb clauses are introduced by _____ _____.

13. Noun clauses are introduced by _____ _____.

14. Adjective clauses are introduced by _____.

15. In regard to adjective clauses, the introductory words *who, whom, which,* and *that* are examples of relative _____; *whose* and *which* are examples of relative _____; and when and *where* are examples of relative _____.

✎ **EXERCISE B** Identify the function of the phrases in **dark print** by writing *N* (noun), *Adj.* (adjective), *Adv.* (adverb), or *V* (verb) in the blank. If the phrase is a *noun phrase*, tell how it is used by writing *S* (subject), *DO* (direct object), *PN* (predicate nominative), *OP* (object of a preposition), or *A* (appositive) above the phrase. If it is an *adjective* or *adverb phrase*, draw an arrow to the word it modifies.

1. _____ My goal, **to complete the manuscript**, will take several months.

2. _____ **Being an ardent fan**, he followed the team tenaciously.

3. _____ The ship **sailing the high seas** was heading for safe harbor.

4. _____ By **choosing the path of least resistance**, the sluggard missed many opportunities.

5. _____ **To be a godly example** requires much prayer and meekness.

6. _____ Their ideology is hard **to define in absolute terms**.

7. _____ Professor Carson enjoys **reading theological tomes**.

8. _____ **Being a merciful person** gave her the capacity to love the unlovable.

9. _____ The secretary of state **will be meeting** with the Saudis over the next few days.

10. _____ **To be an effective leader**, he knew he had to earn the people's trust.

✎ **EXERCISE C** Underline the dependent clauses in the following sentences. Double underline any signal words found in noun clauses. In the blank, write how the clause is used in the sentence. Use the following symbols: *S* for subject, *DO* for direct object, *OP* for object of a preposition, *PN* for predicate nominative, *A* for appositive, *Adj.* for adjective, and *Adv.* for adverb.

___*S*___ 1. Whom the pastor married was the most godly couple in the church.

_____ 2. Peter told me about what you did.

_____ 3. Although he was reluctant, he still sang in the chorus.

_____ 4. My question is whether you are ready to meet the challenge.

_____ 5. The most direct route, where we take I-294, was the most crowded.

_____ 6. You must play smart, if you are going to win the game.

_____ 7. She will be the one who is carrying the briefcase and wearing a scarf.

_____ 8. That we are always in the dark is obvious.

_____ 9. The report that you filed was the wrong one.

_____ 10. He could not discern which person was telling the truth.

Unit 10
Sentences

Some word groups are expressions that are incomplete and must depend upon other words or groups of words to make their thoughts complete; these are called **phrases** and **clauses**. Some word groups express ideas or thoughts that are complete in themselves; these are called **clauses** and **sentences**. In this unit, you will work with the latter.

LESSON 74: COMMON SENTENCE ERRORS

SENTENCE FRAGMENTS

A group of words is a complete sentence only when it includes a *subject* and a *verb* and expresses a complete thought. A group of words that is missing one or more of the parts needed to make a complete sentence is called a **sentence fragment**. Sentence fragments become a grammatical error when they are used in written compositions as if they were complete sentences.

A sentence fragment may simply be the result of omitting words necessary to complete the meaning of the intended sentence. It may also result when a dependent clause, a verbal phrase, or an appositive is separated from a nearby sentence to which it is related.

☞ **EXAMPLES:**

Fragment:	In the spring primary, the incumbent. (*lacks a verb*)
Complete:	In the spring primary, the incumbent ran as a tax-relief candidate.
Fragment:	Is always dissatisfied. (*lacks a subject*)
Complete:	The vain child is always dissatisfied, though his parents indulge his every whim.
Fragment:	Under the impression. (*lacks both subject and verb*)
Complete:	The employees were under the impression they would get a raise each year.
Fragment:	Soldiers wounded in battle. (*still lacks a verb—wounded in battle is a participial phrase describing soldiers; it is not a verb*)
Complete:	Soldiers wounded in battle did not always receive medical treatment in time.

■ *Phrase Fragments*

Remember that a *phrase* is a group of related words, containing neither a subject nor a predicate, which functions as a single part of speech. Regardless of what kind of phrase it is (prepositional, verbal, participial, gerundial, or infinitive), it is only *part* of a sentence and must not be separated from the sentence where it belongs. If it stands alone, it is a fragment. This error can be corrected by attaching the **phrase fragment** to the related sentence.

☞ **EXAMPLES:**

Fragment:	The business trip was scheduled for early April. At the beginning of a busy season.
Corrected:	The business trip was scheduled for early April, **at the beginning of a busy season**. (*The prepositional phrase fragment modifies scheduled and belongs in the sentence.*)

Fragment:	Last summer, we visited my grandparents. Living in Florida.
Corrected:	Last summer, we visited my grandparents **living in Florida**. (*The participial phrase fragment modifies* **grandparents** *and should not be separated from the sentence*.)
Fragment:	He finally persuaded his friends. To stop hounding him about going to college.
Corrected:	He finally persuaded his friends **to stop hounding him about going to college.** (*The infinitive phrase fragment modifying* **persuaded** *belongs in the sentence*.)

■ *Dependent Clause Fragments*

Another error regarding fragments is the dependent clause that is wrongly separated from the sentence where it belongs. Remember that a dependent clause does not express a complete thought and must not stand alone. Be sure to connect a dependent clause to the appropriate sentence.

☞**EXAMPLES:**

Fragment:	She entered the classroom just after the instructor had handed out a quiz. Which did not give her time to complete it.
Complete:	She entered the classroom just after the instructor had handed out a quiz, **which did not give her time to complete it.**
Fragment:	The jury was anxious to hear the defendant's account of the alleged felony. Because so many questions remained unanswered.
Complete:	The jury was anxious to hear the defendant's account of the alleged felony **because so many questions remained unanswered.**

RUN-ON SENTENCES

A run-on sentence is a grammatical error consisting of two or more sentences written as if they were only one sentence. Run-on sentences are not necessarily always long. Even short expressions, when improperly joined, can form a run-on sentence. If only a comma is used between two complete sentences (instead of a period, a semicolon, or a conjunction), the writer has created a run-on sentence. An even greater error is to omit *any* punctuation between them.

☞**EXAMPLES:**

Waiting in line can be annoying, there are so many other important things you could be doing. (*wrong punctuation between sentences*)

Waiting in line can be annoying there are so many other important things you could be doing. (*worse error—no punctuation at all!*)

Run-on sentences can be corrected in several ways:

Rule 1	Separate the sentences with a semicolon if the thoughts are closely related.

Run-on:	So many people entered the contest we were amazed at the response.
Better:	So many people entered the contest; we were amazed at the response.

Rule 2	Separate the thoughts with a comma and coordinating conjunction if the thoughts are closely related.

Run-on: Please turn in the first draft of your research paper, send it with your outline.

Better: Please turn in the first draft of your research paper, and send it with your outline.

Rule 3	Separate the thoughts into two sentences if the ideas are distinct.

Run-on: You may need to update your Web site, new data is always becoming available.

Better: You may need to update your Web site. New data is always becoming available.

Rule 4	Put one of the thoughts into a dependent clause if the ideas are closely related but not of equal grammatical rank.

Run-on: The going gets tough, the tough get going.

Better: When the going gets tough, the tough get going.

✎ **EXERCISE** Identify the following expressions as run-on sentences (*R*) or sentence fragments (*F*). If the expression is a fragment, correct the error by making the sentence complete. Revise run-on sentences using the four ways explained above.

_F_   1. He who laughs last.

   He who laughs last laughs best.

____   2. Trust in the LORD with all your heart, lean not on your own understanding.

____   3. The elder who oversees missions.

____   4. Remember our trip to Australia what a wonderful time we had!

____   5. Using all those suggestions.

____   6. The transplant surgery that Dr. Koffron performed.

____   7. Whatever you were about to do.

____   8. Perhaps you should take that course, it meets one of your graduation requirements.

____   9. Jesus wept, then the Jews said, "See how He loved him!"

____   10. The bald eagle majestically soaring through the sky.

LESSON 75: CORRECTING FAULTY COORDINATION

COORDINATE IDEAS

When there are two or more ideas or clauses in a sentence, the ideas will be either equal or unequal in rank. ***Coordinate ideas*** are equal in rank (*co-* means "equal"; *ordinate* means "ranked"), that is, they have equal emphasis in the sentence. A *coordinating conjunction*, therefore, links together these words, phrases, or clauses of equal grammatical rank.

The conjunction a writer chooses to connect the coordinate ideas in his sentence should make clear the relationship between the two ideas. There are four common kinds of relationships between coordinate ideas. They are *addition*, *contrast*, *choice*, and *result*.

Addition

☞**EXAMPLES:**

David wrote most of the Psalms, **and** Paul wrote much of the New Testament.

My wife **and** kids love traveling abroad; **likewise**, my mother-in-law enjoys coming along.

COORDINATING CONJUNCTIONS OF ADDITION			
also	furthermore	besides	moreover
and	likewise	both … and	then

Contrast

☞**EXAMPLES:**

Lying lips are an abomination to the Lord, **but** those who deal truthfully are His delight.

Renee and her sisters often bicker; **however**, they are still good friends.

COORDINATING CONJUNCTIONS OF CONTRAST				
but	still	nevertheless	however	yet

Choice

☞**EXAMPLES:**

Straighten your room, **or** I will decrease your allowance this week.

Tell the truth; **otherwise**, you will be under God's chastisement and man's discipline.

COORDINATING CONJUNCTIONS OF CHOICE			
either … or	neither … nor	or, nor	otherwise

Result

☞**EXAMPLES:**

The Lord loves His people; **consequently**, He delivers them from all their troubles.

The President committed perjury—the willful telling of a lie under oath; **hence**, he was impeached.

COORDINATING CONJUNCTIONS OF RESULT			
accordingly	hence	consequently	therefore

■ *Choosing the Right Conjunction*

If you want to write effectively, it is important to choose connecting words that *clearly* express how the ideas in your sentences are related. Pay attention to the logical relationships of your ideas; otherwise, your intended meaning may be obscured.

☞**EXAMPLES:**

Not clear:	Andrew had to take his pet to the vet, and it did not seem to mind.
Clear:	Andrew had to take his pet to the vet, **but** it did not seem to mind. (*relationship of* <u>contrast</u>)
Not clear:	Jason spent nine weeks at boot camp, but he is a disciplined soldier.
Clear:	Jason spent nine weeks at boot camp; **consequently**, he is a disciplined soldier. (*relationship of* <u>result</u>)

Note: The preceding examples show that, in joining coordinate clauses, the connecting words *and, but, yet, or,* and *nor,* are usually preceded by a **comma.** The words *besides, likewise, furthermore, moreover, however, nevertheless, otherwise, consequently, therefore, hence,* and *accordingly* are usually preceded by a **semicolon** and followed by a **comma.**

✎ **EXERCISE A** Determine the logical relationship between the clauses in the following sentences by writing *addition, contrast, choice,* or *result* in the first blank. Then choose an appropriate connecting word from the lists in this lesson to make the meaning perfectly clear. Use correct punctuation.

_____ 1. Shape up _____ ship out!

_____ 2. Jed planned the expedition _____ Art was his right-hand man.

_____ 3. In 1893, economic depression caused widespread unrest _____ this prompted calls for a more pervasive government role in managing the economy—the seedling of our modern welfare state.

_____ 4. Call a meeting of the board immediately _____ I will resign my position.

_____ 5. The fear of the Lord is the beginning of wisdom _____ the knowledge of the Holy One is understanding.

_____ 6. The Red Cross brought disaster relief to many victims of catastrophes _____ they still received numerous requests for help.

_____ 7. God has justified believers by faith _____ they have peace with Him through Christ.

_____ 8. The professor gave the class detailed instructions _____ the students did not understand.

SUBORDINATE IDEAS

Subordinate ideas in a sentence are those that are of lower rank—they are not the main thought of the sentence (*sub-* means "under" or "lower"; and as stated earlier, *ordinate* means "ranked"). The most important thought is expressed in an *independent* clause and the secondary thought is expressed in a dependent or *subordinate* clause.

☞**EXAMPLES:**

The mountain guide, who was an experienced climber, taught us how to use our equipment safely. (*independent clause—greater emphasis:* **The mountain guide taught us how to use our equipment safely**; *subordinate clause—lesser emphasis:* **who was an experienced climber**)

Even though a thunderstorm was forecast, the farmer decided to plant the corn. (*independent clause—greater emphasis:* **the farmer decided to plant the corn**; *subordinate clause—lesser emphasis:* **Even though a thunderstorm was forecast**)

■ *Adverb Clauses*

A *subordinating conjunction* connects a dependent (subordinate) clause to an independent clause. In linking a subordinate **adverb clause** to an independent clause, the subordinating conjunction you choose should make clear the relationship between the two ideas. The four possible kinds of relationships between subordinate ideas and independent clauses could be described as *time, cause* or *reason, purpose* or *result,* and *condition.* These generally correspond to the questions that adverbs answer: when? why? how? how often? to what extent?

Time

These conjunctions express a time relationship between the clauses.

SUBORDINATING CONJUNCTIONS OF TIME			
after	before	until	whenever
as	since	when	while

☞**EXAMPLE:**

Our dog barks menacingly **whenever** *the mailman approaches.*

Cause or Reason

These conjunctions introduce an adverb clause that expresses a causal relationship to the idea in the independent clause.

SUBORDINATING CONJUNCTIONS OF CAUSE OR REASON			
as	since	because	whereas

☞**EXAMPLE:**

We stopped for a bite to eat at the next exit **because** *Dad was getting drowsy at the wheel.*

Purpose or Result

These conjunctions introduce an adverb clause that expresses a purpose or result of the idea in the independent clause.

SUBORDINATING CONJUNCTIONS OF PURPOSE OR RESULT		
that	in order that	so that

☞**EXAMPLE:**

Thy word I have hid in my heart **that** *I might not sin against Thee.*

Condition

These conjunctions introduce an adverb clause that expresses the condition under which the idea in the independent clause is true. The conjunctions *though, even though, although,* and *while* mean "in spite of the fact that." They are used to introduce a condition *in spite of which* the idea in the independent clause is true.

SUBORDINATING CONJUNCTIONS OF CONDITION			
if	provided that	unless	while
though	even though	although	

☞**EXAMPLES:**

If *you are faithful in doing your chores,* you will learn good work habits.

Although *all His disciples fled in fear,* Jesus loved and died for them. (***Although all His disciples fled in fear*** states the condition in spite of which Jesus loved them.)

✎ **EXERCISE B** Determine the relationship of the subordinate clause to the independent clause in the following sentences by writing *time, cause, purpose,* or *condition* in the first blank. Then choose an appropriate subordinating conjunction from the lists above to connect them.

_____   1. You will not be saved, _____ you repent of your sins and believe in Christ.

_____   2. Please clear your things off the table _____ I can set it for supper.

_____   3. _____ everyone had arrived, we started the Bible study.

_____   4. We had to return home quickly _____ we forgot to lock the door.

✎ **EXERCISE C** Revise each sentence below by *adding a subordinate clause* at the beginning or end of the sentence. Use a different subordinating conjunction each time.

1. Revival comes to the church.

   When the Holy Spirit awakens His chosen ones to repentance, *revival comes to the church.*

2. I will not be able to go on the winter retreat.

   _____

3. Mark began to organize a work day for the church.

   _____

4. The Cassidys decided to have a family reunion.

   _____

5. The pastor encouraged his congregation to vote in the next election.

   _____

6. Pro-life activists may be barred from protesting.

   _____

7. Missionaries need to learn the local dialect.

   _____

■ *Adjective Clauses*

The preceding exercises used subordinate clauses that functioned as adverbs. A writer may also make use of *adjective clauses* to subordinate one idea to another, depending on which information he wishes to emphasize or de-emphasize. The following two sentences can be arranged in one sentence according to which idea the writer wants to emphasize and which one he wants to subordinate.

☞**EXAMPLE:**

> The Heidelberg Catechism was known as the Palatine Catechism.
> The Heidelberg Catechism was written at the request of Elector Frederick III.

1. The Heidelberg Catechism, which was also known as the Palatine Catechism, was written at the request of Elector Frederick III.

2. The Heidelberg Catechism, which was written at the request of Elector Frederick III, was known as the Palatine Catechism.

Both are equally good sentences. The only difference is one of emphasis. Use adjective clauses to make clear the relative emphasis you want to give the ideas in your sentences.

✎ **EXERCISE D** Revise the following sentences by *reversing* the emphasis. Place in a subordinate *adjective clause* the idea which is now in the main clause.

1. Elector Frederick III, who governed the Palatinate, was one of the most powerful German princes.

   _____

   _____

2. Zacharius Ursinus and Caspar Olevianus, who formulated the Heidelberg Catechism, were two theological professors at Heidelberg University.

   _____

   _____

3. The catechism, which was later divided into fifty-two sections for exposition during Sunday services throughout the year, was approved by a synod in Heidelberg in January 1563.

   _____

   _____

4. The Heidelberg Catechism, which was also approved by the Synod of Dort in 1618–1619, soon became the most ecumenical of the Reformed catechisms.

   _____

   _____

5. The catechism, which is the most translated of all Reformation catechisms, is the most widely used and most warmly praised catechism of the Reformation period.

   _____

   _____

CORRECTING FAULTY COORDINATION

We might say that a sentence is "uncoordinated" when two *unequal* ideas are given equal rank (joined with "and") instead of one placed subordinately to the other. Although the word *and* is the most frequently used conjunction, it should not be asked to do the work that a subordinating conjunction can do more properly. There are three ways in which a writer may place ideas of lesser emphasis in a subordinate position.

1. Place the lesser idea in a subordinate adverb or adjective clause.

☞EXAMPLE:

Faulty coordination: John Bunyan was born near Bedford, and he wrote an allegory of the Christian life entitled *Pilgrim's Progress*.

Corrected by an adjective clause:

John Bunyan, **who was born near Bedford**, wrote an allegory of the Christian life entitled *Pilgrim's Progress*.

2. Place the lesser idea in a modifying phrase.

☞EXAMPLE:

Faulty coordination: Anne was playing the flute, and she achieved an elegant, fluent tone.

Corrected by a modifying participial phrase:

Anne, who was **playing the flute**, achieved an elegant, fluent tone.

Faulty coordination: Northwestern Memorial Hospital is on Chicago's Gold Coast, and it is one of the nation's foremost academic medical centers.

Corrected by a modifying prepositional phrase:

Northwestern Memorial Hospital **on Chicago's Gold Coast** is one of the nation's foremost academic medical centers.

3. Place the lesser idea in an appositive.

Remember that an *appositive* is a word—with or without modifiers—that follows another noun or pronoun to help identify or explain it.

☞EXAMPLE:

Faulty coordination: Christ is our representative, and He is therefore the means by which God can show us His grace.

Corrected by an appositive:

Christ, **our representative**, is therefore the means by which God can show us His grace.

✎ **EXERCISE E** Correct the faulty coordination in the following sentences using the three ways described above.

Place the subordinate idea in a subordinate adjective or adverb clause:

1. Iraq is located along the Tigris and Euphrates rivers, and it was once under British administration.

    _____

    _____

2. Mr. Morello taught high school art for a number of years, and now he owns his own gallery.

    _____

    _____

3. She waited at the dentist's office for an hour, and the doctor finally called her.

    _____

    _____

Place the subordinate idea in a modifying phrase:

4. The call was to surrender, and it came from General Lee.

    _____

    _____

5. The congregation accommodated the rich and powerful, and it teetered on the edge of demise.

    _____

    _____

6. Steve was looking for an employee, and the applicant must be willing to work fast and furiously.

    _____

    _____

Place the subordinate idea in an appositive:

7. Joshua is joining the pro-life alliance, and it is an extremely vital association.

    _____

    _____

8. Grisham's latest novel is *The King of Torts*, and it is written in the same propelling style that has made his legal thrillers so accessible.

    _____

    _____

9. Mrs. Castle is our grandmother, and she emigrated from Luxembourg over twenty years ago.

    _____

    _____

LESSON 76: PRONOUN AND ANTECEDENT AGREEMENT

Remember from your previous study that an *antecedent* is a noun, pronoun, or other noun-like expression to which a pronoun refers.

☞**EXAMPLE:**

Tatya asked Dad for more financial assistance, but he would not give it to her.
(*Tatya is the antecedent of her; Dad is the antecedent of he; assistance is the antecedent of it.*)

Since the meaning of a pronoun is clear only if the reader knows what it refers to, a writer must make sure that there is a clear antecedent for each pronoun he uses. Learn how to avoid three types of unclear references: *ambiguous reference, general reference,* and *weak reference.*

AMBIGUOUS REFERENCE

An ambiguous reference is one in which the reader is unsure to which of two possible antecedents the pronoun refers.

☞**EXAMPLE:**

Ambiguous: Mrs. Whiting chose Renee to sing the solo because she realized what an important part it was.

The pronoun *she* could refer either to Mrs. Whiting or to Renee. The confusion can be cleared up by revising the sentence in either of two ways:

Clear: Mrs. Whiting, realizing what an important part it was, chose Renee to sing the solo.

Clear: Because Renee realized what an important part it was, Mrs. Whiting chose her to sing the solo.

In order to clear up an ambiguous reference, it is sometimes necessary to replace the pronoun with the correct noun.

☞**EXAMPLE:**

Ambiguous: The friendship between Jonathan and David was strengthened after he spoke well of him before the king.

Clear: The friendship between Jonathan and David was strengthened after Jonathan spoke well of David before the king.

GENERAL REFERENCE

A general reference is one in which a pronoun refers confusingly to a general idea in a phrase or clause, rather than to a specific antecedent. The pronouns *which, this, that,* and *it* can cause confusion if they do not refer back to a specific antecedent.

Sentences with general references can be corrected by the replacement of the pronoun with a clear noun, but it may sometimes be necessary to rework the entire sentence.

☞**EXAMPLES:**

General: Some recipients of the Gospel are supported by missions in a way that encourages dependency. It brings negative results. (*It is unclear what the pronoun It exactly refers to. A definite noun makes the meaning clear.*)

Clear: The **system** brings negative results.

| General: | The youth group served dinner to the homeless at the Wayside Mission, which gave the teens great satisfaction. (*The pronoun **which** refers to the general idea of serving dinner; however, the pronoun is placed so that it appears to refer to **Wayside Mission**.*) |
| Clear: | The youth group served dinner to the homeless at the Wayside Mission. The **work** gave the teens great satisfaction. |

WEAK REFERENCE

A weak reference is one in which the antecedent has not been stated at all, but is assumed in the writer's mind.

☞**EXAMPLES:**

Weak:	The Indy 500 is exciting to watch; they are awesome. (*There is no antecedent for the pronoun **they**. The writer meant the pronoun to stand for the noun **drivers**.*)
Clear:	The race car **drivers** are exciting to watch; **they** are awesome.
Weak:	She spent the morning at Borders, but it was not in stock. (*The intended antecedent [book] is "hidden" in the noun **Borders**. When the antecedent is hidden in a modifier or verb form, the reference is too weak to be clear.*)
Clear:	She spent the morning looking for a particular **book**, but **it** was not in stock.

INDEFINITE USE OF PRONOUNS

When we speak in everyday conversation we use the pronouns *it*, *they*, and *you* in an indefinite sense. In writing sentences, however, avoid the indefinite use of these pronouns.

☞**EXAMPLES:**

Indefinite:	In the last verse of the hymn, *it* implies that there will be no death in heaven.
Better:	**The last verse of the hymn** implies that there will be no death in heaven.
Indefinite:	In this soccer tournament *they* use volunteer referees.
Better:	In this soccer tournament **volunteer referees** are used.
Indefinite:	In France *you* call French fries "pommes frites."
Better:	In France **the people** call French fries "pommes frites."

✎ **EXERCISE** Revise the following sentences by correcting the pronoun/antecedent errors.

Revise by correcting ambiguous references:

1. I overheard Gavin talking to Ethan about his new Diggler's Dirt-Dawg.

   _____

   _____

2. The dry cleaner removed the stains from my suits and pressed them.

   _____

   _____

3. Rita had met the new doctor previously, but she did not remember her.

   _____

   _____

Revise by correcting general references:

4. Since Dad never gets around to fixing the dryer, Mom cannot do the laundry; and she is tired of it.

    _____

    _____

5. The girls fight like cats and dogs, which their father abhors.

    _____

    _____

6. Missionaries showed a film of their work, spoke of the desperate plight of the believers in Sudan, and challenged us to help. This moved the congregation.

    _____

    _____

Revise by correcting weak references:

7. After teaching a year at the mission school, Esther decided she didn't want to be one.

    _____

    _____

8. The Great Barrier Reef was well worth seeing, but it would take several days.

    _____

    _____

9. Intoxicated by the rocky Mediterranean landscape, Cézanne painted prolifically; but he was increasingly unable to detach himself from them, owing to his passionate temperament.

    _____

    _____

Revise by correcting the indefinite use of *it, they*, and *you*:

10. According to an article in the *Guardian Unlimited*, it claimed that, after the UN weapons inspectors left in 1998, the sole source of intelligence concerning Saddam's regime was the Iraqi National Congress—a London-based, dissident group.

    _____

    _____

    _____

11. During the Dark Ages, they lived under miserable conditions.

    _____

    _____

12. In polite conversation you don't talk about the problems you face at home.

    _____

    _____

LESSON 77: PLACEMENT OF MODIFIERS

Unlike some other languages, English often depends on the *arrangement of words* in a sentence to convey the proper meaning. It is normally assumed that words placed near one another in a sentence are logically related. Writers must therefore be careful to place words, phrases, and clauses in a logical order that will not confuse the reader. The general principle to follow is to place all modifiers as near to the words they modify as possible and to avoid placing them near words to which they are not properly related.

MISPLACED MODIFIERS

Misplaced modifiers are those which are located in such a way that they appear to be modifying the wrong word. The results can be quite humorous, but the bottom line is that the writer's idea will not be communicated clearly to the reader.

☞**EXAMPLE:**

Confusing: Ariel divulged her plans to leave the mission field while we chatted suddenly.
(*The adverb **suddenly** modifies **divulged**, not **chatted**, and should be placed closer to **chatted**.*)

Clear: Ariel **suddenly** divulged her plans to leave the mission field while we chatted.

Clear: While we chatted, Ariel divulged **suddenly** her plans to leave the mission field.

The most common way to correct a misplaced modifier is to move it next to, or closer to, the word it modifies. Another way, however, is to move an adverb clause (*while we chatted*, in the example above) to the beginning of the sentence.

Confusing: Pastor Ryan thanked the congregation for their help as he neared the close of his sermon.
(*The congregation was not helping the pastor near the close of his sermon, were they? By moving the adverb clause **as he neared the close of his sermon** to the beginning of the sentence, the meaning will no longer be confused.*)

Clear: **As he neared the close of his sermon**, Pastor Ryan thanked the congregation for their help.

✎ **EXERCISE A** Improve the clarity of the following sentences either by placing the modifiers near the words they modify or by placing adverb clauses first in the sentence.

1. On Wednesday evening, the church offers an Awana program for children starting at 6:30.

2. One of my buddies went to Aspen with his new gear where he could go rock climbing.

3. The students began to have major conflicts about the scores they received with their teacher.

4. Brett finally admitted "borrowing" Anne's car after we confronted him.

   _____

   _____

5. The animated classic is about a poor little girl who lives in an orphanage named Penny.

   _____

   _____

6. The lawyer digressed from the argument he had developed by underestimating his opponent.

   _____

   _____

7. At Tuesday's meeting, the treasurer discussed the considerable cost of repairing the townhouse roofs with the association members.

   _____

   _____

8. Jan followed the controversy over the expansion of O'Hare International Airport with concern.

   _____

   _____

DANGLING MODIFIERS

A second way in which modifiers can be incorrectly written—the ***dangling modifier***—is slightly harder for an inexperienced writer to detect, but it nonetheless causes confusion. Dangling modifiers are those which have no word in the sentence to logically modify; thus they are pictured as "dangling"—not logically connected to any word in the sentence.

☞**EXAMPLE:**

> **Dangling:** Shopping at the mall, our packages seemed heavier with each step.

When an introductory participial phrase is used, *shopping at the mall*, it must modify the noun or pronoun **directly following it**. In this case the phrase seems to be modifying *packages*. Since packages cannot shop at a mall, the phrase cannot logically modify it. The modifying phrase "dangles."

> **Corrected:** Shopping at the mall, **we** felt that our packages seemed heavier with each step.
>
> **Corrected:** As **we** were shopping at the mall, our packages seemed heavier with each step.

A dangling modifier can be corrected in either of two ways:

Rule 5	Add a word that the phrase can logically modify.
Rule 6	Change the phrase to an adverb clause by adding to it a subordinating conjunction and a subject and verb.

Study how these sentences have been changed to pin down the "danglers."

> **Dangling:** Following the crowd, the celebrity could barely be seen by us.
>
> **Clear:** Following the crowd, **we** could barely see the celebrity.
>
> **Clear:** **As we were** following the crowd, the celebrity could barely be seen by us.

Dangling:	Flying over the ocean, the waves became imperceptible.
Clear:	Flying over the ocean, **we noticed** that the waves became imperceptible.
Clear:	**While we were** flying over the ocean, the waves became imperceptible.

✎ **EXERCISE B** Revise the following sentences to correct the dangling modifiers. One of the sentences is clear and needs no revision. Simply write "clear."

1. When learning a new software program, the menus must be explored.

2. After listening to the Pharisees' remarks, the reply of Jesus was astonishing.

3. Standing near the mechanic, a metal burr struck the man.

4. Driving to church, the traffic lights were all green.

5. Having promised to be home by 10:00, my father was concerned when I arrived at midnight.

6. Encouraging each other with hymns of praise, Paul and Silas endured their hours in prison.

7. Embarrassed by her childish attitude, her opinion changed by week's end.

TWO-WAY MODIFIERS

A third way in which modifiers in a sentence can cause confusion is if they are placed in a position where they could *logically* modify two different words. The reader cannot tell which meaning the writer intends. These are called two-way modifiers.

☞**EXAMPLE:**

Two-way: Mr. Lindstrom stated during chapel Grace sang divinely.

Since the modifying prepositional phrase "during chapel" could logically modify either *stated* or *sang*, the meaning is not clear. Did Mr. Lindstrom say this during chapel or did Grace sing divinely during chapel? The prepositional phrase should be relocated in either of two ways according to the meaning intended.

Clear:	**During chapel**, Mr. Lindstrom stated Grace sang divinely.
Clear:	Mr. Lindstrom stated Grace sang divinely **during chapel.**

EXERCISE C Revise the following sentences to correct the two-way modifying phrases.

1. Mr. Bennett wanted to know before the vote was taken what the officials said to his opponent.

    _____

    _____

2. Tell Scott when he finishes the lawn I want to talk to him.

    _____

    _____

3. Mr. Jordan told his son after the sixth inning the game gets more exciting.

    _____

    _____

LESSON 78: PARALLEL STRUCTURE

EXPRESSING PARALLEL IDEAS GRAMMATICALLY

When we speak of parallel structure in sentences we mean that two or more equal and closely related ideas are expressed in similar form. It is important to express parallel (paired) ideas in the same grammatical form—a noun with a noun, a verb with a verb, a gerund with a gerund, an adjective with an adjective, an infinitive with an infinitive, a phrase with a phrase, and a clause with a clause. If you keep ideas of equal rank in parallel grammatical form, your writing will be smoother and more clearly understood.

To illustrate, note the corrections made to the following sentences to make the structure grammatically parallel.

☞**EXAMPLES:**

Not parallel:	He is an outstanding athlete in golf, polo, and *on the tennis court*.
Parallel nouns:	He is an outstanding athlete in **golf, polo**, and **tennis**.
Not parallel:	A pastor must study the Scriptures, train elders, and *he must be a wise counselor*.
Parallel verbs:	A pastor must **study** the Scriptures, **train** elders, and **counsel** wisely.
Not parallel:	For fun Renee likes watching movies, playing video games, and *to view professional sports*.
Parallel gerunds:	For fun Renee likes **watching** movies, **playing** video games, and **viewing** professional sports.
Not parallel:	Matt was handsome, good-natured, and *exhibited humor*.
Parallel adjectives:	Matt was **handsome, good-natured**, and **humorous**.

Not parallel:	Working a double shift on Tuesday, she had little time to exercise or *fixing an elaborate meal*.
Parallel infinitives:	Working a double shift on Tuesday, she had little time **to exercise** or **to fix an elaborate meal**.
Not parallel:	The class spent philosophy class going over yesterday's test, learning new material, and *they studied for the final exam*.
Parallel phrases:	The class spent philosophy class **going over yesterday's test, learning new material**, and **studying for the final exam**.
Not parallel:	His campaign speech revealed *pro-life convictions* and that he would be fiscally conservative.
Parallel clauses:	His campaign speech revealed **that he had pro-life convictions** and **that he would be fiscally conservative**.

✎ **EXERCISE A** Make the following sentences grammatically parallel by choosing either a or b.

1. If I had my druthers, I would rather go skiing than _____.

    a. snowboarding   b. to the snowboard hill

2. The school must decide whether to use the extra funds in the budget for new computers or
    _____.

    a. if they should remodel the science labs   b. for remodeled science labs

3. Mountain climbing does not interest me as much as _____.

    a. to go explore caves   b. cave exploring

4. The drinks at the new coffeehouse are aromatic, full-bodied, and _____.

    a. inexpensive   b. they cost less

5. The day before Jeff left for the Bible conference, he mowed the lawn, packed his suitcase, and
    _____.

    a. the dog was taken to the kennel   b. took the dog to the kennel

6. Her anecdotes were known more for their humor than _____.

    a. their significance   b. what they signified

EXPRESSING PARALLEL IDEAS IN PARALLEL FORM

In addition to stating parallel ideas in the same grammatical form, there are several other ways to insure that the ideas in your sentences are expressed in a parallel manner.

1. **When stating parallel ideas, repeat an article, a preposition, or a pronoun whenever necessary to make the meaning clear.**

☞**EXAMPLES:**

Before the retreat I talked with the organizer and host.
(*This could mean either that the writer talked with **one** person who was both organizer and host, or that he talked to two different people. If the latter is the intended meaning, repeat the article **the**.*)
Before the retreat I talked with the organizer and **the** host.

Jeremy showed more interest toward his little brother than Cousin Freddie.
(*This could mean either that* **Jeremy** *showed more interest than* **Cousin Freddie** *did, or that* **Jeremy** *showed more interest toward* **his little brother** *than he did toward* **Cousin Freddie**. *Add a preposition or an appropriate verb to make the intended meaning clear.*)
Jeremy showed more interest toward his little brother than **toward** Cousin Freddie. [*add preposition*]
Jeremy showed more interest toward his little brother than Cousin Freddie **did**. [*add extra verb*]

King Herod declared that Bethlehem must be searched, that infant boys—two years and younger—must be killed, and he would not rest until it was done.
(*In a series of parallel clauses using the relative pronoun* **that**, *repeat the introductory pronoun in each clause for the sake of clarity.*)
King Herod declared **that** Bethlehem must be searched, **that** infant boys—two years and younger—must be killed, and <u>**that**</u> he would not rest until it was done.

2. Place the correlative conjunctions *both ... and*; *not only ... but also*; *neither ... nor*; *either ... or*, immediately before the parallel items they introduce.

If a part of these two-part correlative conjunctions is placed before the wrong word, the meaning will be inaccurate. Keep each part of these conjunctions directly before the word it logically introduces.

☞**EXAMPLES:**

Wrong placement:	The Covenanter's stand for political and religious liberty not only established the beginning of persecution but also the end of French Catholic influence in Scotland. (**Not only** *wrongly precedes the verb* **established**, *whereas the second half of the conjunction*, **but also**, *precedes the noun* **end**. **Not only** *should come before* **the beginning** *to make the parallel structure and meaning clear.*)
Corrected:	The Covenanter's stand for political and religious liberty established **not only** <u>the beginning</u> of persecution **but also** <u>the end</u> of French Catholic influence in Scotland.
Wrong placement:	Enemy soldiers could neither force Covenanter John Frazer to profane his God nor to betray his Lord, King Jesus.
Corrected:	Enemy soldiers could force Covenanter John Frazer **neither** <u>to profane</u> his God **nor** <u>to betray</u> his Lord, King Jesus.

3. In the second part of a parallel construction add any word(s) necessary to make the parallelism clear and complete.

☞**EXAMPLES:**

Incomplete parallel:	Pastor Dave's sermons are easier to grasp than Pastor John. (*This sentence leaves the reader feeling that something has been omitted because it wrongly compares* **sermons** *with* **Pastor John**.)
Corrected:	Pastor Dave's sermons are easier to grasp than **those of** Pastor John.

✎ **EXERCISE B** Correct the faulty parallel construction in the following sentences by using the three methods explained above.

1. You may either choose the short-term mission trip or the summer survival camp.

_____

_____

2. Bach's "Little Fugue in G Minor" was a much harder piece for me to play than Ellie.

    _____

    _____

3. The sight in my left eye is better than my right eye.

    _____

    _____

4. Meals cooked at home are much tastier than the hospital.

    _____

    _____

5. Growing up in South America is different than North America.

    _____

    _____

6. The view from Mt. Rainier, Washington, is even more awesome than Mt. Whitney, California.

    _____

    _____

7. I talked to the president and manager before I made my decision.

    _____

    _____

8. Thad likes "diggling," the new bike-board sport, better than Chad.

    _____

    _____

9. George Washington not only led the colonial army but also the Constitutional Convention.

    _____

    _____

10. Jesus both healed the lame and the blind.

    _____

    _____

LESSON 79: UNNECESSARY SHIFTS IN SENTENCES

If a writer changes from one subject to another within a sentence or from one verb tense to another, these are unnecessary "shifts" that result in an awkward style. Although some shifts are appropriate for expressing a writer's intended meaning, the following two shifts are not appropriate.

■ *Shifting From One Subject To Another*

☞**EXAMPLE:**

Awkward: A *teenager* should read Solomon's proverbs daily so that *you* may learn wisdom. (*The shift in subject from* **teenager** *to* **you** *is awkward and affects the smooth flow of the sentence.*)

Smooth: A teenager should read Solomon's proverbs daily so that **he** may learn wisdom.

■ *Shifting From One Verb Form To Another*

Rule 7	Do not shift from active to passive voice or from passive to active voice within one sentence.

Remember that when the subject of a verb is doing the acting, that verb is in the *active "voice."* When the subject is acted upon (receives the action of the verb), that verb is in the *passive "voice."*

Active: Ben **won** three trophies. (*subject acting*)

Passive: Three trophies **were won** by Ben. (*subject receiving the action*)

If you shift within one sentence from active to passive, or vice versa, the subject also shifts.

☞**EXAMPLE:**

Unnecessary shift: The girls *organized* the bake sale, and the signs *were painted* by them. (*Because of the shift from active to passive voice, the subject has also shifted from* **girls** *to* **signs**.)

Shift avoided: The girls **organized** the bake sale and **painted** the signs.

Rule 8	Do not shift from one verb tense to another within one sentence.

Awkwardness also results when a writer shifts from present to past tense or past to present tense in the same sentence. Be careful to continue the same tense with which you started.

☞**EXAMPLES:**

Unnecessary shift: King David *gazed* triumphantly at the slain Philistines on the battlefield and *gives* thanks to God.

Shift avoided: King David **gazed** triumphantly at the slain Philistines on the battlefield and **gave** thanks to God.

Unnecessary shift: Martin Luther *nails* his ninety-five theses to the door of the church and *received* the wrath of the pope.

Shift avoided: Martin Luther **nails** his ninety-five theses to the door of the church and **receives** the wrath of the pope.

■ *Acceptable Shifts of Verb Tense*

An exception to the above rule would be an *appropriate tense shift* from present tense to future tense, or from past tense to future tense.

☞**EXAMPLES:**

The first graders **have eaten** their lunches and **will** soon **have** recess.

She **made** that mistake in the past and **will be** careful to avoid making it again.

Another instance in which it is appropriate to shift verb tense is when *expressing a general truth* such as a scientific or geographical fact. General facts such as these should always be stated in the present tense.

☞**EXAMPLES:**

Professor Howard **told** us that plankton **has** [not *had*] many uses.

The Bible study group **was** not **aware** that the Dead Sea **is** (not *was*) 1,360 feet below sea level.

✎ **EXERCISE** Revise the following sentences to correct the awkward shifts in subject, in verb voice, or in verb tense.

1. When you "Hike for Life," Christians have an opportunity to demonstrate Christ's love to unborn children and their mothers.

    _____

    _____

2. A young child must learn God's Word, obey his parents, and godly behavior ought to be pursued.

    _____

    _____

3. When the rice comes to a boil, cover the pot and the heat should be reduced.

    _____

    _____

4. Father says that we were all too emotional to think clearly when the family began to quarrel.

    _____

    _____

5. After you return from the retreat, they should start a Bible study for their own spiritual benefit.

    _____

    _____

6. He planned to go into business for himself, but he changes his mind and becomes a CEO for IBM.

    _____

    _____

7. Do you like to read Reformation history or was the history of missions more appealing?

    _____

    _____

LESSON 80: SENTENCE CONCISENESS

When you write, make sure that every word is carrying a *load*. By that we mean that every word you use should be necessary to convey your meaning. One of the most obvious signs of an unskilled writer is the use of more words than are needed to accomplish the writer's purpose. This fault is called *wordiness*, and its solution is *conciseness*.

Conciseness is not necessarily the same as "shortness." Sometimes it takes many words to express a thought completely and precisely. But the writer should use no more words than *necessary*. The word *concise* means "cut off," as in cutting out of your sentences all the "do-nothing" words that only clutter up your composition and make your ideas harder to find and follow. Keeping your prose "lean and mean" requires discipline, one of the hardest traits for a writer to learn. This lesson will teach you how to work toward that goal.

UNNECESSARY REPETITION

Eliminate the unnecessary repetition of ideas and redundant words.
☞**EXAMPLE:**

Wordy:	After a tedious, wearying journey trekking through the dense woods and forests of Big Bear Lake, the mountain biking club members approached the final mile, coming closer to the end of their trip.
Concise:	After a wearying trek through the dense woods of Big Bear Lake, the mountain biking club members approached the final mile of their trip.

Some writers make the mistake of packing their sentences with extra adjectives that are synonymous with ones already used. *Tedious* and *wearying*, *woods* and *forests*, and *approached* and *coming closer* all mean essentially the same thing. Repetition of ideas and redundant words tend to dull the impact of a sentence and actually make it harder to follow.

✎ **EXERCISE A** Revise the following sentences, removing any unnecessary words or redundant ideas you can find.

1. It goes without saying that it is a common observation that you may add fuel to the fire, that is, make a tough situation worse, with those remarks and comments.

    _____

    _____

2. In my opinion, I think that liberal, radical policies need to be exposed and laid bare for what they are.

    _____

    _____

3. Harvey took a huge, deep breath and stepped up and walked to the podium, or lectern, at the Chicago Marriott Downtown, in the heart of the city.

    _____

    _____

4. "Diggling" has the potential, or possibility, to do to mountain biking, or riding a mountain bike, what snowboarding, or riding a snowboard, did to skiing ten years ago, that is, a decade ago.

    _____

    _____

5. When Melissa saw her thirteen-year-old brother, who just became a teenager, driving and steering the tractor, she was dumbfounded because she could not believe it.

    _____

    _____

6. I asked Renee to repeat again what she said, or tried to verbalize, because it was inaudible to my
    ears; I could barely hear it.

    _____

    _____

7. As Sam read through the Bible, he was amazed and flabbergasted by all the commands and laws
    that God prescribed, or laid down, for His people, the body of Christ, to obey and follow.

    _____

    _____

8. The course title *Applications of Grammar* means that now, in our everyday writing, speaking, and
    talking, proper grammar—the study of language—should be rightly applied and practiced.

    _____

    _____

REDUCTION

A writer can use **reduction** to make wordy sentences more concise and still convey his meaning
effectively. There are three ways to reduce a bulky sentence: *reduce a clause to a phrase, reduce
a clause to an appositive,* and *reduce a clause or phrase to a single word.*

1. Reduce clauses to participial, gerundial, or infinitive phrases.
☞**EXAMPLES:**

Clause:	*When they were frightened into the halls and down the stairs,* the World Trade Center employees tried to escape.
Participial phrase:	**Frightened from their offices,** the World Trade Center employees tried to escape.
Clause:	*If you win this debate,* you will get to the championship round.
Gerundial phrase:	**Winning this debate** will get you to the championship round.
Clause:	*So they could finish all the tasks,* the girls worked fast.
Infinitive phrase:	**To finish all the tasks,** the girls worked fast.

2. Reduce clauses to appositives.
☞**EXAMPLES:**

Clause:	My friend Harry, *who is an avid bird watcher,* can imitate over twenty birdcalls.
Appositive:	My friend Harry, **an avid bird watcher,** can imitate over twenty birdcalls.
Clause:	One of the most opulent tourist destinations is Bangkok, *which is the capital of Thailand.*
Appositive:	One of the most opulent tourist destinations is Bangkok, **the capital of Thailand.**

3.   **Reduce clauses and phrases to single words.**

☞**EXAMPLES:**

Clause:	The gangbangers *that had been jailed* were irate.
Single word:	The **jailed** gangbangers were irate.
Clause:	This is a pogo stick *that will never break.*
Single word:	This is an **unbreakable** pogo stick.
Phrase:	Her home *in the jungle* was destroyed by a flood.
Single word:	Her **jungle** home was destroyed by a flood.
Phrase:	The guide dog helped his blind master *in a faithful manner.*
Single word:	The guide dog helped his blind master **faithfully**.

✎ **EXERCISE B** Omit wordiness in the following sentences by reducing the italicized *clauses* to phrases, appositives, or single words. Reduce the italicized *phrases* to single words. You may change the word order if needed.

1.   After hearing the concert, I listened at home to three more cantatas *that were composed by Bach.*

_____

_____

2.   Our drive in the Blue Mountains, *which are situated near Sydney, New South Wales, Australia,* would have been perfect if it had not been for our tire *that went flat.*

_____

_____

3.   Our daughter, *who is the most adorable toddler this side of the Mississippi,* turned three today.

_____

_____

4.   *After she became paralyzed in an accident which occurred while she was diving,* Joni Eareckson Tada faced a period of rehabilitation *that was challenging.*

_____

_____

5.   *While he was imprisoned in Scotland,* Samuel Rutherford, *who was a faithful pastor,* wrote hundreds of letters *that were insightful and sympathetic.*

_____

_____

6.   The films directed by Alex Kirby dramatized three books *from the Narnia series,* but not always *in an accurate manner.*

_____

_____

LESSON 81: COMBINING AND REVISING SENTENCES

In this unit's previous seven lessons, you have learned various ways to write complete sentences that express coordinate and subordinate ideas accurately, state antecedents clearly, place modifiers correctly, produce sentences that are parallel in structure, avoid unnecessary subject and verb shifts, and are concise in nature.

Now we will shift our focus away from the individual sentence and consider some *issues of style*—namely, how to correct either a *choppy* style or a "*stringy*" style in your writing.

CORRECTING A CHOPPY STYLE

A choppy style of writing is the result of too many short, single-idea sentences that follow the same pattern—subject first. Compare the following two accounts of the same paragraphs, taken from "Does Yoga Conflict with Christianity?" The first is written in a *choppy style* in which each idea is presented in the same predictable grammatical pattern and in which no idea is subordinate to any other idea.

☞**EXAMPLE OF A CHOPPY STYLE:**

Phil Catalfo is a senior editor of *Yoga Journal*. He asks, "Is Yoga a Religion?" in a sidebar. This is an easy one. No. This is like asking if prayer is a religion. Prayer is a fixed religious practice. Yoga is a fixed religious practice. Catalfo tries to manipulate this fact. He uses an appeal to the standard New Age distinction between religion and spirituality.

What is in Catalfo's mind? A person's "understanding" of the personal and cosmic issues of life can somehow be separated from the "doctrines" of one's religion. Catalfo probably means here that spirituality can be pantheistic. It can be transpersonal. Even while one's religion is monotheistic and interpersonal, it can be. The Jew can recite the Shema. The Christian can recite the Nicene Creed. At the same time, they can somehow have an "understanding." These doctrinal words are not to be read "literally"; God is really the divine in everyone. No one suggests that Buddhists do their chanting and think to themselves that their Buddhist faith really means that they are lost sinners. No one suggests that Buddhists understand that they can enjoy eternal life only through faith in Jesus as their Savior and Lord! This is "cross-fertilization." This argument works only in one direction. The distinction between spirituality and religion is a conjurer's trick; he convinces people that monotheistic religion can and should accommodate pantheistic spirituality. The pantheistic religions may remain safely pantheistic in their spirituality.

Does yoga conflict with my religion? You betcha. Telling people that God cannot bring them ultimate happiness conflicts with my belief. The chief end of human beings is to love God and enjoy Him forever. Encouraging people to worship their yoga master conflicts with my belief. The Lord is God and there is no other. Encouraging people to believe that spiritual fulfillment can be attained in any religion conflicts with my belief. Without Jesus Christ people of all religions (Christianity is a religion, too.) are lost.

Now study the actual, well-written account excerpted from the article and notice how the author has used subordinate clauses, introductory participial and prepositional phrases, appositives, and a combination of active and passive voice. By using all of these tools, the writer has achieved a smooth and appealing style:

☞**EXAMPLE OF A SMOOTH STYLE:**

In a sidebar, Phil Catalfo, a senior editor of *Yoga Journal*, asks, "Is Yoga a Religion?" This is an easy one: of course not. But this is like asking if prayer is a religion. No, but it is an incorrigibly religious practice. The same is true of yoga. Catalfo tries to [manipulate] this fact by an appeal to the standard New Age distinction between religion and spirituality:

> Spirituality, it could be said, has to do with one's interior life, the ever-evolving understanding of one's self and one's place in the cosmos—what Victor Frankl called humanity's "search for meaning." Religion, on the other hand, can be seen as spirituality's external counterpart, the organizational structure we give to our individual and collective spiritual processes: the rituals, doctrines, prayers, chants, and ceremonies, and the congregations that come together to share them.

Apparently, in Catalfo's mind one's "understanding" of the personal and cosmic issues of life can somehow be separated from the "doctrines" of one's religion.... Another translation would seem to be in order: What Catalfo probably means here is that spirituality can be pantheistic and transpersonal even while one's religion is monotheistic and interpersonal. In other words, the Jew can somehow recite the Shema or the Christian recite the Nicene Creed while at the same time having the "understanding" that these words are not to be read "literally" and that God is really the divine in everyone. Of course, no one suggests that Buddhists do their chanting while thinking to themselves that what their Buddhist faith really means "at the deepest level" is that they are lost sinners who can enjoy eternal life only through faith in Jesus as their Savior and Lord! No-this "cross-fertilization" works only in one direction, and the distinction between spirituality and religion is a conjurer's trick to convince people that monotheistic religion can and should accommodate pantheistic spirituality. The pantheistic religions, meanwhile, may remain safely pantheistic in their spirituality as well.

Does yoga conflict with my religion? [Absolutely.] Anything that tells people that God cannot bring them ultimate happiness ... conflicts with my belief that the chief end of human beings is to love God and enjoy [H]im forever. Anything that encourages people to worship their yoga master ... conflicts with my belief that the Lord is God and there is no other. Anything that encourages people to believe that spiritual fulfillment can be attained in any religion … conflicts with my belief that without Jesus Christ people of all religions (even Christianity!) are lost.

—Robert M. Bowman, Jr., "Does Yoga Conflict with Christianity?"[58]

1. Combine short sentences by adding adjectives, adverbs, prepositional phrases, participial phrases, or appositives.

☞**EXAMPLES:**

Three sentences:	Sam ran fast. Sam ran on the path. Sam ran toward the finish line.
One sentence:	Sam ran **fast on the path toward the finish line.** (*combined using an adverb and prepositional phrases*)
Two sentences:	She sampled the chocolate. She placed an order for one pound.
One sentence:	**Sampling the chocolate,** she placed an order for one pound. (*combined using a participial phrase*)
Two sentences:	J. S. Bach was born in Eisenach. He was one of the greatest composers of all time.
One sentence:	J. S. Bach, **one of the greatest composers of all time,** was born in Eisenach. (*combined using an appositive*)

2. Combine short sentences by putting one idea in a subordinate clause.

☞**EXAMPLES:**

Two sentences:	The golfer won the open. The golfer was awesome on the course.
One sentence:	The golfer **who won the open** was awesome on the course. (*combined using an adjective clause*)
One sentence:	**Since the golfer was awesome on the course,** he won the open. (*combined using an adverb clause*)
Two sentences:	Julie wanted to join the drama club. She did not make the tryouts.
One sentence:	**Although Julie wanted to join the drama club,** she did not make the tryouts. (*combined using an adverb clause*)

Remember that two or more choppy sentences may be combined into one smooth sentence by changing one or more of the choppy sentences into a *subordinate clause* or *participial phrase* which begins with one of the following conjunctions, relative pronouns, or participles:

Subordinate Adverb Clauses:	begin with such words as *although, when, because, if, since, after*
Subordinate Adjective Clauses:	begin with *who, whom, whose, which, that* (i.e., relative pronouns)
Participial Phrases:	contain a participle (usually an *-ing* verb form)

Note: Sentences may also be changed into **prepositional phrases** which begin with one of a number of prepositions. (*See the first example under number 1 above.*)

---

58. Robert M. Bowman, Jr. is the director of the Institute for the Development of Evangelical Apologetics (IDEA), P.O. Box 60511, Pasadena, CA 91116. His e-mail address is <robertbowman@mindspring.com>.

✎ **EXERCISE A** Combine the following choppy sentences into one smooth sentence using the methods prescribed.

Combine using *adjectives, adverbs*, and *prepositional phrases*:

1. My friend was kind. My friend encouraged me. She encouraged me by listening.

    _____

2. Philip Emeagwali conducts research. Philip Emeagwali does this vigorously. He conducts research on next-generation supercomputers.

    _____

    _____

3. The girl threw the pillow. The girl was angry. She threw the pillow at her sister.

    _____

    _____

Combine using *introductory participial phrases*:

4. The hurricane swept across southern Florida. The hurricane destroyed everything in its path.

    _____

    _____

5. The computer consultant boarded the aircraft. He was headed for Seattle.

    _____

6. Jesus knelt down with a towel. Jesus washed the disciples' feet.

    _____

Combine using *appositives*:

7. The three friends climbed Mt. Everest. Mt. Everest is the tallest mountain in the world with an elevation of 29,035 feet (8850 meters).

    _____

    _____

8. Jed Smith was a trailblazer of the West. Smith was a Christian gentleman and the greatest of the mountain men.

    _____

    _____

9. John G. Paton was a Scottish missionary to the New Hebrides. He gave to the Aniwan people their first hymnbook and translated the New Testament into their language.

    _____

    _____

Combine using a *subordinate adverb clause*:

10. Parenting is a God-given responsibility. Parents should use it to rear righteous children as God's Word directs.

_____

_____

11. Thick fog blanketed the area. Motorists kept driving.

_____

_____

12. The hepatologist gazed at the blood tests thoughtfully. He quietly turned to the patient with liver disease.

_____

_____

Combine using a *subordinate adjective clause*:

13. I forgot to bring the recipe. It was lying on the kitchen counter.

_____

14. Shannon wrote her research paper on Elector Frederick III of the Palatinate. She learned about Elector Frederick III on the Internet.

_____

_____

15. We met Mr. and Mrs. Ash. They had recently returned from the mission field in Indonesia.

_____

_____

CORRECTING A "STRINGY" STYLE

The opposite of a choppy style is a "stringy" style in which too many ideas are strung together with the conjunctions *and, but, and so,* and *so*. If these connecting words are overused, your sentences will be not only boring but also lacking in logical sense and impact. We emphasize once again the importance of subordinating one idea to another. Remember that subordinate clauses express relationships of time, cause, purpose, or condition (*See page 232*). You will obscure the logical relationship of ideas in a sentence if you connect them only with *and* or *so*.

1. **Correct stringy sentences by using subordinate clauses and participial phrases.**
   ☞**EXAMPLES:**

   Stringy: The Little League teams paraded up State Street, *and* it caused an enormous traffic jam, *and so* the police have denied permission for any more team parades.

   Improved: **Because the Little League teams paraded up State Street, causing an enormous traffic jam**, the police have denied permission for any more team parades. (*The first idea has been placed in a subordinate clause, the second idea in a participial phrase, and the third idea has become the main clause.*)

Stringy:	Nick heard a strange noise in the plane's engine, *so* he was afraid of mechanical difficulty, *and so* he decided not to fly to Milwaukee.

In writing, the use of *so ...*, *and so* is considered poor form. Here is one way to avoid their use:

Improved:	**Fearing mechanical difficulty after Nick heard a strange noise in the plane's engine**, he decided not to fly to Milwaukee. (*The second idea has become an introductory participial phrase, the first idea has become a subordinate clause, and the third idea has become the main clause.*)

2. Correct stringy sentences by dividing them into more than one sentence.

Sometimes a stringy sentence contains too many ideas to correct by subordination and other methods. Find a logical place to end it and begin another sentence.

☞**EXAMPLE:**

Stringy:	Flames burst forth from every direction, *and* the house was in immediate danger, *and so* Mr. Winslow helped his family out the window *so* they could escape the fire.
Improved:	**Because** flames burst forth from every direction, the house was in immediate danger. Mr. Winslow, therefore, helped his family out the window, **where** they could escape the fire.

Keep in mind that a "stringy" sentence may be rearranged by changing one or more of its independent clauses into a *subordinate clause* or *participial phrase* beginning with one of the following conjunctions, relative pronouns, or participles:

Subordinate Adverb Clauses:	begin with such words as *although, when, because, if, since, after*
Subordinate Adjective Clauses:	begin with *who, whom, whose, which, that* (i.e., relative pronouns)
Participial Phrases:	contain a participle (usually an *-ing* verb form)

✎ **EXERCISE B** Revise the following stringy sentences by getting rid of the overuse of *and* and *so*. Use subordinate clauses and participial phrases. If you have used these tools and still find too many ideas for one sentence, divide into two sentences.

1. A survey was sent to registered voters, and the voters were asked to indicate their greatest concern, and national security was their first choice.

_____

_____

2. Philip decided to become a mathematician, and he was fourteen, and he mastered calculus and could even out-calculate his instructors.

_____

_____

3. Iago was Shakespeare's most wicked villain, and he began to awaken suspicions in Othello, and so these suspicions were ultimately converted into jealousy, and his reasons for hating various characters in the play were too obvious though muddled.

_____

_____

4. Adam stood by Eve's side, and he listened to Satan, and he ate of the forbidden fruit.

   _____

   _____

5. It snowed the entire weekend, and huge drifts of snow piled up around the house, and so the Matthews were not able to dig out for several days.

   _____

   _____

6. Martin had learned programming at Harper Community College, and he was a competent programmer, and Martin was never out of work.

   _____

   _____

7. The Waverunner sped around the sharp turn, and it spun out of control, and it overturned in the water.

   _____

   _____

8. The extension of the suburban expressway is a subject of heated debate, and the issues seem insurmountable, and so the people do not anticipate any resolution soon.

   _____

   _____

LESSON 82: UNIT REVIEW

✎ **EXERCISE A** Fill in the blanks:

1. A sentence fragment is _____

   _____.

2. A complete sentence must have a _____ and a _____ and express a complete thought.

3. A _____ is a group of related words, containing neither a subject nor a predicate, and functions as a single part of speech.

4. A _____ clause does not express a complete thought and must not stand alone.

5. A _____ sentence is a grammatical error consisting of two or more sentences written as if they were only one.

6. List four ways the sentence described in number 5 can be corrected:

   a. _____

   b. _____

   c. _____

   d. _____

7. A coordinating conjunction is _____

    _____ .

8. The four common kinds of relationships between coordinate ideas are _____ ,

    _____ , _____ , and _____ .

9. A subordinating conjunction is _____

    _____ .

10. The four possible kinds of relationships between subordinate ideas and independent clauses are

    _____ , _____ , _____ , and _____ .

11. List three ways faulty coordination can be corrected:

    a. _____

    b. _____

    c. _____

12. With respect to pronoun-antecedent agreement, define the three types of unclear references
    that should be avoided:

    Ambiguous: _____

    _____

    General: _____

    _____

    Weak: _____

    _____

13. The _____ use of pronouns, such as *it, they*, and *you* should be avoided in writing
    sentences.

14. _____ modifiers are those which are located in such a way that they appear to
    be modifying the wrong word.

15. What is the most common way to correct the modifier described in number 14?

    _____

    _____

16. List two ways the modifiers described in number 14 can be corrected:

    a. _____

    b. _____

17. _____ modifiers are those which have no word in the sentence to logically
    modify; they are not logically connected to any word in the sentence.

18. What is the best way to correct the modifiers described in number 17?

    _____

    _____

19. _____ modifiers are those which cause confusion when they are placed in a position where they could *logically* modify two different words.

20. When two or more equal and closely related ideas are expressed in the same grammatical form in a sentence they are said to have _____ _____.

21. List three ways parallel ideas in a sentence may be expressed in a parallel manner:

    a. _____

    b. _____

    c. _____

22. What two unnecessary shifts in sentences result in an awkward style?

    a. _____

    b. _____

23. State the two rules regarding verb-form shifting which you must always follow:

    a. _____

    b. _____

24. What are two acceptable shifts of verb tense within a sentence?

    a. _____

    b. _____

25. What is the best way to change wordiness to conciseness in a sentence?

    _____

26. List three ways you can reduce a bulky sentence.

    a. _____

    b. _____

    c. _____

Note: The following two questions deal with *style*, rather than individual sentence *structure*.

27. How can *choppiness* be changed into a smooth and appealing style?

    a. _____

    b. _____

28. How can a *stringy* style be changed into an interesting and logical one?

    a. _____

    b. _____

✎ **EXERCISE B** The following paraphrase has been adapted from an article (entitled "Venerable Vision") written by Linda Shrewsbury for *WORLD* magazine ("The Buzz," May 31, 2001). On the lines provided, rewrite the article using the rules and principles outlined in this unit.

Black history month founder was pre-pc

When in 1926, the year artist Claude Monet died, black historian Carter G. Woodson instituted and founds Negro History Week. (The forerunner of today's Black History Month.) Celebrated across America every February, he wasn't kowtowing or fawning to the idols of multiculturalism—of, relating to, reflecting, or adapted to diverse cultures. Woodson's hope and trust, in fact, of generating respect and admiration for the contributions and offerings of blacks, or African Americans, to American society predated and comes before political correctness by more than half a century, over fifty years. He is born into a poor Virginia family in 1875, and both his mother and father were former slaves, but Woodson isn't able to attend school regularly. Still by age 17 years of age he had mastered the fundamentals and principles of common everyday school subjects, largely through his own efforts, and hard work.

For years and years and years, he toiled and labored in Virginia's coal mines to helped support his family. At age 20 Woodson is able to enter high school. He earns his diploma in less than two years. He worked after earning a degree at Berea College in Kentucky as a teacher and writer and then earned and received a Ph.D. in history from Harvard University in 1912.

Woodson's studies convinces him himself that American history books ignored—and sometimes misrepresented and belied—the black experience in this country, the United States of America. He sets out to change that: In 1915, he founded the Association for the Study of Negro Life and History. Which operated today as the Association for the Study of Afro-American Life and History. In 1916, he launched and established the *Journal of Negro History*. In 1921, he founded a publishing printing company to print books and texts about black life that didn't interest or attract mainstream publishers and printers.

He first conceives of Negro History Week, and Woodson chose the second week in February to coincide with the birthdays of two persons who had dramatically and histrionically affected the lives of black Americans: Abraham Lincoln and Frederick Douglass, the former slave who became a leading abolitionist, one who fosters abolition. Fifty years later during America's 1976 bicentennial 200th anniversary celebration and so the week-long observance was expanded to include the entire month.

This month marks points to the observance's diamond seventy-fifth anniversary, but for many Woodson's vision of greater and more respect, regard, and understanding between black and white, African and Caucasian, Americans still seems far away—in the distance.

_____

_____

_____

_____

_____

_____

_____

_____

_____

Appendix

Present	Past	Past Participle	Present	Past	Past Participle
(to +)		*(have, has, had+)*	*(to +)*		*(have, has, had+)*
arise	arose	arisen	pay*	paid	paid
bear	bore	borne, born	prove	proved	proved, proven
beat	beat	beaten	put	put	put
become	became	become	rise	rose	risen
begin	began	begun	ride	rode	ridden
bid (auction)	bid	bid	ring	rang	rung
bid (command)	bade, bid	bidden, bid	run	ran	run
bite	bit	bitten	say*	said	said
blow	blew	blown	see	saw	seen
break	broke	broken	set	set	set
bring	brought	brought	sit	sat	sat
build	built	built	shine (gleam)**	shone	shone
burn	burned, burnt	burned, burnt	show	showed	shown, showed
burst	burst	burst	shrink	shrank, shrunk	shrunk
cast	cast	cast	sing	sang	sung
catch	caught	caught	sink	sank, sunk	sunk
choose	chose	chosen	sleep	slept	slept
come	came	come	speak	spoke	spoken
cut	cut	cut	spend	spent	spent
dig	dug	dug	spring	sprang, sprung	sprung
dive	dived, dove	dived	stand	stood	stood
do	did	done	steal	stole	stolen
draw	drew	drawn	swear	swore	sworn
drink	drank	drunk, drunken	swim	swam	swum
drive	drove	driven	swing	swung	swung
eat	ate	eaten	take	took	taken
fall	fell	fallen	tear	tore	torn
feel	felt	felt	think	thought	thought
find	found	found	throw	threw	thrown
flee	fled	fled	wake	waked, woke	waked, woken
fly (sail)**	flew	flown	wear	wore	worn
forecast	forecast, (-ed)	forecast, (-ed)	weep	wept	wept
forget	forgot	forgotten	win	won	won
freeze	froze	frozen	wind	wound	wound
get	got	got, gotten	wring	wrung	wrung
give	gave	given	write	wrote	written
go	went	gone			
grow	grew	grown			
hang (object)**	hung	hung	*lay, pay, and say may also be considered regular verbs in
know	knew	known	that they use the regular ending -d to form the past and
lay*	laid	laid	past participle—after changing the final "y" to "i."
lead	led	led		
lend	lent	lent	**Other meanings have regular parts:
let	let	let	fly (hit baseball)	flied	flied
lie (recline)**	lay	lain	lie (tell falsehood)	lied	lied
lose	lost	lost	hang (by the neck)	hanged	hanged
meet	met	met	shine (polish)	shined	shined

Glossary

Active voice
The form of an action verb which tells that the subject is the doer of the action.
> **EXAMPLE:**
> George *mowed* his lawn.

Adjective
A part of speech that modifies or limits the meaning of a noun or pronoun. An adjective usually answers one of the following questions about the noun or pronoun which it modifies: *which one? what kind? how much? how many?* A *simple adjective* is generally located immediately before the word it modifies. A *predicate adjective* is usually located after a linking verb and modifies the subject of that verb.
> **EXAMPLES:**
> the *happy* people (simple adjective)
> The eggs are *rotten*. (predicate adjective)

Adjective clause
A dependent clause used to modify a noun or pronoun.
> **EXAMPLE:**
> The car *which you rented* must be returned tomorrow.

Adverb
A part of speech that modifies a verb, adjective, or another adverb. Adverbs used as transitional devices in sentences may modify the entire thought of the sentence.
> **EXAMPLE:**
> We are, *however*, planning to visit you shortly.

Adverb (adverbial) clause
A dependent clause that modifies a verb, adjective, or adverb.
> **EXAMPLES:**
> Mary quit her job *because she preferred her role as a mother*. (Modifies verb)
> The test was harder *than most others were*. (Modifies adjective)
> I think more sharply *after a good night's rest*. (Modifies adverb)

Agreement
Sameness in number, gender, and person. Agreement in number is required between a subject and predicate. Pronouns must agree with their antecedents in person, number, and gender.

Antecedent
The substantive (noun or pronoun) to which a pronoun refers.

Appositive
A noun or noun clause added to (usually following) another noun or pronoun to further identify or explain it. The appositive signifies the same thing as the noun or pronoun it seeks to identify or explain.
> **EXAMPLES:**
> One economic system, *socialism*, is a proven failure.
> A basic socialist premise, *that all people deserve an equal share of the world's material substance*, is a false assumption.

Auxiliary verb
Also called a *helping verb*. A verb used to "help" another verb in forming voices, tenses, and other grammatical ideas. The most common are forms of *be, have, do, can, could, may, might, shall, should, will, would, must, ought, let, dare, need*, and *used*.

Case
The forms that nouns or pronouns have (nominative, objective, possessive) signifying their relationships to other words in a sentence.
> **EXAMPLES:**
> The *car* was new. (Nominative)
> The subject of the *speech* was crime. (Objective)
> The *children's* story hour was always popular. (Possessive)

Clause
A group of words including a subject and a predicate and forming a part of a sentence. All words in a sentence must be part of a clause. Clauses are classified as to their *use* (adjective, adverb, noun), their *character* (dependent, independent, elliptical), and their *necessity* (essential [restrictive], non-essential [non-restrictive]).

Complement
A word or expression used to *complete* the action or idea indicated by a verb. Predicate *complements* include predicate nominatives (noun or pronoun) and predicate adjectives following linking verbs and describing, identifying, or modifying the subject.

Compound pronoun
A pronoun with the suffix *-self*. There are two types: reflexive and intensive. (See entries for *reflexive pronoun* and *intensive pronoun*.)

Conjugation
Changes in the form and use of a verb to signify *tense, voice, number, person*, and *mood*.

Conjunction

A part of speech used to connect words or groups of words such as phrases and clauses. Conjunctions are classified as *coordinating* when they link equal elements or *subordinating* when they link unequal elements.

EXAMPLES:
I like apples *and* bananas. (Coordinating conjunction linking two direct objects)
My hair is brown, *whereas* Mary's is blonde. (Subordinating conjunction linking an independent clause with a dependent clause)
(See also *Conjunctive adverb*.)

Conjunctive adverb

An adverb used as a coordinating conjunction connecting two independent clauses.

EXAMPLE:
The picnic was cancelled; *nevertheless*, we had a pleasant afternoon in the park.

Coordinating conjunction

A conjunction linking words, phrases, or clauses of equal grammatical rank, importance, or value.

EXAMPLE:
Do your duty, *or* turn in your badge.

Correlative conjunction

Coordinating conjunctions used in pairs. Each member of the pair must be followed by words of equal grammatical value. The most common are: *either°or, neither°nor, both°and,* and *not only°but also*.

EXAMPLE:
Neither my grandfather *nor* my grandmother was born in America.

Demonstrative pronoun

A pronoun pointing to, pointing out, identifying, or calling attention to: *this, that, these, those,* and *such*.

Dependent (or subordinate) clause

A clause that does not express a complete thought in itself but which depends for its full meaning upon an independent clause in the same sentence. The three use-related classifications of dependent clauses are: *adjective, adverb,* and *noun*.

Direct object

See Object.

Direct quotation

Stating the exact words (all or part) of a writer or speaker.

Future perfect tense

The time of a verb's action beginning in the present and reaching completion sometime in the future.

EXAMPLE:
He *will have finished* his work by this time tomorrow.

Future tense

The time of a verb expressing action or state of being after the present time.

EXAMPLE:
She *will be* ten years old next Tuesday.

Gender

The classification of nouns or pronouns indicating sex: *masculine, feminine, neuter,* or *common*.

Gerund

A verb form used as a *noun*. Like nouns, gerunds can be used as *subjects, direct objects, objects of prepositions, predicate nominatives,* and *appositives*. The gerund ends in *-ing* most often. Sometimes gerunds end with *-ed*.

EXAMPLES:
Walking is now a popular sport.
(Gerund used as a subject)
She enjoys *teaching*.
(Gerund used as a direct object)
Wisdom comes from *meditating* on God's Word.
(Gerund used as an object of a preposition)
Their greatest battle involved *fighting* Satan with the Word of God.
(Gerund used as a predicate nominative)
Her struggle, *overcoming* fear, ended when she claimed God's promises.
(Gerund used as an appositive)
Jesus healed the *crippled*.
(Past gerund used as a direct object)

Helping verb

See Auxiliary verb.

Indefinite pronoun

A pronoun with an implied antecedent but referring to no specific person, place, or thing: *one, someone, everyone, somebody, everybody, each, none, no one, nobody, everything, nothing,* etc.

Independent clause

A clause that expresses a complete thought in its context and could, if necessary, stand alone as a complete sentence.

EXAMPLE:
If she is chosen next Friday night, *Kim will be the first Chinese homecoming queen in the school's history*.

Indirect object

A noun or pronoun preceding a direct object of a verb and indicating a recipient of the object of the verb. An indirect object usually could have the prepositions *to* or *for* placed before them.

EXAMPLE:
I sent *Mother* a birthday card. [I sent (to) *Mother* a birthday card.]

Infinitive

A verb form which is the first principal part of a verb, equivalent to the first person present tense. The infinitive has the function of a verb (as part of the predicate) but can also be a verbal or in a verbal phrase, commonly used as a noun, adjective, or adverb. As a verbal it is preceded by an introductory *to*, either expressed or implied. The infinitive may also serve as the predicate of an infinitive "clause."

Interjection

An exclamatory word expressing strong feeling or surprise and having little or no grammatical connection with other words in a sentence.

EXAMPLES:

Ouch! That hurts. *Oh,* what a lovely day!

Interrogative pronoun

A pronoun used in a question: *who, which, what, whoever, whatever.*

Irregular verb

A verb whose past and past participle forms are different in spelling from the present (infinitive) form and do not follow the regular pattern of having the last two principal parts formed by the addition of the letters -*d,* -*t,* or -*ed.*

EXAMPLES:

see, seeing, saw, seen; drive, driving, drove, driven; lose, losing, lost, lost; set, setting, set, set.

Linking verb

A non-action verb that expresses a state of being or fixed condition. It "links" a subject to a noun or adjective (or equivalent phrase or clause) in the predicate. The most common linking verbs are forms of *be, look, seem, appear, feel, smell, sound, become, grow, remain, stand, turn, prove.*

EXAMPLES:

She *is* small. His theory *proved* correct. You *look* better today. That dog *smells* bad. The Word of the Lord *stands* secure.

Modify (Modifier)

To describe or limit. Adjectives and adverbs *modify* other words.

EXAMPLES:

sang *happily* (describes); the *only* child (limits).

Nominative case

The *case* of nouns or pronouns used as subjects or predicate complements.

EXAMPLE:

He is Lord. This is *he.*

Noun

A part of speech that names a person, place, thing, idea, action, or quality.

EXAMPLES:

John, sky, table, capitalism, eating, ugliness

Number

The form of a noun or pronoun showing whether one or more than one is indicated. Nouns and pronouns are either *singular* (one) in number or *plural* (two or more) in number. Verbs have singular or plural forms corresponding to the number of the nouns or pronouns that perform their action or state of being.

EXAMPLES:

The *boy sings.* (Singular noun and verb)
The *children sing.* (Plural noun and verb)

Object

The noun, pronoun, or noun clause following a transitive verb or preposition.

EXAMPLES:

Larry ate the *cake.*
(Noun as object of a transitive verb)
Put the cake on the *table.*
(Noun as object of a preposition)
She gave him *what he wanted.*
(Noun clause as object of a transitive verb)

Objective case

The *case* of nouns or pronouns used as objects of prepositions or as direct or indirect objects of verbs.

EXAMPLES:

I gave *him* some advice. Tell your problems to *me.* She loves *us* very much.

Participle

A verb form functioning either as a verb in a predicate or as an adjective. Participles have three forms: *present participle, past participle,* and *perfect participle.*

EXAMPLES:

I am *enjoying* my lunch.
(Present participle in a predicate)
I have *finished* my lunch.
(Past participle in a predicate)
A *steaming* bowl of soup would make a good lunch.
(Present participle as adjective)
Having finished my lunch, I returned to work.
(Perfect participle used as adverb)

Parts of speech

A classification for every word in a language. In English, the primary parts of speech are: *noun, pronoun, adjective, verb, adverb, preposition, conjunction,* and *interjection.*

Passive voice

The form of a verb telling that the subject is not the doer of the action but the entity which is acted upon.

EXAMPLE:

The song *was performed* by the choir.

Past participle

The fourth principal part of a verb used as part of a predicate or as an adjective.

EXAMPLE:

I have *eaten* my breakfast. (Fourth form of the verb *to eat*: eat, eating, ate, eaten)

Past perfect tense

The time of a verb beginning at a point in the past and ending at a later point in the past.

EXAMPLE:

She *had said* the same thing before.

Past tense

The time of a verb before now. The third principal part of a verb.

EXAMPLE:

She *baked* a cake.
(Third form of the verb: *bake, baking, baked,* [have/had] *baked*)

Perfect infinitive

Formed by the auxiliary *to have* and the past participle.

EXAMPLE:

to have loved

Perfect participle

Formed by the auxiliary *having* and the past participle.

EXAMPLE:

having loved

Person

The form of a pronoun (and corresponding form of a verb) indicating whether the "person" or "thing" represented by the pronoun is the one speaking or writing (*first person*: I/we worship), the one spoken or written to (*second person*: you worship), or one spoken or written about (*third person*: he/she/it/they worship).

Personal pronoun

A pronoun referring to the speaker or writer, the person spoken or written to, or the person spoken or written about.

EXAMPLES:

I, you, he, she, it, we, they, me, him, her, she, us, them

Phrase

A group of related words not containing a subject and predicate.

EXAMPLE:

The sound *of the old church bell* brought back many memories.

Plural

The classification of nouns, pronouns, subjects, and predicates indicating a number of two or more.

EXAMPLES:

cows, they   The *animals graze.*

Predicate

The verb or verb phrase in a sentence that makes a statement about the subject. A *simple predicate* is the verb or verb phrase alone. A *complete predicate* is the verb or verb phrase plus its object(s), indirect object(s), and all of their modifiers. A *compound predicate* consists of two or more verbs or verb phrases in a single sentence.

EXAMPLES:

She *wrote the letter yesterday.*
(*Wrote* is the simple predicate. *Wrote the letter yesterday* is the complete predicate.)
She *sealed* the envelope and *stamped* it.
(Compound predicate)

Predicate adjective

An adjective placed in a predicate after a linking verb and used to modify the subject of a sentence or clause.

EXAMPLES:

Children are *happiest* when they know that they are *loved.*

Predicate nominative

A noun, pronoun or equivalent clause used in a predicate after a linking verb to identify the subject.

EXAMPLES:

God is our *Father.*
This is not *what it seems to be.*

Preposition

A part of speech "positioned before" a noun or pronoun showing the relationship of that noun or pronoun (object) to some other word in the sentence.

EXAMPLES:

at school, *under* the couch, *behind* the house, *across* the ocean

Prepositional phrase

A preposition plus its object and related words. The preposition usually precedes, but sometimes follows, its object in the phrase.

EXAMPLES:

They crawled {*through the dark and damp tunnel*} {*to the other side*} {*of the cave*}.
What is the world coming to?

Present participle

The second principal part of a verb. The present participle is the *-ing* form of a verb and is used as part of a predicate or as an adjective.

EXAMPLES:

He is *working* at a local factory.
(Part of predicate)
This is the *working* part of the engine.
(Adjective)

Present perfect tense

The time of a verb beginning in the past and ending just now or still in progress in the present.

EXAMPLE:
I *have been studying* all morning.

Present tense

The time of a verb showing action or state of being now.

EXAMPLE:
God *loves* me.

Principal parts

The four primary forms of verbs — *present (infinitive), present participle, past, past participle* — from which all other forms and uses (tense, mood, tone, voice) of verbs are created.

EXAMPLES:
(to) love, loving, loved, (have/had) loved; (to) burst, bursting, burst, (have/had) burst; (to) swim, swimming, swam, (have/had) swum.
(See also *Irregular verb* and *Regular verb*.)

Progressive (tense) tone

A verb form, sometimes referred to as *progressive tense* and sometimes referred to as *progressive tone*, expressing on-going action or state of being. The progressive tense or tone consists of an appropriate form of the auxiliary verb *to be* plus the present participle.

EXAMPLES:
Jody *is going* to the store. Bill *was playing* golf this morning.
Darlene *will be helping* her mother clean the house.

Pronoun

A part of speech used to replace a noun, often to prevent undue repetition of a noun.

Pronouns include:
I, me, you, he, him, she, her, it, they, them, who, whom, which, that, etc.
Pronouns are classified as:
personal (he),
relative (which),
reflexive (she gave *herself*),
interrogative (Who?),
demonstrative (these),
intensive (he *himself*),
indefinite (all),
reciprocal (each other)

Reciprocal pronoun

A pronoun indicating interchange. English has only two: *each other* (interchange between two) and *one another* (interchange among more than two).

Reflexive pronoun

A pronoun ending in *-self* and referring back to the subject. It usually comes after the verb and is essential to the meaning of the sentence.

EXAMPLE:
She told *herself* not to be afraid.

Regular verb

The most common type of verb in English, which forms its past and past participle forms by adding
-d, -t, or *-ed* to the present form.

EXAMPLES:
move, moved, (have/had) moved; mean, meant, (have/had) meant;
laugh, laughed, (have/had) laughed

Relative pronoun

A pronoun connecting or *relating* an adjective clause to its antecedent. They include *who, whom, which,* and *that.*

Restrictive or essential

A modifier, usually a phrase or clause, that limits or identifies the word modified.

Singular

The number classification of nouns, pronouns, verbs, subjects, and predicates indicating a quantity of *one.*

EXAMPLES:
a *girl*, the *cowboy*, a *truck*
One *game* of tennis *makes* me tired.

Subject of a sentence

The noun, pronoun, noun phrase, or noun clause about which a sentence or clause makes a statement. A *simple subject* is the noun or pronoun alone. A *complete subject* consists of a simple subject and all its modifiers. A *compound subject* consists of two or more subjects in a single sentence.

EXAMPLES:
The *President* of the United States spoke on television. (Simple subject)
The President of the United States spoke on television. (Complete subject)
George Washington and *Abraham Lincoln* are two well-known Presidents. (Compound subject)

Subordinating conjunction

A conjunction connecting a dependent clause to an independent clause.

EXAMPLES:
because, that, since, if, although
I have been lonely *since* you left.

Substantive

Any word, phrase, or clause that has the qualities and uses of a **noun** (which names a person, place, thing, quality, or idea). In its capacity as a noun, a substantive can be used in the following seven ways: *subject, direct object, indirect object, object of a preposition, objective complement, predicate nominative* (subjective complement), and *appositive.*

Tense

The time of action or state of being expressed in a verb: *present, past, future* (simple tenses), *present perfect, past perfect, future perfect* (perfect tenses). The *progressive* form of a verb is sometimes called a *tense* and sometimes a *tone* within some of the other six primary tenses.

Tone

A characteristic of verb tenses indicating *progress, emphasis,* or *simple* time.

EXAMPLES:

am eating (progressive tone), *did eat* (emphatic tone), *eat* (simple tone)

Topic sentence

A sentence which expresses the central idea in a paragraph.

Transitional sentence

A sentence which serves as a link between one paragraph and another. It connects what has already been expressed with what will follow.

Verb

A part of speech expressing *action* or *state of being,* or *helping* another verb complete its meaning.

EXAMPLES:

construct (action verb), *is* (state of being or linking verb), *have* built (helping verb)

Verb phrase

A group of words consisting of a verb and its helpers.

EXAMPLES:

has spoken, did speak, will have been spoken

Verbal

A verb form used as another part of speech: *participles, gerunds,* and *infinitives.*

Voice

The form or use of a transitive verb indicating whether its subject is the doer (*active* voice) or receiver (*passive* voice) of the verb's action.

EXAMPLES:

The buck *stops* here.
(Active voice)
The book *was written* in the 19th century.
(Passive voice)

Index